To: Yolanda

Please be encouraged as you
go in that class to touch
one of God's children. May
God bless you c̄ that degree.

God
Bless
Veryl

God Hears A Teacher's Cry

By Veryl Howard

Edited by
Audrey J. Hinton
Virginia H. Howard, Ed.D.

Table of Contents

Preface

The educational arena has dropped in value over the past two decades. Even though it was never a profession for teachers that offered a lot of money, it was one that offered respect. Professionals in this arena were once looked up to, like judges and doctors. With the constant destructive changes in our society, the teaching profession has suffered tremendously. It has become undesirable to many college graduates and looked down upon by society. It is ultimately blamed for every problem that revolves around criminal activity. Over the years, the school has been blamed for broken homes, low income, low aptitudes, ineffectiveness in the corporate world, and basically for any issue that may be a hindrance to our society. Unfortunately, the blame is passed down the totem pole and laid at the feet of the teacher.

The teaching profession has not been elevated nationally, which hurts our students. There is a lack of adequate supplies, funding for salaries, and security funds, as well as respect. In the United States, the teacher is still expected to do the same job at a competitive level as compared to teachers in other countries. The teacher is expected to be the parent, psychologist, friend, pastor, security guard, counselor, and thus wear any hat. However, this is expected without support from the parents, the system, the students, or society.

Every teacher is expected to work along with the principal,

create miraculous situations, and compete with teachers in other countries. Many times the teacher does not have a supportive situation even with the "boss," which again leaves the teacher alone. The teacher has very few rights in the classroom. Students curse you out as if you were an enemy on the streets. Students challenge you daily with threats just for reprimanding them. Students of today have an "I don't care" attitude and will jump at the opportunity to sue the teacher if given a chance. What is so sad is that the student is initially always assumed to be right. All in all, the school system on the whole is under constant ridicule while very little emphasis has been placed on increasing funds to better educate the children of this era.

The student of today is unique in character. Many are from foster homes, broken homes, cracked-out parents suffering with AIDS, abusive homes, a generation of welfare recipients, and are looking for a way out. Some don't even know their parents. Many don't view themselves as making it to the age of twenty; better yet, sixteen. Conditions of the world have not dictated nor offered them anything more than welfare or prison. Death is knocking at their doors daily in their circle of friends; many are pregnant, suicidal, on drugs, and downright confused. Is this the responsibility of the teacher?

Students have little hope for careers and are just trying to survive by any means. This is a result of what society has produced, while at the same time, it expects the schools to educate and/or babysit. It is a situation that will sadden your heart. It is one that will require frequent visits to the school environment in an attempt to understand these fears.

With the lack of funds and little emphasis on the importance of education, these students are affected even more. There are few to no facilities to work with to keep their interest in the classroom. The student of today needs supplies of today which are not available. Students work on antiquated equipment that you can't even buy parts for. This is especially true of computers, which are hot commodities when it comes to stimulating a student's interest. Ultimately, frustration leads to the same violent activity in the class as it does in the streets. Although this is so, I don't blame the student.

So the bottom line is: What do we do as caring individuals in a corrupt society when a neighbor doesn't even care about a person's hand being cut off? Our students have only become what we as a society have taught them to become. We have allowed our homes to become toxic with what we have exposed them to. We fail to teach our students respect and values. Maybe we just accept their "New Age" way of thinking out of fear. But whatever the reason, it has permeated the educational sector, resulting in the teacher being labeled "the blame." The streets have become the classroom, which grieves my heart and spirit when I look into the eyes of young students who want to learn. Surely, this is probably an emotion that most teachers have experienced at one time or another.

Ultimately, society must find a way to reach our young minds and reiterate the value system of life. Congress needs to implement the importance of education and place funds needed in this arena. For example, security guards are not available because of limited funds. With all the tragedies happening in various schools on a national level, security should be a primary concern. Imagine teaching or learning in fear at every blink of an eye. Recently, I discovered that one of my students had been arrested for murder. Wow, did that scare me! Well, actually, it did not. Either you are tough as an educator or you sink. Something must be done.

As you read these stories, think of ways to help recapture love in a diseased society that is killing our young by the minute. These stories are real-life episodes that required prayer by the second to overcome them. Many of these episodes are so sad that I still ask God to help me deal with the hurt. I never stopped asking him to save our babies and know he will hear my cry.

A Teacher Cries Help!

By Veryl Howard

Staring at an empty chair, droplets trickled down my face.
It was only last week, I thought, when James sat in that
*   chair.*
The room seemed so bare but yet it was noisy.
Frustrated bodies moved about the room preoccupied.
Not at all was a state of mind focused in on my thoughts.
Energy was flowing from me in its highest potential, but
*   only creating a force on few.*
Next week who will be missing, I thought.
Only if that force could keep someone in that chair where
*   James once sat.*
Cry no more, for tomorrow has tears of its own to be shed.
Lord, without you the force maintained would be of confu-
*   sion.*
With you I know I will touch some brilliant minds waiting
*   to blossom.*
I'll use my tears to create productivity.
Maybe they will see my pain in wanting them to succeed.
I'll continue to do my best as the chairs become empty.
But Lord, I can't reach those that stay without you.
Hear my cry oh Lord. In Jesus' name I cry out to you.

1

Leaving the Bus

It was a dreary day. The sky was darkened by the soon-to-be rainstorm. Or maybe it was darkened in my mind because I was to teach in one of the worst sections of the city. The trees blew in synchrony as their stiff leaves fell to the ground. The streets were choppy from all of the pot holes. As I looked through the ragged bus windows, I noticed a school was ahead. This was my new place of employment. I shrilled in my seat as I looked at my job site. In a daze, the bus driver stopped and said, "This is your stop, Miss." So I slowly got out of my seat. I walked towards the door, then stepped down the steps looking at the bus driver with fear in my heart. I was scared and he knew it. As I walked off the bus, I felt an air of wicked mist. Maybe this scared me even more. But this mist had only been a breeze of what the world had become–a cold, cruel place.

I thought about getting another job or just moving to another city. When I left the bus, I had to walk through the neighborhood to get to my destination. I prayed all the way, asking God to restore my car which was dilapidated. Then again, I thought, "Oh well God, it's you and me." This became my phrase each day as I traveled to and fro. But the first week showed me what I was made out of. I was truly becoming equipped with what would be needed in the classroom. I can remember strolling along the cracked sidewalks trying to avoid breaking my heels, when I noticed students sprawled on the outside steps of a big, old, red building surrounded with dirt, smoking cigarettes and basically having a mingling session. They lined the steps like sardines with nowhere to go. I was so scared that I almost left a stream behind me to trail my steps. Some students watched while they drank their beverages from bags. Others browsed up for only a second away from their intense crap game.

"Look at the new teacher. Where did she come from? Africa?" They all laughed as I kept walking. I sucked in any statements that had reached my mouth and kept walking until I reached the inside of the building. Before I left my home, I recalled wondering how my welcome would be on that morning. Prior to this day, only teachers were allowed to frequent the building. The idea of students being present created a different perception of what this antiquated building would be like with their presence.

This was one of the most ambivalent days of my life. I was indecisive because I knew that whatever move I made, I had to "come correct." As a new teacher, I would feel the tension from all the old fogies that were waiting for retirement. I knew my walk, my talk, weren't going to be good enough for the traditional style teacher from ancient times. I must have changed clothes ten times before leaving my house, making sure I didn't come in as an outcast on the first day. My clothes had to be strong enough to win over the oldest teacher in the building but cool enough to win over the toughest child. I indeed had a challenge set out for me.

Well, the day began. I entered what was called a school by the standards of the system. It was an old, red, beat-up building where my father had taught when I was a child. The doors were of heavy steel that could keep a prisoner out. I was scared to see the inside of the building. Students were draped along the inside of the building waiting to cut on every teacher who walked by. Any minute I was to be their next victim. Since I experienced this outside, I put on my toughest face, dressed in a suit that I really didn't like and dared one of them to open his or her mouth. Heck, I grew up in the ghetto, too! Well, not really, but my neighborhood had its aspects of the ghetto. I knew all the lingo and could break down a sumo wrestler if need be. But inside I was praying that no one said a word. After all, it was my first day and I had to learn to be strong, but not ignorant.

The halls were dark and gloomy as if I were in the basement of a warehouse. The walls had mounds of chipped paint that dropped off as you walked by. The atmosphere was that of a dungeon. I thought, "Lord, how in the world do you expect me to teach science in this mess?" But, hey, I needed a job so I had to deal with the situation. After all, it wasn't like I had a choice of a location. It was teach in the rodent hole or not teach at all. Fortunately for me, God had given me an assignment that I was soon to learn about. With that in mind, I just decided to teach as if I was teaching in paradise. So I continued on my little tour of the antiquated building, hoping to reach my classroom soon.

I had to trot to the back of the building where my class was located. This really scared me. I had thought, "Suppose something happens to me where there's no security, no intercom, no lights, and a door for walk-ins to enter freely." I wondered how long I could actually survive in this rodent-infested dungeon in this system called a school. But again, like most teachers, I needed a job. I kept asking God, "Why do you want me here? Lord, this is punishment." His answer was the same, "THIS ISN'T ABOUT YOU; THIS IS ABOUT THE CHILDREN." So I obeyed and kept walking. For a brief moment, I thought I wasn't up to the job or maybe the Lord chose the wrong person. But who can argue with God? I was new in my Christian walk and was learning how to hear God and give up my selfish ways. But, truly, I wasn't there yet. God is God, so slowly I approached my room. It was a small beat-up classroom with what looked like ten-year-old paint, and two doors that overlapped each other instead of locking together. The chalkboard was chipped, the heat didn't work, and half my windows were nailed down. There were no supplies, the chalk was a fossil, and I was to teach in this room. I immediately thought to myself, No wonder our kids are killing themselves selling drugs and can't read past the fifth grade level.

There was not a modernized spot in the whole school or even one that resembled modernization. I wanted with all of my heart to write the superintendent but I knew from past experience that you can't complain or you are fired, or better yet, labeled and black-balled. So I knew that I had to do back flips in my room to reach even one child. The Lord was truly going to work his miracles because I knew I wasn't with this program.

Young Veryl and Ben Ben Howard
Both teachers
Learning at home

2

Learning the Ropes

Well, the year started out. Most of my children were from deprived homes where 6 or 7 kids lived in a 2-bedroom apartment. Most of them came from different fathers or had no knowledge of who their parents were. It was sad! It seemed as if most of my students carried guns, knives, fingernail files, or whatever worked as a weapon. But the sad part was that I couldn't blame them. I often wondered just how long it would be before I starting toting a weapon. I, myself, had just come to know the Lord and was not without a whole lot of sin in my own life. Therefore, I wondered if I would transform to the environment in view of the large amount of time I spent in it. Even though I thought this, an inner voice kept telling me that it was all a test and not to be used or fooled. Again, this isn't about you, Veryl. So I dropped the thought–temporarily.

Reality showed me on a daily basis that the gloominess in my students lives moved with them from home to school. The school presented no change in environment. The presence of poverty was exhibited not only in the state of the building, but in the attitudes of everyone there, including the mentality of the staff with their low expectations of the students. I had to cry out to God by the minute, just to overcome the defeatist negative principalities of the air (Ephesians 6:12). I didn't want to get complacent or laxed because my students were not from a so-called elitist economic background. Only God could keep showing me how to instill hope. Boy, was this a challenge. I refused to set low expectations for them. They had the world to do that for them. These students needed a ray of hope.

Well, although, the school year started out pretty rough, I eventually peeled off my expensive suits and introduced my body to sweatsuits and jeans. After all, clothes do not make the teacher. This was a traditional corporate mindset and I was by no means traditional. I was learning God's style for me as a teacher and I knew it was a contemporary approach. But my style, though functional, presented problems for my principal. It was truly not her cup of tea. Complaints became a part of my assessment sheets even though my technique was working and reaching the students. Isn't that what education is all about? Without a doubt, I was beginning to understand that God had it all in control so why was I worrying? I had to prepare for battle in the spiritual sense while I was learning more about releasing the desire to resolve matters in the physical sense. This was one of my toughest tasks.

On any given day, I would have to break up a fight and designer clothes weren't cutting it. Initially, my suits were useful in establishing my aura, but they were not a necessity. The students learned that Ms. H didn't play. Once the respect is granted, half the battle is over. Then you can teach. My students knew I cared and that I was really there to teach them. Eventually the discipline became a little easier as the students grew to like me. By this time I had paid my dues and earned their respect.

Today's system doesn't even bear any resemblance to that of ten years ago. It needs to be studied. Old tactics of the seventies and eighties just don't work. A teacher almost has to pretend to be a thug covered up with education. If you weren't a thug, the students would just run all over you. It was all about respect. The teacher had to learn how to be kind–a sweet thug that left little room to be challenged. One reason was that the system did not protect them on security matters, inside or out of the classroom.

Many times teachers are tired and burnt out from the system

that doesn't value the teacher. Therefore, a lot of teachers have adopted a phased-out existence. This means to phase out the true discipline problems and not get stressed out. Unfortunately, this attitude would surface after endless hours of effort put forth by the teacher to reach a student. This was done with little support from the system or society. Therefore, the teacher's sanity was maintained through ignoring reality. I don't knock this rationalization but I knew it wasn't for me. After all, God quickly reminded me when I was obedient to his call, that teaching was not about me.

So I stepped into the boxing ring refusing to let another child pass through the system with few to no reading skills. Heck, I was young, full of energy for that moment, and wanted to make a difference. I knew that God and only God could sustain the energy needed to run the race. But little did I know that the system was designed to burn my flame out, too. Most of the teachers were older and had fought the system to save that one child. It was obvious that at some point they had plenty of spunk, but later became tired and burnt out. It was now all about a pay check and retirement. But who is to blame them after being stripped of all dignity and self worth. The system coupled with all the discipline problems could definitely render this end result. It was one lacking empathy and it wasn't because they didn't care but because they were too tired to care. Most of these teachers had two and three higher level degrees and were making no more than the secretaries. It was insulting and did not emphasize the importance of education. That was a big price for society to pay as the outcome is reported daily in criminal statistics. I thought to myself, "Self you will not be in this system long." There I went again, limiting God and what he can do.

The days went on, some good and some bad, but I was progressing, considering my non-traditional style. I began to get used to being different. My principal never had a kind word and I got used to that. I knew, like many in similar positions, it wasn't about the students. It was about the fluff and drama that made the school look exceptional. Individual students were really not concerned unless it resulted in a plaque for the school. This saddened me. If you had a mission, you were on your own as a teacher. I can recall numerous episodes where I was reprimanded for doing my job in situations that could have resulted in violence. On numerous occasions, I had to plead for my job and was questioned when I had to write up a student. It was against the rule to suspend too many students even if they were threatening your life. This would send too many bad reports downtown and that was a no-no. I quickly learned my legal rights as a result of the constant accusations for protecting the lives of others. It was unbelievable.

One day, I recall being summoned to the principal's office without reason. When I entered the office, I saw a six foot, two hundred pound, masculine-looking woman waiting for me with anger in her eyes. There was no doubt at that moment that she had decided to release her anger on me. It was also obvious that the principal already had this notion, too, before I was called to the office. This parent was responding to a complaint that I submitted based on her child threatening my life, not to mention that he stayed in what were said to be drug-trafficking altercations which supposedly ultimately lead to his death. Well, the principal just sat there propped up in her plush office that she hid in. She let the parent harass me and get in my face. Now at this time, I was running a little low on my Christian attitude. I thought that at any given minute, this woman would sling me across the floor like a rug. But, I said to myself, "I'm not scared." After all, I taught drug dealers and gang members daily. I could tell from the look on my principal's face that she did not have my backbone. Again, I was on my own. It was as if my principal had bet on the fight and was waiting for the outcome. She seemed as if she had a ringside seat. How professional is that?

So I snapped. I couldn't take another accusation for doing my job. What was I to do, phase out a life-threatening situation? The child of this parent would have killed me or a student so I wrote an anecdotal account before a tragedy came to pass. I broke this parent down in tears. Yes, all two hundred pounds. Here I was with enough degrees to give away and I "read her" like a bad school girl from the ghetto. I was rail thin and dared her to touch me. Without foul language, I cut her up with my mouth and the same aura I had learned from teaching, which was to be professional, caring, and strong. The principal was indeed stunned. She discovered that day that I had some spunk and was not your typical teacher. She also showed in her facial expressions that she knew that I was aware of her non-supportive attitude. With this in mind, she dismissed the parent as if the incident never happened. Precious time had been wasted in regard to my class that remained upstairs. I had been rudely disrupted in the middle of my routine. But that didn't surprise me. So I proceeded back to my domain with a smile. Even though I hadn't been the most Godly, my statement was made about the success of the students and their safety. I knew in time God would help me with my newly-established, tough disposition. But, in the meantime, I was trying to survive, too. This was the beginning of learning to take my own security battles into my own hands. I was in a public facility where I, the teacher, was supposed to be protected, I was not!!

Ms. Howard milking cow on farm trip

Dr. Howard at work

3

The Bully

Time progressed and I was beginning to establish a relationship with my students. I was learning their style and they were learning my teaching style. I knew that it was only God and God alone who was going to use me as the instrument to touch a few. I was beginning to understand that all my students would not be reached, therefore I zeroed in on special appointments I knew God had given me. But I still gave my all, with all of my students.

There was this one child in particular who really touched my heart. She was a bully that half the school was afraid of. But bully and all, she became like a child of my own. I thought, "Lord, only you know why this child has become like a child to me." This student would beat up the other students, carry weapons and curse out any teacher with threats on one of her good days. But despite all her anger, there was something about this student that was special. I began to view her as dealing with her problem the best way she knew how. I didn't know her problems, but I knew that she really didn't want to be so bad. It was all a front to hide her true feelings. So I began to reach out to her. God had told me that she was one of the reasons I was teaching. He said that with his guidance, I would be able to reach her, but it wasn't going to be easy.

Initially, she rebelled against any disciplinary measures I dished out. She would disrupt the flow of my class with threats towards me. But I knew in time that God's word would come to pass. So I prayed, humbling myself while God went to work. Eventually, she began to come around. She joined the dance class that I taught after school and became one of my most skillful dancers. There were times when other teachers came to me to report the problems they were having with this student. I had officially become like a mother to this student. She began to listen to me but I was smart enough to know that I didn't do it; God was the ruler. It was God, who was moving the mountains. God was transforming this tyrant into a spirit-filled young lady right before my own eyes. Therefore, I just sat back and watched God mold this new person as he was also molding me.

I began to notice that on certain days this student was absent. Like an adopted mother, I began to question until I found out that she was extremely ill with a blood disorder. Her days absent increased until finally she told me that she desperately needed new kidneys. Now this really scared me. I cried endlessly wondering how such a young child could be in such an ill state. Many days were spent in hospitals having her kidneys filtered. Her hours became long and painful while she frequented the hospital to be hooked up to machines. But through it all, she never stopped her dancing. I guess this freedom allowed her to still be a child with normal desires.

As time progressed, God instructed me to invite her, along with other students, to my church and that I did. She began to frequent the church and eventually joined. At that time, my pastor assured me that I had now acquired a new responsibility. That was the responsibility of following through on what I started, monitoring and aiding in the students' attendance to church. I had now become bus service for all the students that joined. But, hey, if God said do it, I was "down for the cause." This bully began to transform into one of God's bright lights. I was beginning to understand the scripture which speaks of God's servants being the salt of the world. It was amazing. I watched darkness being energized into light. This bully was quoting scriptures, praying for people, and dancing her little heart out. She became the most talented dancer despite her sickness. People began to notice her change as she and others led teenagers to the Lord. She became an inspiration to all of us. My problems became magnified with every second. The school and the church had now become one in this child's life. God used her to merge two worlds from opposite descents.

Days went on and she began to miss more days out of school. Eventually, most of her time was spent hooked to a machine. Occasionally she would blow up physically because fluids backed up in her body. But somehow she would find a way to leap in dance class. Her disease worsened to the point where she had to be hospitalized. Nights were spent in the hospital by her bedside as she fought for her life. My church family became her family, and I was a mother watching my child die. But little did I know that God wasn't quite finished with this little servant of his. She periodically went in and out of the hospital.

This girl grew stronger in the Lord even though she was dying. Each hour became a bout with death until eventually she died. But until her last breath, she was witnessing to those present. She witnessed to many lost souls up until the time of her death. This child knew her duty was complete with the Lord and she accepted death. She was ready to be with the Lord. Here I was, a grown, confused woman, and yet this thirteen-year-old knew her purpose on earth. What a dichotomy! God showed me and others how he can purge out the dirty weeds and transform them into beautiful sunflowers for his kingdom. I knew I had a long way to go. I was still in the wilderness myself, being a part of the fields of weeds. But I had hope knowing that God could renew me, too. Like my student, I had to exercise some faith and give it my best shot. I wanted God to say to me, "Well done my faithful servant." Her faith was an eye opener for me.

Well, this story was a sad one that turned out to be good. As a result, many souls were touched. Other students became evangelists in the school, holding their own Bible studies with the other teens. They were giving students, who had no hope, hope. It was indeed the work of God. My student's funeral gave them a new perspective on life. Many of them learned that they didn't want to die and that God could give them life. They learned that the lack of spirituality destroyed their physical being, which created a life of drugs, alcohol, crime, and depression among teens.

4

Ex-Cons

Incidents began to multiply even though I was growing in the Lord. God was by all means giving me testimonies. I remember teaching class one day when I noticed a metal anklet around one of the student's legs. Now this student was about sixteen years old and in the seventh grade. He had features of a grown man. His body was mature in structure. His muscles bulged as if he lifted weights daily for competition. He had a small area on his face symbolizing a beard. He looked as if he were thirty. He was tall and brown-skinned with bushy hair. Combat boots with army fatigues were a part of his fashion decor. He had a taste for the latest fashions. His first day in my class was one that tickled my defense mechanisms. His appearance alone scared me.

Even though this student was older-looking, he was always respectful. But there was something about his demeanor that established a point of demarcation for me. I knew he could only be pushed so far. He struggled to maintain his politeness. But I was not going to take him to his limit. Well, on this day, I asked him about his anklet. I remember thinking to myself, "Okay, what new fashion is this?" When I asked the question, the class silenced. They obviously knew something that was a mystery to me. They respected this student as if he was a captain in the army. Better yet, the ringleader in a prison. So we all sat still while I waited for an answer. It was as if we were in a Catholic chapel confessing our sins with a whisper. Well, the young man looked at me and said that he had just been released from prison. The anklet was a house arrest anklet that would signal the student's whereabouts to the police. Now, I didn't dare ask how he became a prisoner at some point in his life. Again, I knew my limit. His piercing eyes spoke for him. They were not to be taxed.

I thought to myself. "Self, when was the school going to let me in on this treasured secret?" Here I was on a human shooting range, trying to teach ex-cons and not even being warned. At least I could have purchased a bulletproof vest. I was a sitting duck with no clues or options. Again, I had been left alone. "This isn't the profession for me," I thought.

Fortunately for me, God had placed his angels around my personal space. Wisdom was placed in my spirit in regard to how far I could go with disciplinary actions with this student. It was a blessing to me that this young man liked me as a teacher. Heaven forbid if I had raised my voice or even questioned him about his homework, I might not be here now to tell about the real deal of the school system that is supposed to mold our children. The same school system that is supposed to provide a safe environment for all there. What a joke!

Too many times there were situations where teachers were left in the dark. We were teaching murderers, drug dealers, thieves, gang members, and various forms of criminals with no–and I repeat, no–supplies. We were expected to do this with very few personal funds as well. Here I was educated and all, barely making $20,000 a year. I, myself, was struggling to survive so I knew every dollar I spent on supplies tapped into my rent money. But what was I to do with students whose attention span did not exceed ten minutes? Creatively, I had to make my funds stretch from my personal life into my work arena. This was a must to teach science to students who had little to no interest in any form of education. Classes had to be designed with non-stop hands-on lessons that kept the students' interest. My class had to provide a world of fun while learning. Many times skits were incorporated with a revolving door—one that turned constantly allowing new ideas to permeate my class. I refused to give any second to being a target. My own survival depended upon the uniqueness in every lesson I taught.

Despite the ridicule from the principal along with the lack of respect from the world, I kept creating new ways to teach and reach my students. Each day was a challenge. God's angels were truly protecting me. I had incidences, regardless of my creativity, where I could have been stabbed, shot, robbed, raped, or just plain violated. Sometimes I was not so fortunate. But I knew God allowed incidents to happen to build the Christian character in me. So, I flowed with God's program regardless of the pain. I remember one incident like it was yesterday. A student threw scissors at my face while I was teaching. The scissors were thrown less than one-half inch from my eyes. We were required to keep our doors open while teaching which left teachers as targets. We were written up if we locked our doors.

On this day, the door was open when I experienced the scissors being slung across my face from a hand in the hallway. So immediately I ran out of my room chasing down the culprit. Remember security was a joke. When I caught the student (a known drug dealer), I nearly choked him to death. The other students had to pry my fingers off of this student's neck one by one. I had slammed him on the floor so hard that I thought the floor was cracked. The student was a drug dealer who had threatened my life on numerous occasions. My rage was a result of built-up assaults coming from him. So I thought it was justifiable. I remember choking him so hard that the other students cried out, "Ms. H, you are going to hurt him." I thought, did he think of that when he almost took my eye out? No, I think not. So I practiced the phase out mode. I phased their voices right out of my brain until I realized that I had lost it. I had taken security into my own hands and that resulted in my gaining more respect. Sad as it may seem, this is what it took.

God told me in a chastising voice that my actions were not of God. I said back in my mind, "Well God, you gonna have to find another way because this is the way I choose to deal with the situation." I told God that he would have to change me or someone really was going to get hurt. Respect was all a teacher had in the classroom. So by all means, I was not going to let the students control me, whatever the cost. As a new teacher, I had a lot to learn.

I guess, like most teachers, the learning process never stops. The students were becoming more corrupt daily and you had to be a genius to outwit them. Even veterans have tremendous problems in the class. Just recently a teacher was arrested for punching a student in the face after the student pinched her. This teacher had been teaching for over twenty years and I am sure had suppressed a lot of tension from various assaults in the past. Finally that one day came when she lost it, too, defending herself. Even though the student hit her, she was arrested. It's funny. The student is always initially viewed as being right. What a system. But this is only one of many cases that hit the news. The school system has a way of sweeping the real problems under a rug and leaving the surface to be cleaned. When I talk to teachers on a national level, the problems are the same. The only difference may be the available funds.

I remember questioning my brother about his school to see if my episodes paralleled his. As a man, he had experienced situations that would challenge his manhood. He shared an incident with me that nearly made me quit that day. This incident along with the others I had experienced or heard about from other teachers were just not made known to the public. But this incident was ranked very high on the Richter scale when you speak of danger.

One day a student, who was a known kingpin drug dealer, reported to my brother's class. Though he was involved in illegal work, he was a gentleman. He came daily to class with a bulletproof vest. Knowing this, my brother warned him about his activity and putting the other students' lives in danger. On this day a hit man came to my brother's class looking for the student. However, this was later on that day. By the work of the Lord's hands on my brother's life, he was able to resolve the situation. He told me that day really scared him until he experienced the next episode. That time a student entering the room with a loaded gun asked for him. He was sitting at his desk when another student passed him a gun under the desk to defend himself. Now, why was another student sitting in class with a loaded gun? Regardless of the reason, the student's loyalty was to my brother as the teacher. I'm sure this was established only after my brother had gained the student's respect. Anyway, he was able to get out of that situation as well. He discovered that the student looking for him was his cousin who once attended the school. He was a drug runner himself who had only visited the class to become acquainted with my brother. He was a cousin who had heard of my brother teaching in the school and was very proud of his association with my brother. The drug runner wanted my brother to know that he was covering his back in the school and that my brother had nothing to worry about. Now I thought, "Okay, this level of violence and ignorance has really hit home." My own cousin was a part of the generation that the world feared. Yet he thought my brother needed protection in the classroom.

After hearing about these episodes, I wondered how I would have made it out alive. After all, the situation I had with the drug dealer almost ended in tragedy.

That young man became one of my projects. I found out that he really did like me and throwing scissors was his way of getting my attention. I tried to forgive him and move on. But when progress seemed to take place, the student dropped out of school. I don't think he ever made it out of junior high school alive. Even though he was bright, he never expected to finish school anyway. He informed me that he made more in one day than I did in two weeks. I had to laugh myself because he was right. College was a pseudo world to him. Heck, *high school wasn't even in his vocabulary.*

Most of my students who were similar in character had no intention of attending high school. They had their lives all mapped out. They would come to school long enough to stress out their teacher and reach the maximum required age to leave school: sixteen. Most of my students were runners until they worked their way up to the top. So why did they need school? Most of my students kept more money in one day than I had in a two-week period. My salary to them was a joke and offered no exciting future for them. They often asked how I survived and I had to almost laugh with them, wondering the same thing.

There were times when my students would pull out hundreds to offer me money when I didn't have lunch money. I thought to myself that on one hand they would shoot me but on the other hand give me their last dollar. There was a level of love that existed in what seemed to be such cold hearts. What a dichotomy. My students knew my salary and that I was struggling just to stay afloat. Many times they offered me rent money, food money, or just whatever I needed. Though tempted, I never took from them. It was funny; my students pitied my life style while I prayed for theirs.

All my students needed was love. They would seek attention the best way they knew how—even if it meant assaulting me. Sometimes it meant jumping a friend or knifing another student. Whatever the tragedy, they would perform it. My task was definitely set out for me. Many of my students expressed their fear of dying soon and their visions of their friends who had died. So how was I to convince them there was life after age fifteen? Heck, here I was too educated for the job and could barely pay my rent. My salary was furloughed constantly and I had very little hope for myself. So what did I do? I increased in my hope with God. God was all I had to hold on to. So I let my students know that he was my only hope. Regardless of the system, society, or even the world, God would always be there.

But hope is something you can't see or feel. Teenagers, like some adults, want a quick fix. God could not get them out of poverty quickly enough for them. But drugs could, even if it meant at the expense of their lives. They could die having had a thick gold chain or the latest fashions. It was hard to make them understand the intangible feeling of hope. It was hard when they watched my pain daily while they stripped me of all dignity. They could feel my inner cries and pain through my tough-skinned exterior. But it was the joy that came after the tears were exemplified. It was the joy that reached a suffering soul. It was the joy that caused tears to roll down my eyes with their accomplishments. It was the joy found when my class and I stuck together as a team. They became my friends, my support system, when they grew to love me as their teacher. They dared anyone to even attempt to harm me. They even protected me against the administration when they attempted to destroy my character. My students and I became inseparable and were able to feel hope in someone believing in them.

But this hope was established after long, sleepless nights as a result of all the initial trials the students put me through. A bond was formed once my physical and mental state had been drained. But the bond helped to regenerate all the energy lost. This helped me keep fighting the battle to reach my students. But I knew the battle had to be won before their ripe old age of sixteen.

One day life tested me again to see what I was made of. I was talking to one of my students about her consistent state of depression. After all, that wasn't abnormal. The teacher was the mother, father, psychologist, and friend when allowed. I was invited to be the friend this time as my student let me into her world of inner depression. I was concerned because she was bright but wouldn't do her work. I had done all I knew to do as a teacher. I had visited her house, called her parents, reported her, and nothing worked. It was time to be her friend with her approval. I had earned her trust. Honestly, I almost avoided listening to her problems. Some of her problems in the past had been so devastating that I was afraid to hear the latest.

This student revealed to me that she was being sexually abused by her father or live-in stepfather. I'm not sure of the nomenclature. The man was basically the man of the month who was making frequent visits to her bedroom as well as her mother's. What was so sad was that the mother didn't seem to be disturbed by the situation. This child was in the seventh grade, and somewhat mature in statute. However, her personality was that of a newborn kitten who was forced to be a cat.

Anyway, the student informed me that she visited graveyards as a way of finding peace. Of all things, I was not ready for that response. "Graveyards?" I asked her. All I could think of was that she identified death with peace. But whatever the reason, I thought the whole idea was rather spooky and sick. I don't even visit graveyards when someone dies and here she was hanging out there like it was a playground.

When the student told me this, I didn't know how to react. I didn't know how to respond. I didn't know what to say or even if I was to say anything. I thought to myself, "What next?" I have truly heard it all. I cried out to God to give me the words to say. I had never heard of people–especially children–hanging out around graveyards. The only time I had ever heard of any interaction with living human beings and a graveyard was to bury the dead or to steal from them once they were buried. Lost for words, I became speechless for a moment. Here I was in a position to share the intangible through education and this student had already picked out her coffin. After being speechless, God eventually gave me the words to utter. To this day I do not remember what they were. However, I do remember my thoughts about this student having a death wish. I know Satan was becoming real to me and was working hard to kill our babies as early as possible.

After this spiritually trying episode, I wondered who I could talk to in regard to getting help for this young lady. Her parents basically didn't seem to care. The mother's only concern was to remove the student from the house when it was time for her to stroke her man. The student became a vital part of the home only when it was time to babysit the other siblings.

Eventually this student did what I feared she would do. She stopped coming to school. Being concerned, I questioned and questioned until I received answers. I found out from the students that she had attempted suicide and was living in a home for runaways. She had almost died from an overdose and that didn't surprise me. Though not alarmed, I was mad. I was mad at myself and at what I could have done. After all, I had seen all the signs and did nothing but ponder what to do. Anger struck me like lightning hitting an iron pole in a pool of water. I was mad at the devil as well as all the other teachers who saw signs like I did but were too busy phasing them out to be concerned. Sad, isn't it ? As I taught class, I often thought the whole crazy suicidal attempt could have been avoided. I was driving myself crazy thinking about this student and all the newly-developed events that had surfaced with my other students. God in so many words told me to get a grip and pray. All I could do was pray that she would be kept alive because of God's grace and mercy. I didn't know how to rebuke the wickedness of the devil from her life but I did know that prayer worked. So pray I did, holding God to his word which says, "And whatsoever you shall ask in my name, that will I do that the Father may be glorified in the Son." Not saved long, I knew that I could ask God to have mercy on this student and that it was not God's will for any human being to commit suicide. Therefore, I prayed realizing that again it wasn't about school but survival in a cold, cruel, wicked world.

Weeks went on before she returned to school. Her graveyard visits had meant more to us than any of us could imagine. When she returned to class the students along with myself let her know that we loved her and missed her. I had already requested the students to treat her with love and not pity. Teens can be so cruel to each other so the seriousness of what had happened had to be stressed. Sad as it may seem, this student was looking for praise as if she had done something daring but yet heroic. By all means, I did not allow this train of thought to permeate the class too long.

With time, this student went in and out of homes for runaway teens. She struggled to come to school wearing whatever she could scrape up. Because our teens are so driven by materialism , I knew that it was just a matter of time before she would stop coming to school altogether. Not to my surprise that day came and I wondered if she ever made it past the ripe old age of fifteen. I thought, "There goes another one lost to a dying world."

Years had passed and I had forgotten about this particular student in my short-term memory. However, her well-being played a role in my long-term one. Ironically enough, I ran into her this year on the street. I was so happy to see her alive. I didn't dare ask her about school–just life. She was just as excited about seeing me and wanted to tell me about all of her success–that being an eighteen-month-old baby and her new live-in man. She looked every bit of thirty years of age. I calculated that she was only about eighteen at the time. She told me that she had a good job and was now trying to raise a family. Her accomplishment, like that of many students, was the baby and her new apartment with public assistance. All I could do was thank God for saving her life and ask him to continue to keep her. Only eighteen, she had now found a reason to live. She had a baby, a man, and rent. As cold as this may sound, this all brought a smile to my face.

There were many instances where I ran into my former students. It was a blessing because most of the ones I ran into were my hardest students to teach. Regardless of the stress that was generated from teaching them, they always greeted me with love when they saw me. Some of them even thanked me and wanted to stay in touch with me. The reunion with my students was very touching for both sides and I never knew how they were going to receive me. But each time God saw fit to make our reunion one of love.

Unlike a lot of teachers, I lived near the school where I taught. I was a down-to-earth teacher according to the students, though I was stern. The students knew where I lived and respected the fact that I lived in their neighborhood. Many of them would stop by on their own to say hello if they saw me in the yard. Most teachers lived in huge plush homes in the suburbs. I can't say that I blamed them because they were seeking a change from their work environment. Unlike the veteran teachers, I couldn't afford a change of environment. Where I lived was middle-class but within walking distance of the ghetto. I myself was a city girl and didn't mind the city. But I was hoping that it wouldn't take twenty years to one day get my dream house.

All in all, living near my students made a better working relationship with my students if they weren't trying to harm me. My students thought that I had a better understanding of their lifestyles. Though my home was a step up for them, I was still from the hood. In Washington, D.C., one can live in an exclusive neighborhood which stands one block from the ghetto. However, most choose the peace of the suburbs. Well, I guess I lived in the transitional area that resulted in respect from some of my students.

There was this one student who became very fond of me as his teacher. No one seemed to be able to reach him or maybe they just didn't care to. He was one of the eight students that God had assigned to me to pick up for church every Sunday. I would go into their world with my beat-up truck every Sunday. Many weekends my students would pile in my truck just to get away from their homes. Though I was ready to be married and have children of my own, God would ordain these students to be a part of my weekends. I had no life and God made it clear that these were his precious children. I was to be the vessel that he would use at this time and there was no running away from the assignment. Therefore, my life was sacrificed daily as God taught me that Christianity wasn't about being selfish. Someone had to pray for me while at the same time I exercised patience. Therefore, I stuck it out.

One day I came home and this young man was sitting outside of my house. I walked up with another teacher and we couldn't believe our eyes. I was glad that someone else was there to witness this. I asked him how he got to my house and why was he sitting on my front porch.

He said, "Ms. Howard, I walked." Now he had to make a twenty- to thirty-minute trip by foot. He said "Ms. Howard, I knew you would understand."

I thought to myself that this was my free weekend. It wasn't even Sunday. I began to get a little angry with God. I murmured under my breath to the Lord, "Darn. Am I ever going to have a life?" But I could see the sadness in this little boy's eyes. He was crying for help.

This little boy or young man was twelve years old and about two hundred pounds. He was almost six feet tall and threatening in his physical appearance. However, he had a baby face and young disposition. He was a child, just a big child, who was scared. My other students used to tease him about his weight. It was very hard for him to stay clean because he owned few clothes. Many times my mother clothed him for church out of her own pocket. My family assisted when needed with this student as well as others. But this day he was a child who did what he felt he needed to do to survive—even if it infringed on my time.

He told the other teacher and me that he was tired of all the gunshots in his building. He said he couldn't sleep at night and was scared. A dead man had even been found on the front porch of his apartment. Now I was young and could barely take care of myself and was by no means prepared to take care of someone else's child on a full-time basis. Many times he was kept up at night because of the gunshots or arguments in his building. I looked at my colleague, baffled. So I let him vent his problem with the two of us. During this time his parents didn't even know he was missing.

I told him that he should have told his mother where he was going. She knew and trusted me. I took him to flight lessons on Thursdays and church on Sundays but never without her permission. I explained all of this to him and assured him that I would take him home once he cleared his head. As a teacher, you are a sitting duck in many ways. I, by all means, wasn't going to give anyone a reason to throw lawsuits my way. Therefore, I contacted his mother immediately assuring her that her child was safe and would be returning home soon.

The other teacher and I let the student wash and clean our trucks to earn lunch money and free his mind. He came from a family of twelve who lived in a two-bedroom apartment. I taught many of his other sisters and brothers, too, so the family welcomed me into their living quarters. Well, the little money we gave him couldn't put a dent in what he needed but it was a start. Many times we would let him help us at school to earn lunch money. But today was truly a day to help him occupy his mind with thoughts that did not resemble tragedy.

After finishing the trucks we prayed that he could stay sane, at least until the age of eighteen. I knew I would see him that Sunday for church which offered a couple of hours of peace, but I cried thinking about the other sad hours of his life. He, along with other students, really became a part of my life. If you care as a teacher, you take your work home which scared me for I'd turn off my husband-to-be. Many times the stories were so sad that I felt like giving up. I was single and a lot of times I thought the pressure was too great for me alone. But it was that still, quiet, voice of the Lord's that kept me going. Many times God would give these students the right word to say just when I felt like throwing in the towel.

Fortunately for this little boy, he became a success story. He joined church, continued with his flight lessons and eventually became a leader in the ROTC. He began to develop pride despite the accusations made about his size. His self-esteem skyrocketed and he began to have hopes about getting out of the ghetto. I always wondered about him after graduation until one day I ran into him. He was working as a security guard and seemed happy. Like my other students, I was just happy to see him alive. My dream for all of them was to go to college and establish a career. Just seeing them alive was enough for me. For students like this young man, society only suggested failure.

Often when I feel my world is crumbling, I reflect on how this young man along with many others pulled through despite the obstacles. The hardest climb up their mountain was over because they had made it past the ripe old age of fifteen.

It was so hard for some of these students to get to the point that this young man had reached. Realistically, the school system didn't believe in them and teachers were doing all they could to instill some hope. To the school system, success of students meant funding. Once there was funding teachers could be hired based on the number of students. With the teachers and students in place, administrators could be hired which meant there had to be a school board which kept this educational family in place. Ultimately, this led to high-profile jobs for a superintendent's team who only visited a school to ridicule it and those involved who were lower on the totem pole. Basically the educational ladder was something to laugh at. The student, per se, was not the main concern, the almighty dollar was.

The theme behind the idea of education was totally in opposition to what God was teaching me. Students were passed through the system without being able to read to avoid embarrassment for the city. Test scores were low when compared to national ones; oftentimes they were altered. Students were handed off from person to person while they became a new problem each year. Put the blame on someone else seemed to be the school system's motto. But regardless of where the blame was placed it ultimately landed on the teacher.

I often thought about other cities and school districts. We seemed to have a new superintendent at the blink of an eye. We never received raises and there was always a budget crunch when it pertained to teachers' salaries. After talking to various teachers across the country, I concluded that the problems among the students were similar, but none could top the city administration ones.

The issues we were perplexed with were the do's and don'ts. They included: Do get good test scores or else; don't fail too many students; do have good attendance regardless of your records, don't defend yourself though a child struck you; do change grades to appease parents; don't complain about your working conditions; do spend your own money; don't buck against the system; do write or call parents weekly. There are so many I can't recall them all. The bottom line was: Do be a puppet on a string and deal with the circumstances.

Well, I became tired of all the do's and don't. The system was teaching me to be uncaring and to lie and cheat. I had a problem with that because that was not what God had dictated to me. But I was not alone after conversing with other teachers. We were all merely a part of the funding cycle, which irritated me. We were not looked at as professionals or people having unique characteristics that contributed to the survival of this educational ring. All in all, our existence was to be a part of the master educational puzzle that rendered dollars.

After years of conversing with teachers all over the world, I discovered that teachers are multifaceted individuals. Teachers are like flowers that need the proper nurturing or they will turn into wilted weeds. Teachers are composed of massive energy and talent that often go unnoticed. Their talent is frequently suppressed by the system or an individual in a high-profile job. A teacher can become a stunning flower blossom if allowed. But this would take the support from a system that thinks about dollars only. The creativity of the teacher becomes stifled which ultimately hurts the growth of the students. Teachers become frustrated because they do not get the support they need to reach today's students and many of them just leave the system. If they don't leave, they practice the phase out mode or continue to fight against the grain until they burn out.

This in return means the system keeps control. The teacher must produce or be fired. That's the bottom line as harsh as it may seem. Most teachers across the border have come to this realization. Teachers understand that one of the reasons our reading scores are so low nationally is because enough emphasis is not put on the importance of education. Society has accepted that all students cannot be successful and those that die or get caught up in drugs are a loss we, as a people, are willing to take. This does not govern a solution or hope for new young teachers. Many of these young teachers stay in the system long enough to discover that IBM or MCI can offer a rewarding future. Many give all they can for a few years and decide it's not worth sacrificing their whole lives for. That is what it would take. Only a teacher would really understand the price paid to reach a small number of today's students.

The teachers who hang in there are troopers if they are being effective. They thrive on very little income or praise. The reward comes when a teacher sees a former student as an adult who has succeeded. Then their jobs make sense. It justifies the daily punishment the school system dishes out. It makes the day of retirement seem a little closer. I knew for me the age of sixty-five was too far away. My job was an assignment for me. I didn't know that in the beginning. I didn't know God's plans, but I knew God wanted to use me while I had a burst of energy. Regardless of the roughest hour, God assured me that I could make it as long as I trusted in him with my assignment. When the job was done, God would let me know when to move on. But in the interim, he was my strength as I was learning he would always be.

After comparing notes, stories, and unbelievable incidents with other teachers across the nation, I picked up my roll book realizing that Monday was to come. There was another week that awaited me with many trials and stories. These are stories that I share with you in hope that one day the truth will surface about our educational hierarchy. Hopefully this revelation won't be too late.

Ms. Howard and students do workshops.

*Students build homes in
engineering class.*

5

Babies Having Babies

Being pregnant at the age of thirteen is quite fashionable these days. This seems to make the student a hot commodity. I learned that students tried to get pregnant as soon as their menstrual cycles began. It is a fad that makes a teen-aged female feel like she is an adult. Many of the students feel that their value is in being fertile at an early age. Students as young as the sixth grade would come to class for months with clothing under clothing to give the appearance of being pregnant. I could not get used to this. On the other hand, the boys became studs after and only after they had fathered a child. Folks, we are talking about middle school. Whatever the reason for this trend, I found it to be a hindrance in the student's life.

I had an encounter with a student who put the "d" in the word disrespect. She was an extremely intelligent student who had a bright future ahead of her if she wanted it. She had a face that was deceiving. This student came from a respectable middle class moralistic single-parent home. She had a hard-working mother who gave her the best and raised her in the church. Her mother was one of the few who would come to the school to check on her child's well-being. Prior to meeting the mother, I expected a different parent. Her mother was kind, polished, and very spiritual. I was shocked as a result of the street behavior her child had displayed.

When I had my first encounter with this student, it was not a pleasant one. It occurred in the main office when I discovered the student munching on a piece of chicken. I noticed that no one seemed to mind that she was eating her lunch in the middle of the office where people come and go. I also noticed that no one seemed to mind that this student was always in the office when she belonged in class. When I questioned this student about her where - abouts, she was quite nasty. She told me in rather harsh words that it was none of my business. Now I thought it was any teacher's business in the building to be concerned with any student cutting class. Had I forgotten my job description as an educator? Obviously, from her response, I was out of order according to her.

Weeks later to my and the student's surprise, she was placed in my class. Her schedule had been revised multiple times because no teacher could control her. I was one of her last options. I was used to hard-core students at this time so this didn't faze me. I knew from the past that problems are just passed on and not dealt with. I was willing to work with this student. As intelligent as she was, I refused to let her not give setting goals a try. While taking on this challenge, I knew that her quick thinking could also get her in trouble.

Time went on as I tried to work with this difficult case. I told this student that when she cut classes, it was a reflection on me as her homeroom teacher. I also told her that her tardiness daily insulted me as her teacher. Little did I know that at this time she was experiencing morning sickness which caused her to come to class late every day.

Once in class, she caused confusion. She antagonized all the students. For some reason her pregnancy (that I knew nothing of at the time) gave her clout. While in class, she would run back and forth to the window to look for her baby's father. He was an ex-con who was said to have been involved in a murder. Because of this student's connection to the gang world, she would start fights consistently knowing that no one would dare touch her. Remember, this was while she was pregnant. On numerous occasions I had to keep her from fighting as well as keep her from wanting to get high. One day in particular, I found her in the hallway with a scent of fresh-smoked reefer. When I questioned her, she was wiping her mouth as if the reefer was detectable. She knew I caught her seconds after the action. She denied everything and went on her way. In leaving she left a trail of an upset stomach on the floor. Now, note that I had no idea that she was pregnant.

Am I blind or did I just not know what a pregnant thirteen-year-old should look like? Though this was not new to me, I didn't want to accept it. Well, neither did her mother. Weeks later, we both discovered that she had been hiding her pregnancy for six months. Her mother was almost in tears as she told me she had found out when I did. Her mother had done all she could to provide a better life for her child than what she had. She worked hard to give her the finest things and support. But this era had already had a tight hold on her daughter.

When the mother sat in my class and told me how she felt about being a grandmother in her thirties, I almost cried. She assured me that she had done all she could to raise a respectful child. All, she exclaimed, she got in return was a street girl who was fascinated with sex, criminals, and disrespect. The rage was so escalated in this mother that I could tell she wanted to just give her a street whipping to make up for all the ones she missed. I felt this mother's pain and put myself in her shoes. I can't say that I wouldn't have wanted to do the same. But it was too late for that. The world had already tainted her once-sweet little girl. Only God could whip her into shape with his love (Hebrews 12:6-11).

After gasping for air as a result of the excitement, the mother apologized to me for her daughter's rude behavior. She told me herself that she almost wanted to give up, so she felt sorry for her child's teachers. Well this statement was encouraging. When she left, I wondered what we are supposed to do with so many cases like this where the student isn't even manageable at home. What would happen to this student's baby, I wondered?

One day I was teaching my class with the door open and I heard screams bounce off the dirty hallway walls. I taught with the door open because it was a requirement regardless of the lack of adequate security. How could any of us forget the scissors incident mentioned earlier as a result of an open class door? Anyway, I could also hear feet scuffling down the hall at what seemed to be a rapid pace. There was some sort of event daily; therefore I thought it was just another one of those days. But for some reason this emergency was different. I could hear teachers talking among themselves with concern. I can remember wondering where their students were at this time. The chatter among the teachers began to get louder as the teachers began to display a nervous tone in their voices. I tried to listen as I continued to teach my class through the noise.

A student raced in my room while I was teaching and begged me to leave my class and join the other teachers. I was told at that time that a student was having a baby in the teachers' lounge and that my assistance was needed. A teacher had pushed the girl out of her class to the teacher's lounge in a chair that had wheels on it. She then centered the pregnant girl in the middle of the teachers' lounge. The student's water broke and the girl was about to have her baby when my presence was requested. Now the girl was only in the ninth grade and fourteen years old. I thought it was rather brave of her to stay in school, that long, pregnant.

So I went to the lounge, not knowing what to expect. Teachers were circling the girl asking each other what should they do. My first reaction was to help the girl. She was in a lot of pain and the baby wasn't waiting on us to make any decisions. So I proceeded to go near her when a colleague pulled me to the side and said, "I wouldn't touch her if I were you." He was a brilliant science teacher who had been burnt by parents and the system before. I usually listened when he had something to say.

He told me that if I touched her I could become liable for any mishaps that could occur. Therefore, he was just observing even though he could have delivered that baby. I said to him that the girl was about to drop the baby any moment. He reminded me that the teacher is everyone's dart board. So why would this day be any different? If anything, this situation would be magnified. He said I had to learn not to act on emotions and put myself in vulnerable situations. The bottom line was I had no friends in this career except other teachers. Many times that wasn't even the case. Teachers were conned by the system into backstabbing each other even if they didn't want to.

Parents continuously looked for ways to sue the teacher. We taught in the heart of the ghetto and parents seemed to think that we were their tickets out. Little did they know, we were fighting to get out, too. But given the right opportunity, the teacher could be sued. As stated before, there was little to no support from some principals or the superintendents' team. Reflecting on this, I paused in my steps and took his advice. I couldn't touch her or even say any kind words. Mental or physical abuse could have been a charge. So as hard as it was for me to phase out this event, I did. I knew he was right. That day was really rough for me and I felt like I turned my back on that child. What I did was exercise some wisdom based on reality.

But oddly enough, it didn't take that teacher twice to warn me. I knew the power in the parent's word versus the teacher. I knew the power of anyone's word versus the teacher. The student though only fourteen gave birth to a healthy boy. Eventually, the school was able to locate her very young parents and rush her to the hospital. The school waited until her father was contacted to take her to the hospital. It was a good thing that the baby was on CP time. In other words, as the Black community would say, "Colored People's Time."

I immediately reflected on an incident that almost put me in jail as a result of trying to help a student. Therefore, I ruled out the teachers' lounge that day. I didn't look back to avoid any tears that tried to surface. As I strolled back to my class, I recalled again the parent who wanted to have me arrested. I can remember thinking how pitiful our students are as a result of their parents. In many cases it was not the student's fault but the parents who provided no hope for the students.

Veryl Howard,
Val Brooks,
Heidi Doss
SECME teachers

Mrs. Howard teaching dance

6

The Forbidden Parent

There was a student in my room who had an extremely low self-esteem. Her behavior showed signs of a possible abusive situation at home. Her mother was a white Muslim and her father was a black dictator. Her mother showed signs in her disposition–physically as well as mentally–of being a victim of domestic violence. Other teachers had noticed this problem and we were trying to help the family as much as they could. The student was deprived of basic needs such as glasses. She was extremely bright but was unable to see the board. Her vision could have been mistaken for a deficit, intellectually, but it wasn't. The teachers were very in tune to her demeanor.

I invited the student to join the dance team. Other teachers along with me attempted to get her involved in extracurricular activities to boost her self-esteem. Many times we could reach our students this way. Outside of the class, they would view us differently. We were expected to teach the whole child, therefore we all thought dance class would bring this child out. I, along with the other teachers, was hoping to get to the root of her problem.

The little girl was excited about being in the dance group. She began to open up to the other students. This was what I had prayed for and I thought God heard my prayers. She began to feel proud about herself and acquired friends within the dance group. I had never seen her bond with anyone in the class and was happy about her progress. This student was one of my most gifted students, but was always too shy to express herself. She seemed to be in a world of her own. But dance was allowing her to express herself and let others into her hidden secrets. The dance group began to penetrate her comfort zone as she slowly revealed her painful secrets to the group.

As this student developed confidence in the group, she began to do the same in the class. Her parents began to let her perform all over the city with the group after school. I thought to myself one day that she was really on her way to deliverance. I began to celebrate prematurely, negating the fact that the devil was always busy.

One day the dance group was scheduled to perform after school. I did my normal routine, which was to load up my truck and drive to our destination. The parents had become used to us being little celebrities in our own right around the city. But regardless of their casual disposition, I always asked for permission, remembering the word of advice from the veteran science teacher. Most of the parents began to look for me to take their children out to perform. They knew that if they were with Ms. H., it had to be positive. I had begun to love my students as if they were my own children. Many of the parents thanked me for having such a caring attitude and were glad their children weren't out in the streets. I then learned that not all parents were out to sue the teacher; just the vast majority were. However, there were some who were extremely supportive of me after they learned to trust me. Anyway, this evening was a typical one for all of us after a performance.

I always walked my students to their doors, making sure that they arrived safely and were left in their parents' care. The other students would wait in my truck watching me as if they were my bodyguards until I dropped them off. They all thought I was pretty brave to walk in their neighborhoods at night. But it really didn't have anything to do with being brave. I truly cared about my students and God was showing me how to rebuke fear, even if it meant guns.

As the students watched me approach the front of this student's apartment building, they saw the same silhouette that I saw on the porch. It was the shadow of a man holding an object under the porch light. The student and I walked closer to the man as he held this long object in his hand. As we walked closer to the porch, the face of the man became clear, as did the object. He held a long, wide, leather belt in his hand. It had a big buckle on it that could hurt someone if struck with it. He popped the belt back and forth in his hands as if he was ready to whip the skin off someone.

The student began to cry as we walked closer to the man. She recognized him before I did. The man was her stepfather. The fear on this student's face was as if she had seen a stranger in a dark alley. The expression on her face made me very nervous and helped explain all the bruises she had in the past. The students in my truck watched us, not knowing what was really going on.

When we reached the porch, the man yelled at me and the student. He grabbed her and pushed her in the doorway behind him. He threatened to tear her to pieces the second I left. The little girl's face became pale with fear. My heart started racing and I could feel her beating that was to come. But I couldn't understand why. This was a typical night after a performance. We had permission and I didn't know why he was outraged. But the anger in the man only solidified that he was truly responsible for all the scars I had seen on her in the past.

The man stared me straight in the eyes, as a master would do a slave. He didn't even blink. At that time he must have forgotten that I was not his wife nor his child who would accept his insane behavior. He kept flapping that belt in my face and continued to yell at me. I tried not to flinch. He acted as if I was his next victim. I remember this as clearly as if it were yesterday. I thought he was crazy and I knew only the Lord could get me out of this situation. I just stood there as if I was packing a gun myself. I thanked him for letting his child participate, hoping this would lessen her whipping. I told her she was really progressing in school but that didn't seem to matter.

The man showed me with his response that he had had a bad

day and he was obviously going to take it out on me, too. I thought to myself that night, "This is why teachers don't go the extra mile." By this time the students in the truck knew that I was in danger. They became restless and I could see them moving in the truck. These students were about to join me in my defense. So I cried out to God and asked him to help me get out of this potentially fatal situation. This man let me know that I deserved a beating, too, according to him. Somehow God gave me the words to utter from my lips which scared the man off, though he was still angry. I slowly turned my back, trusting in God, and proceeded to walk back to my truck. I had to believe God and keep my cool at the same time.

I trembled as I walked to my truck, not knowing what the man was going to do. Again, I asked God to protect me with his angels, not knowing what I asked (Hebrews 13:5-6; Hebrews 1:14). When I approached the truck, the other students asked me if I was okay. I smiled with a solemn grin saying, "Yeah, I'll be okay." I told them to pray for their friend that night because I was afraid of what might happened to her.

When I reached home there were numerous messages on my answering machine from my principal. Prior to dropping off the student, without my knowledge, her stepfather had called the police on me. The principal who knew that we performed around the city was in alliance with the parent. I was not surprised. The principal rarely if ever supported the teachers in their efforts. She totally disregarded the existence of the program when the police were called. Knowing this, I became really upset but not shocked.

Many times we performed for the sick and shut-in, homeless, and more. We were a community outreach group that was well-loved around the city. Though this night we were not acknowledged, our programs were used to help the school's evaluations. We were merely a disposable group to the principal when it was not the end-of-the-year evaluation time. Though disturbed about this, that didn't affect my desire to reach these talented students. God was working on me as I helped them.

Surprisingly enough, the little girl returned to school sooner than I had expected. However, she was all banged up. Her bruises began to multiply with explanations as time progressed. I reported her appearance but nothing was done about it. All of the teachers were concerned but there was really nothing we could do. The student would deny being hit. Therefore, we were forced to turn our backs on a tragic situation. Sometimes this was a decision that had to be made to continue to reach the other students. The system wins again, I thought, but I was not ready to give up.

Battered situations were common in the building. Many of the parents took their frustration out on the students and there was very little the teachers could do without evidence. The student would have to admit to the abuse and a lot of times they wouldn't. The teacher would be left alone trying to point out a problem that society, as well as the school system, could care less about. With this mentality, I asked God to never let me get cold-hearted.

There was a student of mine who wasn't willing to stay silent after multiple beatings from her mother. The student was struck frequently with a baseball bat by her parents, which eventually led to her speaking out. Usually the students are torn between being homeless and living in a dangerous situation with a roof over their heads. Many times the roof is chosen. This student, who was rather sassy in her ways, decided to fight back. Though sassy, her punishment was inhumane.

My church reached out to this student and fought to have her placed in a safe environment. She was one of the students I took to church on Sundays. She had become a part of my church family and her happiness was important to us. During the battle, the church was able to place her in one of our church member's homes at least until restrictions were put on the parent. This issue became one that eventually resulted in a safe environment while the parent was monitored. Despite the scarring, this student found happiness in becoming a mother while still in high school. Like some of my other students, I was just happy to see her alive.

Unfortunately, a vast majority of the students I taught were products of cracked-out parents. The parents were young and still trying to find themselves. There were parents that were my age and I was in my twenties. My brother even told me about a great-grandparent who was in her late thirties. He taught her great-grandchild. Now hearing this, I was outdone. We were teaching children whose parents we could have gone to school with, even though we were fresh out of college ourselves.

One of my first encounters with a cracked-out family was in my first couple of years of teaching. After that it was everyday life. There was this one student I had who seemed to always have a clothing problem. She was bright, talented, and well known. Most of the other students loved her but yet feared her. One of the reasons was her big sister, who stayed in reformatory schools or jail for misbehaving. Her sister had done everything from stabbing people to breaking in homes. As a matter of fact, when I first started teaching, her sister was in a jail or a prison for teenagers. Regardless of her location, every student in the school knew of this girl's sister and wouldn't dare bother her. Even teachers were scared to correct her. I guess I had to find out the hard way. I was never one to be scared unless the situation was life-threatening. Because of the grace of God, many incidents were dangerous, but God kept me from being fearful (2 Timothy 1:7).

This student joined my dance group and began to go to church with the rest of my appointed church crew. She was becoming a young lady trying to deal with her problems at home. Her family, like many of the others, became a part of my life. Her family consisted of grandparents who were very old from the beatings of society. They struggled to take care of her and her sister who was in and out of jail. There were never any parents in the picture.

I soon discovered that her parents were crack addicts. As with many of my other students, this was not uncommon at all. Her parents were the epitome of crack-heads. Her father was in jail for being a drug dealer, and her mother stayed drugged-out on crack, heroin, or any drug she could get her hands on. This student had practically grown up with no parents. I was soon to become her adopted mother/teacher.

Well, my family had taken her under their wings. We helped her with clothes, money, or whatever she needed to go to school.

It was nothing for my family to take her home after church or after one of our dance performances. One day I went by her house to pick her up for one of our performances in the community. While I and another student waited on this student, the police knocked on the door. There were teenagers sitting on the porch when I entered the house. One of them was her big sister who had just been released from jail. Now the police asked for whom I thought was her big sister. Knowing that she was on the front porch, I wondered why they came into the house. Did they miss the teenagers on the porch that they had to step over just to knock on the door?

The grandmother told the police that she didn't know where her other granddaughter was. The police had obviously been made out to be incompetent. When they asked the teenagers on the porch about the where-abouts of this student's big sister, they all said they didn't know where she was. Now the teenager they asked was the one they were looking for. I guess I didn't really know how God had been protecting me. The sister was able to escape while the police were in the house talking to the grandparents.

In time, due to all the stress from life, this student's grandfather died and her grandmother struggled to hold on to her life. The mother was found dead from an overdose and the father was released from jail only to go right back. The big sister stayed on the run creating a new identity for herself. This girl had no one. Some how, this girl was able to graduate and go on to high school. The teachers were instrumental in pulling together to help this student graduate.

Though she graduated from middle school, this student soon became a mother in high school, as did her friends. Again, this gave her something to live for when her whole world seemed to crumble around her.

Ms. Howard takes a group of students to National Airport.

Ms. Howard does engineering classes at U.Va. with other teachers.

IRA students go to Canada, May 11, 1994

7

The PTA, The FBI, and the Neighborhood

PTA (Parents Teachers Association) nights were the nights that most teachers dreaded. These were usually long-drawn-out nights that didn't suggest any overtime. Teachers were usually in the building as late as ten o'clock after a long day's work. These nights were designed so that the parents could meet with the teachers and discuss any problems their child or children were having. Usually the parents of the most problematic students didn't show up. If they did they always questioned the teacher's word. These parents didn't want to believe the teacher. So many times the problem was never resolved.

One PTA night outweighs them all. This was when I first started teaching in the ghetto. I was sitting at a table with the rest of the science teachers when an intoxicated parent stepped in front of me. This parent swayed while she talked to me and the smell of liquor reeked from her mouth. She was so loud that everyone turned to listen to what she had to say. The administration and some teachers in this school were always looking for drama. The support system was terrible and teachers thrived on someone else's confusion. Knowing this, I knew that all the eyes in the cafeteria were plastered on me and this parent. So I braced myself with the most professional, cool demeanor I could dig up.

Being cool, Christ-like, and calm, I listened to what this parent had to say while she spit all over me (Matthew 5:39-44). She exclaimed that she was mad over a grade I gave her child. While she hovered over my head as I sat in the chair, I politely told her that her son deserved worse than what I had given him. I was giving him the benefit of the doubt since it was the first semester. This wasn't good enough for her. She became very loud and irate while wanting to fight me. Again, in a very–and I mean very–stern voice, I assured her that I didn't change grades nor fight over them. I respectfully assured her that her threats did not scare me and our conversation was over changing grades.

Teachers had been instructed discreetly to change grades at times. Well, this was not a part of my philosophy. I relayed that to her. I was willing to work out a strategy to help her son get on track and out of trouble, but she wasn't happy with that. Not having anything else to discuss at this point, I kindly went to the next parent, feeling sorry for the son of this one. But this could only be done after I put her in her place once she threatened me. It was all done in a tactful, Christ-like manner.

After this parent's dramatization, I was glad when PTA was over. It was dark, late, and we all needed to prepare for the next day. I proceeded to walk outside with a group of teachers when we all noticed men dressed in black FBI-looking uniforms around the school. They were also circling around the apartment buildings where our cars were parked. They scaled these buildings with long, black objects in their hands that resembled guns. These objects varied in size.

As we walked closer to our cars we asked the men why they were outside with what appeared to be guns. They told us that they were doing a drug bust and that we had to wait to get in our cars. How wonderful, as if the PTA meeting wasn't enough. Well, we followed instructions as we watched. When given the right signal we all dashed to our cars. En route, we saw the men bring one of our student's parents out of the building with restraints. This did not surprise us but saddened us. Most of us taught the student and could only wonder how he would face us and other students that next day. Imagine the community standing outside watching this episode. I can't say what ultimately happened to that child but he was in school for awhile. This type of arrest became quite common in this community. The students were immune to shame after awhile.

I could always count on an episode when leaving or returning to school. I had to either walk though the neighborhood when my car decided not to work, or drive through. I tried to avoid driving because teachers' cars were always being vandalized. Though mine was old, it was not too old to be tampered with. I still had a functioning battery.

One day when driving through the neighborhood, leaving school, a student jumped out in front of my car. He had an object in his hand and put it in my window while I was at the stop sign. The object appeared to be a gun. He said to me, while my heart almost jumped out of my chest, that, "This is a stick up." Now this statement wasn't too far-fetched for this student. He came from a chain of drug dealers and was running drugs himself. I had every reason to believe him. Well, after fighting for my heartbeat to return to normal, he said to me "SYKE," which is a word we all recognized as joking. Again, you could have bought me for two cents. I was so nervous that I couldn't believe it was a joke. The gun was a play one that looked too real to me.

I scolded this boy the best way I knew how while not verbally abusing him or physically abusing him. But I scared him with the stern yet polite words I said. God had truly been working on me. Under normal conditions, prior to salvation, I would have beaten him to a pulp. But because of God, I was able to see the devil in disguise. This was a child who could become lost like so many others. So I spared him my ghetto tactics, thanks to God (2 Timothy 2:24-26). Time went on and eventually he was killed in one if his drug transactions. I told him with my incident that most people wouldn't take his jokes as kindly as I did. Well, I was right, though I didn't want to be.

Ms. Howard in class with students

Ms. Howard building a boat

8

El Salvador Merges
with the System

Just when I felt like throwing the towel in again, another child was reached. It's amazing, when God has a plan it's best to just move out of the way. God is going to be God and his work will be done. Either we submit to his will and do the job he has called us to do or we resist and still the job will get done.

There was a new student in the school who spoke little to no English. He had been in the country less than a week and was already thrown into a school system that could not meet his special needs. I wondered why he was placed in an environment where Spanish classes weren't even an option. But then again the unexpected was always expected. Therefore, I didn't harp on the idea too long. I just made myself available to assist this student when I could. I imagined how I would feel in his shoes.

This student had a homeroom next door to mine. I had taken extensive classes in Spanish and would help his homeroom teacher obtain basic information from the student when applicable. I began to notice that other students picked on him and treated him as if he was mute. It was a trying situation for this little boy. I couldn't believe the system had done such a thing. Within the first week of school, the little boy began to use curse words–some of the worst ones in the book. Of all words that he could learn, he was most fascinated with the curse words. I would hear him walk down the hall sayings these foul words repeatedly. I figured out that this was his way of counteracting all the attacks from the other students.

One day as this boy walked by my room cussing, I stopped him. I addressed him in Spanish, hoping that I conjugated my verbs correctly. He walked over to me with a smile. I guess he felt that someone could identify with his culture. I asked him in Spanish about how he learned all the negative words. He immediately said that the other students taught him the words. He said he remembered the students using those same words to speak to him, so he learned them. He also revealed that the children hit him in class and that he felt tormented being in his new school environment. He said he didn't understand a word of what any of his teachers were saying and felt lost in America. I could feel his sorrow as he spoke.

Well, we made a deal. Even though I was not his homeroom teacher, I would teach him during my free period if he would stop cursing. Also, he had to help me brush up on my Spanish. I would only talk to him in Spanish while he had to learn to reply in English. So this was a deal that we established. His teachers would send all his work to me daily. I would help him in all his subjects and at the end of the day he would take his completed assignments to his teachers. This seemed to work for the teachers as well as the student. But in the meantime I was getting over-worked. Since the school offered no help, we all felt obligated. The teachers knew that they were expected to pass him whether or not he spoke English. The system had already established this for all teachers.

Regardless of the hurdles, the student and I worked hard as he learned English. This little boy had been stripped from his family in El Salvador because of violence in the country. Even though he was safe for now, he was culturally deprived. He trusted no one and thought everyone wanted to harm him.

Within months, he was talking English in bits and pieces. He used to say to me that he wanted to be a professional singer. "Me gusta a cantar," which means, "I like to sing." He had learned a lot of words from memorizing songs he mimicked from the radio. Knowing this, I used singing to teach him English. It wasn't long before he became one of our after-school pack members. He also went to church with this group God had placed in my care for the year. He danced with the dance group and did drama as well. The students began to love him and his sense of humor when he couldn't remember a word. He even told me about a little black girl he had a crush on, though they had a hard time communicating. He really was adapting to his new environment. But this was all done by the grace of God.

All of the administrators thought I was crazy for taking on such a task with this particular student. Like others, they felt this case was hopeless. But what they didn't know was that I served a God who was bigger than a speaking barrier. I served a God who operated on the principle of love that covers all barriers. The ridicule, I reasoned, was a result of a non-caring disposition from the administrative staff. I often wondered why they selected a profession that required more than criticism from them. But I remembered that the test scores and passing statistics were all that were important. What a disfigured society we live in.

Despite the doubt from others and the lack of support, I just kept working with this student as well as the others. I would partner with corporations that wanted to give back to the community. Many times the corporations would provide funding and teaching materials so that these students could be rewarded for their achievements. Like my Spanish-speaking student, many of them were ambitious and just needed an opportunity. After the defensive walls were broken down and the trust was established, progress could be seen in many of them. Many of my corporate sponsors were instrumental in providing me with the tools I needed to take that student to the next level.

The basketball team in the Washington area known as the Bullets would donate tickets to the students. The team was a partner that I established as a means of having an incentive program for those students receiving good grades. When my students excelled,

I would give them tickets to the game and they would meet the basketball players. My mother and I would load up our trucks and take the students to the games as well as other outings. One night away from gunshots really made a difference in a lot of my students' lives.

One weekend we took my Spanish-speaking student with a truckload of other students to a professional basketball game. His parents, who were his big sister and brother, trusted me at this time and were happy he went out with other students. We all agreed that his first experience at a professional basketball game with other students would be one he would cherish for the rest of his life. This experience became one that I would cherish, too. When I think of this weekend I chuckle and a smile comes to my face.

When we went to the stadium, my Spanish-speaking student's eyes lit up. It was so rewarding to me as a teacher to see his joy that he expressed in his face. The other students were astonished too. They had never been to a professional game either. Clinging to my every step I took, this student was sucking in the new environment. I noticed that, though excited, he was scared to let my coat loose. I had become his link to society that night because no one else with us spoke Spanish. Therefore, I established the guidelines early on. He was not to leave my sight. All of these students were my responsibility when I had them with me. By all means, I was not going to lose a student who couldn't communicate his address if need be. I watched all my students as if they were my own children.

The game was exciting and the night was almost over. It was time to go back to my students' real world that they identified with. Each student had been given a partner to be responsible for at all times. The students had to be escorted by an adult even if they wanted to purchase popcorn. Well, the rules were established and we proceeded to exit the building.

Without any warning, a mad rush occurred in the crowd. Still holding on to my group, I led them to the door through the scuffling crowd. Just as we were about to exit, a student expressed the need to go to the bathroom. Knowing we had quite a drive, I suggested that everyone go. Why did I do that? When I turned my back for less than a second, my Spanish-speaking student had disappeared. I can remember asking my mother where he disappeared to that quickly. I was frantic. You could have bought me for one penny this time. I had never been that nervous before in my life over a student. Here I was trying to be as careful as possible and I lost the one child who didn't speak English. He didn't even know his phone number.

All types of thoughts circled around in my mind. They started out with the principal who thought I was crazy, the parents who trusted me, and the child's fear. My mother, the students, and I searched that stadium until security put us out. By this time, I could feel my black hair turning gray. I was sobbing in my inner being but trying to keep my cool. I didn't know what to think or do. I tried to keep a cool disposition so that the other students would not get nervous. But no matter how hard I tried, I was scared and they knew it.

So we all walked to the parking lot still looking for my student. The parking lot was empty except for my mother's van and my truck. We could see from afar. As we walked closer to the rides, I could feel the fear from the other students. They had grown to love this student, and were concerned about their new foreign friend. We were now less than six feet from the rides and who did we see in the dark? Yes, it was my Spanish-speaking student. He was standing at my truck with the biggest smile on his face. He was eating a bag of popcorn as if he did not know that he had been lost. In his eyes we were obviously the lost ones. I learned that day, that even though he was limited verbally his brain wasn't.

He knew where the truck was and in his own way was meeting us there. All I could do was laugh when I saw him. I felt like a mom who had lost her child to an adoption agency and had just been reunited with her child. I wanted to cry. The students and I gave him a hug to let him know that we were worried. It was a happy moment for all of us. We could now go home and prepare for the trials that society had to offer the next day.

Though I don't teach this child any more, I often wondered

about his well-being. I had restless nights one week thinking about his safety. I asked some of his old teachers and the students to see if they knew of his where-abouts. Not to my surprise, his family moved him out of the neighborhood because of the danger he faced daily traveling to school in a strange country. His big sister and brother sent him to live in Maryland with another relative hoping that he would be provided a better education. Even though I knew the school system was better equipped, I wasn't sure about his safety. I knew he was in danger.

This feeling I had in my spirit troubled me to the point of driving to his old apartment and questioning his sister and brother who were raising him at one time. When I saw his siblings, they were surprised to see me. A couple of years had passed and they thought I, like many, had forgotten about my former students. I assured them that I never stop caring. I pray that even as adults they are prosperous and in good health. They were impressed that someone really cared. I was glad that they were so receptive to my popping by. I had taken a chance in hoping that someone still lived there who was related to my former student. To my surprise, they remembered me and were very resourceful.

What I discovered that day really took a toll on my emotions. The sister told me that my former student had been caught in crossfire on his way home from school. He was walking home from school and two students were arguing and shot at each other but hit my former student. He was innocently shot and almost killed over a teenage dispute that he had nothing to do with. As she told me this story over loud Latin music, I began to cry. She told me that he was bed-ridden but was doing better. She called him on the phone so that I could talk to him. I tried to speak to him through my tears. Though hard, I found a way to bring up happier moments—especially those when he tried to sing.

He said to me that he had moved to avoid being killed in the school I worked in. Little did he know that he would be shot on his way home from school in another district altogether. At that point, I realized that though the school system I worked in was unbelievable and unsafe, teenagers today are dangerous regardless of where they live. We as educators really had our work cut out for us and unless the school system regrouped, society was in trouble.

Fortunately for this student, God healed his body. He had been pierced in the stomach by a bullet that almost left him in a coffin. He couldn't eat and had to be waited on. He had missed a lot of school as a result and was just trying to hang on to his life. Now, here is a child that survived the violence in his country which exhibited barbaric behavior, yet he comes to America to get shot. What a dichotomy.

Well, I closed out with this student with words of encouragement. I told him that one day I would try to visit him and that I knew God would restore him. I hung up knowing that I would pray for him when God placed him in my heart to pray for. But by all means, I never dreamed that the school system would ever place a non-English-speaking student in an English-speaking public school again. Boy, was I wrong.

This past year I experienced another student who only smiled if you asked him a question. He hadn't even had science in his native country. How was he to pass a standardized test at the end of the year, I thought? This wasn't just any standardized test, either. This was a test that would determine if the teacher was fired and not based on the student's performance. All I could think was that the system was designed for the teacher to fail.

SECME, Sept. 26, 1996

Ms. Howard wins award as runner-up in National Teacher of the Year (SECME). From left: Dr. Howard's mother; Delores Braxton; Dr. Calvin Brooks; Dr. Howard.

9

In Retrospect of the Good Old Days

All of my days weren't bad. There were some good ones generated after a lot of hard work. Students began to shine on their tests, in contests, and in extra-curricular activities. Though they were poverty-stricken, many of them would beat the odds and surpass the upper middle class schools in competitions. Many of them were Percy Julians or Madam C.J. Walkers waiting to be discovered. They were bright but needed a helping hand and someone to believe in them when their families didn't. The teacher was that someone in most cases. But despite some of the worst situations, there was always that one child who stomped on the word "quit" or that one administrator who believed in you even though his or her job was on the line. I experienced this eventually in my soon-to-be new school. There was that one parent who helped you with your events. There was even that one child who could say one word that would brighten your day. All in all, there were some who fought to make a difference in their genecidal dilemma.

Many of my students received scholarships, topped district standardized tests, won national awards, and excelled in all they set out to accomplish. They began to believe in themselves with hope of having a future. Parents were even inspired to finish their education as a result of taking classes with their students. I provided workshops in the afternoons for the parents as well. Many parents became my friends and still stay in touch with me today. Many of my students could even teach me different ways to deliver a lesson which made me proud.

But the most important accomplishment was when those who were gang leaders, thieves, sexually promiscuous, and drug runners turned their lives around to the Lord. These were my happiest moments. To see a sinner who didn't care about life come clean and value life was success to me. My work was not in vain. My students were learning that they were important and regardless of what the world thought, God loved them. God's love was enough hope when there was no hope from man.

Veryl Howard and students with Kellie Williams of "Family Matters"

10

My Father's Death

There was always a ray of hope in my mind about receiving support from the school system. One day I refused to harp on the negative though I was working under a superintendent's team that didn't even want to give teachers a raise. But I always tried to look at the positive when there wasn't one. I refused to believe that teachers were mere toys that the superintendent's team played with on any given day.

The teacher was disposable to the system and that was no secret. Knowing this I still tried to keep a positive look on things. I hoped that one day a revelation would sweep through the superintendent's office–one that would open up the eyes of those who were in authoritative positions to make a change in the teaching profession though they hadn't, thus far. But again I was wrong. Not even in a time of sorrow was there any support. There was a "stoic persona" that seemed to have been embedded in the superintendent's team, administrators, and secretaries. They were all on the same page that the teacher was not privy to. My father's death made this page comprehensible to me even though I wanted to skip past it.

My father, who was a bilateral amputee, once taught in the school system. When I was a child, he taught in the same old, dirty building that I was now teaching in. As a matter of fact, some of the same teachers who taught with him were now teaching with me. It was amazing how his stories years earlier resembled some of mine years later. The system hadn't gotten better but worse. There were solutions still floating in the air from the time when my father began teaching. How sad!! There had even been very little cosmetic adjustment made since he taught at the school. The same drab look the school had when I was a child was still apparent. Children were changing with the times but the school system wasn't.

I remember my father telling me before he died that to be a teacher you had to play the game. He was never a game player and I sure wasn't going to be. He told me that the bottom line was about the old school cliques that ran the school system and not about the children. He knew that I was dedicated to teaching. He told me, "Don't look for any accolades or praise in return. Just go in your class and give it your all. Don't get caught up in the games because the games will come to you if you do your job." In other words, folks are jealous and don't want to see you really do a good job. You must be a part of the clique, the end crowd that takes directions. "Don't be too creative on your own and don't expect a certificate," was what he uttered.

Hearing this from my father did not surprise me. After all, most of his stress was initiated from teaching and trying to make a difference. He was one of many teachers who was brilliant but the system beat him down, never appreciating his gifts. It ultimately drove him to excessive smoking and drinking which left him with amputated legs. I wasn't about to allow the system to strip me of my life as it had done him. Being a pawn in the school system aided in his heart conditions which ultimately took his life at an early age. But the sad part is, the school system had no remorse and I learned this the hard way. So many teachers scraped up every ounce of energy they could find to reach that child the system didn't care about. But yet they died unnoticed.

Knowing that my father had a serious health condition, I alerted my school in case of an emergency. The secretaries knew that I transported my father to and fro and that his days were numbered.

However, the head secretary never had a kind word to say when my father would call for me. She was instructed from the top knowing that my father was ill not to put too much emphasis on his call. But this type of attitude is not unique to any school building. I'm sure many teachers can attest to this. Teachers were never given messages in our building in a timely, professional manner. This went along with the job.

Many times teachers had emergency situations where they would alert those who answered the phone. But because of the lack of professionalism in the D.C. public school system, many requests were ignored, even if they were life-threatening situations. Secretaries were taught from the top that the teacher was at the bottom of the totem pole. The level of respect wasn't even honored from the secretary who basically made more than the teacher. This attitude trickled down into each office throughout the city. When the top sets the tone, everyone else follows.

I remember requesting my principal to have the secretary answer the phone in a professional manner. Too many times people such as my father were harassed when asking to speak to a loved one in an emergency situation. Cruel statements were made to my father up until his death. They all revolved around his physically handicapped state. Though obnoxious statements, they were never addressed by the principal. The reply was always the same: "So what, Ms. Howard? You teach in the ghetto. Worry about the end-of-the-year test scores."

But this cold disposition, which frequents the lives of some administrators, didn't top my principal's ultimate action. After confronting the principal about my emergency call that was not addressed, my father soon died. Now this was the call I hoped not to receive. However, once it happened, I took it in stride, taking only his funeral day off from work. Well, many other teachers, in support of me, put in for a half-day to attend the funeral. To no surprise, they were docked pay for missing school. They were obviously scrutinized for trying to support another teacher and concluded that they taught in a no-win school district. We knew the only support we had was each other.

The docking of pay was a tactic used to create animosity among us. However, we were smarter than that. We were a group of young teachers who refused to let the traditional philosophy keep us from being effective in the classroom. We knew that if we stuck together as a team, we could reach more students as well as an uncaring school system. But in time we were separated when we didn't despise each other's wisdom. A game plan was designed to strategically dismantle a group of innovative teachers to a group of pawns on a chess board waiting to be moved.

Ms. Howard in boat building class

11

Talk to a Teacher

The school system seemed to thrive off the competitiveness and division that could be generated among the teachers. If everyone lived in fear about their jobs, then they would work harder. Well, this was the mind set of the school system. **Pink slip them every year! Don't give them raises! Furlough them every opportunity you get! Create animosity among the teachers! Don't be sympathetic to their needs! Don't give them any supplies! And, last but not least, pay yourself an enormous salary!!!!!!**

Teachers were supposed to be like supermen. We were all warned by our principals that we were to drag into work even if we needed medical attention. Too many absentee emergencies would be reflected in a teacher's evaluation. I questioned the need for substitutes. The school system seemed to never have them available when needed, even when there was a bereavement need. When they did finally come, they were usually overwhelmed by the disrespect of the students as well as the adults.

Substitutes had to be begged to return to many schools, including mine. When they did return, their attitudes were nonchalant because of the lack of support they would receive. Many would let the students destroy a classroom while they sat and accumulated pay. The teacher would usually return to class needing to regroup. This meant everything from fixing up the torn-up room to re-establishing ground rules. But I don't blame the substitutes. I blamed the system which threw a stranger into a room with today's students without the tools needed to reach them. This task was hard enough for the teacher, let alone the substitute. This behavior left the teacher with no room to become ill. A teacher must sacrifice personal needs daily to be successful according to the system.

The message of this book is by no means meant to depress you because there is some hope. This book was written to educate you so that you can do your part in making a difference. We are living in times where people disregard each other as human beings with feelings. Everyone is out to save their own and could care less about the child who lives on the street.

Unfortunately, this attitude is prevalent in the educational arena while the child still lives in the halls. The parents have given their children to a school system that doesn't want them either. This must change. We are denaturing brilliant minds in the schools when we don't challenge them and provide the tools necessary for them to expand. We can no longer sit back and run away from our responsibilities as a society. Continuously ignoring the problems in the educational arena is equivalent to adding another child living on the streets. The teacher is only a small portion of the village needed to raise the child. We all are guilty as a society if we ignore the deceit that exist in our school systems.

If you talk to most teachers, you will discover much of what is being revealed to you in this book. A teacher will tell you in confidence what little the system really has to offer the student as well as the teacher. But this must be done in confidence to prevent the teacher from losing his or her job. The teacher in many cases knows that the profession has become one of short-term status with them and hence will talk. These were teachers who once thought on a long-term basis, but the system redirected their careers.

"Short-term" has become the jargon for most of the new teachers in the nineties. Many college graduates only look at teaching as a transitional job. They graduate from school knowing the disarray and choose to deal with it on a short-term basis until a better job is secured. I can't say that I blame them. What they have done is exhibited a non-loyal attitude to a system that is not going to be loyal to them. Basically they use the system.

Many new teachers acknowledge that the low pay scale in conjunction with all the other problems teachers face is too much for long-term employment. Like many of the students, these teachers look for a short-term reward where their values are appreciated. Nowadays, only those who are fortunate enough to be in lucrative educational systems stick with them if they are new teachers. The others stay because they are still trying to reach that one child or they have been in the system so long they are scared to make a move. Therefore, they put up with the unnecessary abuse until retirement. My reason was because God had given me appointments. He assured me that he would remove me when he was ready. I was learning that daily, even if it meant that my life was on the line during my short-term.

Cory Martin wins science fair award in Ms. Howard's class.

Ms. Howard and student shoot a commercial with other teachers

12

Dance Practice Could Have Ended with a Bang

One day I really thought my life had become short-termed. I found a student perched in a chair with a loaded gun during my dance rehearsal. No one seemed to be shocked or even have the nerve to remove this student who waited to shoot his moving target. One security guard eventually alerted me about the student with the gun. But this was done after a half an hour of dance practice.

It was routine for me to practice with the students after school in the auditorium. Many times other students would want to watch as spectators. Knowing the problems that this could cause, I wasn't having it. Everyone in the auditorium had to have permission and was a part of the dance or drama group. I would put spectators out of the auditorium so the practice could run smoothly. Well, on this day the spectator was a confused drug runner who was toting a loaded gun. I recognized the student from all the tragedies he caused in the building. He was one of the school's hardest cases and many adults feared him. But this day he was to be my problem.

Oddly enough this tyrant liked me as a teacher, even though I did not teach him. Many of the roughnecks would talk to me or even try to harass me when they were troubled. They knew that they could trust me and talk to me when they needed a caring ear. Well, I had been a caring ear to this student before. I would always use a stern voice when talking to him. I did not hesitate to correct him and he respected that. He couldn't believe that a teacher would stand up to him. But even though I held my ground, I knew he practiced dangerous behavior and many times I was nervous. He had in the past displayed borderline psychotic behavior and I knew that. He had homicidal tendencies and this day was not any different. Therefore, I used my most stern voice, not showing him my fear.

I found out the student had the gun after the security guard could not get him to leave the auditorium. The security guard whispered in my ears that he had a gun. I freaked out, not knowing how I was going to remove him. After all, before knowing that he had a gun, I had asked him to leave the auditorium. Of course, he did not budge. I was blessed when I went to him not knowing what the circumstances were. He could have shot up the whole auditorium if he chose to. Here I was again. Me and God.

As I kept asking him to leave, a voice kept telling me not to push him. The voice said, ask him nicely and get on with your practice. I must have spotted the lunacy in his eyes. Well, with the help of the security guard we were able to convince him to leave. But it was not easy. We were able to escort him out and carry on with the practice. It was sad, though. No one was shook up but me. The principal acted as if the whole ordeal did not occur. This scared me even more. I knew the children had become immune to danger, but not the principal. This was an incident swept under the rug, like others.

After this episode, I decided to let the principal know that I was not going to pretend that I taught at a perfect school. No longer was I going to camouflage the incidents that we were faced with. I was becoming intolerant of my principal's denial state and she knew it. I was not willing to play the game like other teachers. This was the same game that my father had warned me about, but this game could cost you your life. There was a time when it only required you to give up your dignity, but today it would cost your life. My job became irrelevant to me after this gun ordeal. The students as well as myself were sitting ducks for a crazy person with a gun. The irony of it all was we waited to be shot in a so-called school environment My survival skills were progressing daily. Just to function, it was almost a must that you wore a bullet-proof vest. God had to really work with me to return to school that next day.

I began to despise the building and all those associated with the big lie. Nothing was as it appeared in the papers. It was all a facade. I kept pressing on, knowing that one day that big lie would send me out the door. But again God would tell me when to leave. Character was still being developed in me. I was learning to sacrifice for another human being and throw selfish thoughts out the window. But in the meantime, I was tired of the big educational lie.

I was tired of being asked to change standardized test papers that I refused to change. I was tired of being given the answers ahead of time to share with the students. I was tired of the administration blaming the teacher for every problem in the building. I was tired of being rejected when I asked for a pay raise that was due to me. I was tired of not getting a response from the superintendent's team when a teacher had a concern. They were unapproachable and invisible to the teacher unless they were degrading the teacher. No longer was I willing to keep my mouth shut in regard to the big lie. I was a walking time bomb like most teachers who are frustrated with the system. School was not supposed to be this way!!

Whatever happened to the teacher who was respected for being a teacher? Whatever happened to the star who acknowledges his or her teacher as someone making a difference in his or her life? Whatever happened to a union that could reach a superintendent's team to express the teacher's concern? Whatever happened to real test scores that reflected the truth about our students' level of achievement? Whatever happened to the moral code of ethics that once existed in the profession? Whatever happened to the team approach to teach that one child? Whatever happened to the supplies that the taxpayers' dollars were paying for? Whatever happened to the safety that once existed in the school building when the parent left the child? Whatever happened to the healthy lunches that were some children's only meals? Whatever happened to the respect among coworkers? Whatever happened to the mission statement that we were taught to learn? Whatever happened to the pay raise that was promised in a teacher's contract? All of these issues were concerns that I did not want to ignore.

My principal knew that I was not willing to perpetrate the lie and therefore I was watched under a microscope. I had become a marked teacher, meaning that I was one who did not play the game with the school system or the students. But though marked, I still relied on God. I knew that I would be able to overcome each trial and circumstance. I also knew that when my assignment was over I was moving on. So I pressed on being honest and continued to teach, correct, and reach out to my students. But that did not mean that the devil was not still busy. Students would still be students of today. With that came a lot of hostile behavior that I constantly prepared for. My faith did have its share of testing with both the students and the school system.

Five years quickly passed even though it seemed like a century. I knew my body and mind had to be in tip-top shape to withstand five more. The teacher had to stay on guard in all situations. Many of the older teachers had shared incidents with me that made mine seem like a piece of cake. I wondered how they dealt with their families. Many of the teachers had experienced serious illnesses triggered from stress and were just hanging on. I had decided that my stress was going to be dealt with each day to avoid any build-up. This was why I chose not to play the game.

13

The Firecracker

As usual, I was teaching my little heart out with the door open when a lit firecracker flew into my face. Some students were running up and down the halls throwing firecrackers into classrooms. Most of the teachers on my back hall either had their doors locked or weren't in their rooms. This was my lucky day. The firecrackers blew up in my face causing a burn on my neck. Now at this time I had a room full of students sitting in my class. But I was standing in the front of the class when the firecrackers flew in the room. The students were sitting down in their chairs facing me. Fortunately for the school none of them were up moving about That would have been a law suit.

Having the firecrackers hit me was enough. I stormed out of my room with the shells in my hand and took them to the principal's office. My body was still shaking from this event. The principal looked at me calmly and shook her head. She knew from the tone of my voice that this time I had had it. I had stood enough of these little bodily harm episodes.

Teachers were threatened constantly in the class. Students had weapons in the building and the principal would not alert the teacher. I had lost all confidence in my principal and wondered what her true purpose was. She must have been in the clique to continue to maintain her job. Some of these tragedies she could not hide. But she played the game well enough to keep her good administrative job. I asked her what was she going to do about this student. Was he going to be ignored, too? She knew that her time was running out with me before I would report her negligence. Therefore, she did all she could to make my days a living hell. But that was all right. I knew in time the truth would surface. Just like it says in the scriptures, I had been learning whatever is done in darkness will come to light. Living a lie was darkness to me. I knew it would be resolved in God's time.

Time went on and nothing was done about the young man who had thrown the firecracker. But that didn't surprise me. But what did amaze me was an episode that had occurred in the building with another teacher whom the principal and school system wanted to ignore. A teacher was sexually harassed by some students after an aide had been raped in our building. The teacher spoke out about her fear on this issue, but she was ignored by the system, though not ignored by the news. Parents just couldn't have known all we dealt with in this building as teachers. I knew that I had to get out of there as the truth was busting out of me.

The teacher couldn't get any other teachers to speak up on her behalf. They wouldn't even speak on incidents that happened to them—much less those that happened to someone else. I told her she was basically on her own but I would support her about all the safety problems we were being faced with. So the two of us wrote the union while other teachers gave us encouraging words in secret. We asked the union to look into some of these threatening problems that the school had. It was no secret that we wanted a safe environment to teach in.

After numerous letters to the superintendent, union, and principal, absolutely nothing was done. Again it was as if nothing ever happened. The news even found our stories outrageous but that didn't trigger a change in the superintendent's or the principal's mind. But I knew that it was a matter of time before their high paying jobs that took the place of students' supplies would snare them eventually. Therefore, I left them to God while I continued to support what I thought was justifiable.

Meanwhile, the school system continued to deny many instances of violence in the schools. My environment became more of a challenge as my principal put restrictions on me. I began to notice spots on my neck where the firecracker hit me as well as on other parts of my body. I also began to bleed to the point of needing steroid medication. The doctor had told me that all the trauma I had endured was taking a toll on my physical condition. I then remembered my father and all the other broken-down teachers who let stress tear up their bodies. I wasn't about to be another statistic. I was in my twenties, single, and falling apart physically. My doctor told me, "I know you love your students but you need a break. Get another job or go on sick leave."

The teacher who was fighting against the sexual assault incident begin to suffer from hair loss and eventually had a nervous breakdown. The system harassed her for fighting for her rights. She eventually moved away from the city for a year to regroup. But her cry was never heard. Everyone, even the other teachers, began to disassociate from **those teachers who didn't play the game**. This rejection was typical and I had been prepared by my father. I knew that I could lean on the Lord with all my problems though they were magnified. However, I felt the pain of this other teacher who was once an energetic young asset to the school system. Like many before her, she had been stripped of her self-worth by the system. Though struggling, I refused to be stripped of mine. It did not come from man but from God and I knew this.

Two of Ms. Howard's dance students

Students make silly putty in Ms. Howard's class

14

My Volunteer Transfer

The system was successful in breaking down a voice that supported me, too. I was at the point of being alone again. The Lord again instructed me to lean on him because he heard my cry. No man on earth could comfort the pain I was experiencing. I was so drained at this time that I was not physically able to do the work I was called to do. I needed a rejuvenating period to keep my thoughts and body back in shape. I wanted to be a good witness and being physically dilapidated wasn't cutting it. I had experienced what was truly called spiritual warfare. It was part of Satan's plan to destroy my walk and witness to others. Realizing this, I prayed and prayed. I asked the Lord to remove me from this situation and place me in a more conducive one. I thought no school could be this bad. But I was forgetting that all the schools operated under the same superintendent team.

But God being the God he is, answered my cry. I cried not in vain. I asked God to give me a change of environment because this assignment was over. God transferred me when he saw fit. However, he did not force me to do anything against my own free will. God gives us that option and I opted to relocate, acknowledging that there would be a different set of issues at another school. But whatever the circumstances, I was ready for the new scenery as long as God permitted.

That next year I was transferred at my request. Even though my paperwork went through and I was accepted by another principal, there were still problems. My former principal refused to release me or update my salary. This would cause problems for me later on. Now I couldn't understand her logic after all the abuse she delivered to me.

With an outstanding rating every year, I was still under the microscope. I just knew she would be delighted to lose me as a teacher. But I was wrong. She knew I worked my fingers to the bone and that I was honest. I was also very instrumental in providing evidence of teaching being done in the school when it came to test results. My hustling to reach the students was evident in all that I did. She was clever enough to know that she was losing an outstanding teacher. Even if she wanted to harass me she wanted the benefits of my teaching in her building. Well, God didn't see it that way.

Even I went on to another school with hopes of actually being able to teach. Though I was being held up financially in my salary, I still had hopes in teaching. My former principal neglected to acknowledge all my recent degrees and classes taken while teaching. My status as a permanent teacher was overlooked by her which carried on into the new school. I had moved but was still fighting an old battle.

At this point I had so many degrees that I could give them away. I made it my business to stay abreast of the latest science material. Since I did this, it was the responsibility of the school system to advance my pay as well. However, a lack of inserted paper work by my first principal to an already deficient school system only prolonged this process for years. But I made the move anyway, hoping to one day have this mistake of the system's corrected. I didn't let the lack of pay affect me at that time of transfer. Again I gave the system a ray of hope while I continued to reach those students that awaited.

The new school was located in a lower middle class neighborhood. This in itself was quite different from the former school. However, there were many students who attended this school as a result of their neighborhood school being closed. This made an interesting culture that the teachers had to deal with. There were many territorial fights and gangs. This was something I could identify with.

The school was a science/math school geared towards the technological field. This excited me. But even though this school had a different title, the students faced the same problems as the students that I had just left. The school system was the same system with the same philosophy. The only differences were the houses in the neighborhood and the support of my new principal. She was under the same microscope as the teacher and fought to keep her job, too. Maybe she could still identify with the teacher's struggle. But any streak of support from an administrator made a world of a difference when dealing with other school system problems.

Because schools were merged, gang activity was at an all-time high. My first year was spent working like a referee in a boxing ring. Weapons were apparent and always an intricate part of a fight. I had decided that I would watch the next fight as a lot of the other teachers did. The teachers here were not jeopardizing their safety. Even though they did not talk about it, they didn't make themselves available to be hit, either. Their jobs truly did not extend outside their classroom doors. This group of teachers, though quite verbal, just weren't willing to physically be a stepping stool. Within time I joined the bandwagon when it came to a fight.

Too many times I had almost been trampled in the halls when a fight broke out and students bum-rushed in the halls. So I decided that there were too many other issues that co-existed with the fights that needed my attention. I was tired of being one of the few teachers brave enough to break up a fight. I found out that my energy was needed for the more sophisticated issues that came along with this territory.

Other issues that became prevalent in the schools at this time included: firing of teachers yearly, teacher/student hearings, school fires, teen pregnancy, schools closing, murderers in class, ADHD students, court appearances, student alcoholics and drug addicts, sidity parents who would sue you, and more. The problems had escalated to a higher level. Part of the reason was the educated parents who had students whom they felt could do no wrong. So now a teacher was dealing with the bourgeois parent who opposed him or her and also the stubborn school system.

Ms. Howard takes Senná Minor and brother to church.

15

Students Are Fascinated with Fires

Let's talk fires. This new age '90s teenager is fascinated with destruction. The hot items are fires and bombs. This year alone we experienced six fires, all starting with disgruntled teenagers. Bathrooms were lit, hallways, or whatever was available. I remember one time in which the student was caught. When her shirt was scorched and her hair burnt, she still denied setting the fire. It took a week to get the truth. This was typical. After about the fifth fire, I was ready to leave. The teaching environment was constantly disrupted and I felt my life was truly in danger. Eventually, the students would get it right, I thought. But then I spoke to one of my colleagues who told me her bathroom at school was blown up by students. I thought, "Okay, a bomb I can deal with," or a fire or two. I realized that we taught teenagers with very barbaric behavior whose minds had been poisoned by society. They had no value for life, even if it meant their own. Anyway, I stayed in teaching with the strength of God. It took all the praise for God in me to walk in my class that next day.

16

The Teacher Prepares for Hearings

Along with the fires came the constant threats on many of the teachers' lives. I had to go to court to be a witness for a teacher whose life had been threatened by a student while I was standing there. The student literally tried to beat the teacher down the steps, but I stepped in between the two. This was triggered because the teacher asked this young man to take off his hat in the building. This one question lead to court where we both found out he had threatened his mother's life with a knife and had a track record of violence. What a way to spend your day. But it seemed as if he was pondering murder.

I had another student who was arrested for murder this year. I walked in the class one Monday morning to find out one of my problematic students had been arrested over the weekend for murder. I mean murder! I had heard it all. "What next?" I thought.

Like before the teacher was left in the cold. The students were back in school regardless of their criminal actions. We were left to pick up the pieces again.

Ms. Howard and teachers at workshop

17

Teaching Students with Learning Disabilities

But murder, believe it or not, was only one of many issues. I had never seen so many students with ADHD: Attention Deficit Hyperactive Disorder. Where did this come from? Was this a result of young cracked-out parents or was this the result of their sin? I couldn't tell, but whatever the reason it truly challenged me daily. These students were usually short-tempered, violent, impatient, hyperactive, and impossible to reach without their medicine. When given their medicine, they slept, were sluggish and nonresponsive. I can recall one of my students who didn't have his medicine, flipping out and throwing a fit in class. I thought to myself, "What is wrong with him?"

Little did I know he had a history of violent acts and was being tested with new medicine that made him unstable. Well, when was the school going to inform me that I was in danger? I thought this type of child needed to be in another setting. Along with other ADHD students, he had been mainstreamed with a five-minute attention span, and I was to teach him. Boy, this assignment had graduated me to new depths.

Ms. Howard and SECME teachers, Val Brooks and Heidi Doss, shoot video commercial.

Ms. Howard takes students to DisneyLand in L.A.

18

Jealousy and Competitiveness in the School

But the ADHD students were easy street compared to the competitiveness and jealousy beginning to evolve in the building. Hearing after hearing became a custom for me. Regardless of my effort, there was always an antagonistic person who didn't want to see anyone else succeed. We were not to be super-teachers outshining each other. We were to be like zombies with little hope or energy to instill in the students. But I worked for a higher power, that being none other than God. So regardless of the reins placed on me, God steered this horse.

There were hearings initiated by staff members who used innocent parents to point the finger at other teachers. These were life-threatening situations placed before me as a teacher. Parents and students were being used to attack my character. Every day there was a new attack with new obstacles. I can even remember being reprimanded for saying "Jesus" to myself in the halls. I almost lost my job when Jesus was my only reason for even being there. But all in all, I learned the importance of dissecting hope to give to those young minds I had to teach. I learned that self really wasn't the key issue, but their future was.

I learned through those trials to lean even more on that higher source that the world didn't understand. I learned that regardless of the circumstances around you, God has it all in control. "No matter how dangerous or how trying that trial may be, no weapon formed against me will prosper." But the key was to hold onto my faith and not try to understand the character God was trying to build in me. I learned to accept the spiritual while the natural became confused. It was about trusting God and his judgment as he used me to help mold minds for this season, however long he chose it to be.

As I awaited the hour when God would ordain my next steps, the school system was still lingering in a state of disarray. Principals were being fired, teachers were being reassigned and politics were at an all-time high. Schools were closing and students were suffering. The emphasis never changes. It's said to be on "the importance of producing competitive citizens for society." However, I question that motto and I function within my own purpose, which was to teach those who were said to be unteachable.

Ms. Howard and mother, Dr. Virginia Howard,
after Teacher of the Year Award in Engineering

19

Keeping up Your Credentials

My purpose, like that of many teachers, was defined with different characteristics when pertaining to the school system. I could not be molded into the person the school system wanted to create. I did not resemble what a teacher should be, according to the subhuman standards depicted by the school system. Nor did the treatment from the superintendent's staff, which made up the portion of the school system with power, designate the teacher as a professional. The salad bowl we were thrown in consisted of the teacher, debt, loans, low salaries, abuse, long hours, and more, to say the least. These were the key ingredients of the teacher's life.

As a teacher who had been dedicated to the students and profession, I became appalled with the treatment we received. Once I established status as a teacher, my ratings never fell below outstanding. Though I felt the constant pressure from the school system to succeed, I still maintained outstanding ratings. One would think an outstanding teacher would be compensated for his or her outstanding work. This was not the case in the D.C. Public School system.

It is a requirement to take classes over the years to upgrade one's skills, to maintain one's permanent status, as well as to receive a pay raise. Though I have scraped up funds to stay in school as well as teach, I have yet to see an increment in my steps over a six-year period. Knowing that this negligence was in our system, I began to fight what seemed to be a losing battle. Like many other teachers, I was promised a raise that never came. Now to no avail I would frequent our personnel department only to find out that my credentials, along with hundreds of other teachers' credentials, were lost. Yes, lost. I asked how could a school system be so unprofessional about such important credentials. But then, again, I remembered the nature of the school system I worked in.

Fortunately for me, I had all my paperwork dated back to my first day of work. I kept immaculate files and was able to recreate my paperwork. Sad as it may seem for other teachers, this was not the case. Though prepared, I still rectified this for safeguard measures. After all, we had been told that we would be fired if we didn't rectify the problem, due to lost files and incompetency on the system's behalf. It was explained to us that the system failed to properly certify us in the beginning as compared to other states. Teachers were in an uproar when they heard this news. Many of them were two to three years from retirement and had children in college. To lose their jobs based on a system's problem could be the end of their world.

Regardless of the certification dilemma, I found myself teaching with over six years of back pay raises due to me. Paying bills became almost impossible while at the same time dealing with abuse from the system hurt. It was one thing to deal with the students whom you expect to be on a certain level. But the everyday abuse we as teachers faced from the system was overwhelming. I had to learn to develop patience like that of Job. While I fought and fought over the years for back pay, only to find out that no one really cared, my students' performance on the end-of-the-year standardized test was the school system's primary concern. Barely able to survive, I reached out to those I thought could or would help. However, even in principalships or union positions, these men and women were as powerless as I was. We all reminded the system of failure, and the system did not want to hear us. Rectifying the problems was secondary as were the problems of the teachers, the students, or even our dilapidated school buildings. I thought if the school system can let over 25 schools close down due to antiquated equipment or a lack of students, then as readily would they let a teacher's career collapse.

After years with no results I again relied on God. Though my union was doing all they could to have its voice heard in this issue, it was ignored by the school system. Meanwhile, days went on with me out of my class or on leave as I fought for what was due me. All along I knew I would be black-balled for fighting for what I believed to be right. The battle went on as I worked with the union and my lawyer to retrieve what the system had stolen from me, that being over six years of back pay raises. My own lawyer had to chuckle at the level of abuse we all received. We realized that a laugh would ease the tension when examining the years of negligence from the system on this issue.

There were so many teachers in a situation similar to mine. I say similar because my own union reps could not believe that I was teaching with over six years of back pay raises due me. I had to remind them that I stayed because I had an assignment given to me by God and I cared about my students.

Broke and struggling to pay my bills, I was obedient to God in mastering the art of being patient. I had truly tried to give the system a chance to correct a magnified problem. But each time I requested results, my files were lost or I was rejected. Once I remember being told by the payroll office that I had to wait until all retired teachers and teachers who were pink-slipped received their pay. Now this made absolutely no sense to me. People were pink-slipped constantly and were always going to retire. At that rate, I would never get the money that was due to me.

At engineering workshop at U. Va.

20

The Purpose

Even as I write this story, I am in battle knowing that the battle is really God's. I learned that as Christians we still must exercise wisdom. As a Christian first and teacher second, I learned that the wisdom must be put to use, or you will be trampled on. Even though I have been AWOL, terminated, and black-balled, God assured me that he still had it all in control. Scripture states that the wicked will be rewarded for their wickedness and the righteous will witness it (Psalm 37). Though not excited about anyone receiving punishment, I do understand that justice will prevail in the eyes of the Lord.

Homes and buildings of the future built by Ms. Howard's students

Ms. Howard assists Baxter Brown in boat building.

*Ms. Howard cuts out pieces for
the boat she's building.*

21

Encouragement for the Teacher

One would think that these words were written out of anger or bitterness. By all means they were not, for vengeance is the Lord's. These words were written to tell the truth. As it states in the Bible, what's done in darkness will surely come to light. The system has placed a cloud over teachers for years, and it's time for a rainbow to surface. Teachers, be encouraged. Though you seldom receive a certificate, though you seldom receive praise, God knows your work is not in vain. Prevail until your assignment is over. Overlapping your duty in life could lead to blessings being missed on your behalf. God has given you many talents to be shared by your students.

Teachers, if you become discouraged, remember that child's life that you and only you may make a difference in. Even when you seem to be placed in a pit to teach and no one else cares, that child does. Remember the parents who expressed gratitude when dealing with their difficult children. Remember the principal, if there was one, who stuck by your side and encouraged you as the system beat you down. By all means, stand together with other teachers and lend your hand when needed. Constant competitiveness will only divide the purpose. The master plan of the system is to keep control.

But remember the love that teachers shared with you on one

of your most difficult days. Remember the kind word a child uttered when you were down. As a team, the teachers are only as strong as that weakest link. Pray for one another, intercede for one another, and let your attitudes seep into that school system. Ask God for wisdom as Solomon did. Because Solomon did not ask for material items, God blessed him with wisdom and an abundance of material things (1 Kings 3:9-14).

Hold your head up high, for you are God's teacher whom he entrusted with thousands of lives. Don't ever take your assignment lightly. Know when it's time to move on. Be a blessing to others as you share your gifts. This may only be a stepping stone, as God builds strength and character in you. That next assignment could be at your door. But wait patiently and know that your life is in God's hands. God loves you teachers. You are standing in the gap for those souls chosen for his kingdom. In the meantime, I, too, await my next assignment.

Ms. Howard in boat she helped build with Instructor Joe Yoecha
(Alexandria Seaport Foundation)

In Closing

Dear Teachers,

I await the day that the professional mind of the teacher is appreciated. I await the day that the world places emphasis on the importance of education. I await the day that our children's future becomes first priority. But until then, I will continue to bask in God's presence as he uses me for his purpose. Every pregnant thirteen-year-old girl who needs encouragement I will encourage. The fifteen-year-old boy who doesn't know his father I will lift up in prayer. The mother who struggles to hold her family together I will lend a hand to. The father who sits in jail I will bring before the Lord. The politician who doesn't understand I will pray for, and the administrator who doesn't have my backbone I will love. And the world which devalues your character, which needs you—the teacher, for your sake I will bless. Denial of self in a self-actualized, driven world is what is required of you. So again, be encouraged. In due time, your reward will come. But it will come not from man, but from a higher source, from God himself. In the name of Jesus I pray you continue to keep your strength.

God Bless You,

Veryl

The Teacher's Kreb Cycle

ATPs represent the amount of energy used. The total available is 81. Note: Energy is comparable to supplies, salaries, power, stability, respect, and value.

Congress–
The controller of designated
funds–20 ATPs

School Board–Status jobs–15 ATPs

Appointed Superintendent–10 ATPs
(Highly paid position appointed frequently)

Superintendent/Assessment Team–8 ATPs
(Highly paid position, nepotism, etc.)

Administrators–7 ATPs
(The head of a school with little power)

Personnel Staff–A teacher's enemy–6 ATPs

Payroll Staff–A teacher's nightmare–5 ATPs

Secretaries–The bosses in the school–4 ATPs

Parents–The last word–3 ATPs

Union–An overlooked voice–2 ATPs

Students–The money–1 ATP

Teachers/Janitors/Counselors/Aides–
0 ATPs
(The bottom of the
totem pole)

Special Thanks

JESUS, my Lord and savior
My family–Virginia, Ben Ben, Brian, Kim, and Benton
Rhema Christian Center, Pastors Clarence & Doris Givens
Mr. Lamont Murphy–my team teaching partner
Dr. Anne Hilliard–former supportive principal
Harriet Kargbo–former supportive administrator
Darren & Caren Comedy–computer donation, encouragers, prayer partners
Audrey Hinton–editor
Tamera Thompson–friend, donations, encourager, nursery school owner
Gina Thompson–friend, lawyer, encourager, teacher
Judy Johnson–friend, teacher
Val Brooks–friend, teacher, prayer partner
Pam Crocket–lawyer, friend, encourager, donations
Tyrone & Kim Wheatley–friends, encouragers
Denise, Antonio, Antinette Jefferson–parent of former students, friend
Stacey Ward–BET producer/donations to school
Felecia Watkins–BET producer/donations to school
Sita Milan–BET producer/hired my students on show
Bev Smith–BET "Our Voices Show"/students and I invited as guests
Bill Carpenter–Capitol Entertainment/donations
Angie & Debbie Winans–encouragers
Wayne Stevenson–former student
Maurice Douglass–prayer partner, special friend, NFL ballplayer
Dawn Hicks–friend, prayer partner,donations
Darryl Green's Youth Life Foundation–donations
Howard Gibson–encourager
Tiffany Neco–former student
Tameka Marshall–former student
Aerial Booker–former student
Karen Jackson–former student
Dorcus Fields–former student
Gwendolyn Plummer–former student
Latisha Thomas–former student
Cory Miller & Mom–former student
Calvin Carter–former student
Stan Mcknight–encourager
Don & Norma Hernandez–encouragers
Joe Metchum–donation
Dave Rubin–donation
Dart Barton–SECME
Brenda Simmons–SECME
Guy Vickers–SECME
Anne Jackson–SECME
Chloe Garth–SECME
Joe & Karen Mallory–friends

97

Val Tartt–friend
Sandy King–SECME
Kimley Thompson–prayer partner
Vernon Richardson–friend, encourager, donations to school
Vincent Young–Capitol Entertainment, donations
Robert Shanklin–Capitol Entertainment, donations
Don Todd–covered my class, donations
Joyce Maddox–donations
Amber Coles–administrative assistance
Gail Carter–administrative assistant
Dianne Collins, beautician
Korre Twiggs–Teachers Union
John Pope The Bright Light–encourager from New Image Fitness Club
Brother Jimmy–encourager from Rhema Christian Center
Minister Donald Williams and wife Drew–prayer partners
Dr. Derrick Artist–donation of speakers
Yvonne Hefley–NIH, donation of speakers
Aliya & Sena McCullin–former students
Ileana Keith–encourager, math teacher
Lisa McBee–friend, encourager, English teacher, prayer partner
Shirley Lewis–social studies teacher, friend
Carolyn Prue–librarian, donations
Dr. Louis Blackwell–home economics teacher, donations
Mr. Black–science teacher, encourager
Walter Bryant–science teacher, mentor
Blanche Brownley–science coordinator, encourager
Georgette Haden–donations
Sadi William–former student
Robert Atkins–parent, Rhema Christian Center
Bill Cherry–friend
Patria Deshazo–friend
Yvette Downs–friend
Jerry Donahue–supporter
Dewey Reeves–administrative support
Montique Mahan–former student
Mytia Crawley–former student
Tyrone Tarlton–SECME teacher
Mr. & Mrs. Andre Brown–Chicago prayer partners
Harvey Porshai–Chicago prayer partner
Jacquline Coleman–Dudley's, Chicago prayer partner
Betty Clawson–Dudley's, Chicago prayer partner
Ferranda Williamson–professor, Chicago prayer partner
Shari Goodwin–teacher, librarian
Delecia Baker–prayer partner, encourager, radio personality
Danny & Joanne Copeland–speakers, donations
The Civil Air Patrol–speakers

An Educator's Thoughts . . .

I believe that every child is a gift from God. Each one wrapped in different wrapping, possessing unique contents. As a teacher my job is to foster and enhance the content, so that one day they will be able to add, compete and succeed in today's society. Education is the fuel that feeds their minds and drives them for the rest of their lives. It is one of the few things they achieve that can never be taken away. As the state of education moves forth in today's society teachers are becoming less and less valued, making an already difficult job become one of low morale. I just pray that for this "season" as I continue doing the work of God that I am able to touch as many of these gifts as I can. I pray that when my "season" is up I will be able to look back and say, "I touched souls, enhanced self-esteems and changed lives."

Judy Johnson
Special Ed Teacher (high school)
Prince Georges County, Maryland

Education has no boundaries

My profession is noble to those who seek students' success. However, political bureaucracy hampers the academic prowess for our youth. You can't get rich from this tiresome job, but continuing without a break will mark your stone.

There's an old saying [The teachers are afraid of administrators (principals), administrators fret parents. The parents fear their children and the children are afraid of no one.]

Regardless of all the hurdles, the joy is the same when students find you after years to say thanks, whether a business owner, professional athlete, lawyer, actor, or an ex-convict, that's the joy. To hear them say, "You had a positive influence in my life." No economic value is greater than receiving that emotional euphoria.

> Bennie Howard
> High School Coach and English Teacher
> Washington, D.C.

Bennie Howard's Poem

I want to stay until a quarter past four
But now at 3:00 p.m., I wish I could beat the kids to the door.
But I can't.
Though I'm finished with teaching

A Teacher's Day

Do you want to know what makes a teacher's day?
Well, I'll tell you anyway.
A teacher walks out of her house with daughter in one arm, brief-
case and diaper bag in her other hand, gets into her car, drives
fifteen minutes away and realizes she left her lunch on the
kitchen counter.
She drives into construction with only one lane in motion.
She reaches her babysitter's house and it's as quiet as a mouse.
She knocks and knocks and thinks, "Oh, God, my principal is
looking at the clock."
She drives into the school parking lot and without an umbrella in
her car it starts raining and the door is too far.
Her hair gets wet, her clothes are drenched and her perfume now
has a stench.
Her principal is standing at her classroom door. He looks at her
and says, "TEACHER NO MORE."
She walks in her room, tears in her eyes, sits at her desk and a
student walks up to her and says, "Teacher, I like you the best!"

Lisa Williams
English Teacher (junior high school)
Washington, D.C.

I Want To Be More

When I grow up I want to be much more than I am
But judging by the Black man's condition today, I don't stand a chance.
I look at the corners in and around my neighborhood
and I see young men on corners up to no good.
It's not just the boys any more, the girls have joined in as well
Dropping out of school, abandoning babies and filling up the jails.
It frightens me to think of what the future will be
If today's generation doesn't change what seems destined to be.
Recently I saw where a lady hung her baby, not much older than me
And another mother baked hers while watching the baby scream.
Should we pursue and achieve the goals we were put here for?
Yes, for in spite of it all I want to be more.
When the established system of justice works only for a few
It leaves one wondering what should one do.
Rodney King's justice was partial at best
But Blacks have become accustomed to settling for less.
I refuse to accept the crumbs America has set aside for Blacks
It's past time for us to start fighting back.
If you don't help change tomorrow, today,
The dim light of our future is here to stay.
Because even with a good education I could end up sweeping floors.
So I must let you know, I've got to be more.
This kindergarten class wants to see the day when Black is the standard
    by whch others are compared
Rather than the symbol used to represent destruction and despair.
The Clinton administration brought to light that it's time for a change
But even we know a new direction was needed before Clinton ever
    came.
We want to be more and it's up to you
To help shape our future and save yours too.
For we are a direct reflection of the efforts you put forth
Our entire existence depends on your support.

Tamara Thompson Fair
Owner, Pill Hill Development Center and Near the Pier Nursery School
Chicago, Illinois

It Takes a Whole Village

The life expectancy of a black child has been reduced to age 25, largely due to increased gang activity, drugs and random drive bys.

That means statistically, many of us have only 20 years to go. Are we accepting statistics' fate for us? The answer is "No."

On our graduation night, we want to invite you to get involved and collectively, let's work towards a positive resolve.

Ask yourselves the question, "What am I prepared to do?" And remember it takes a whole village to raise a child, and that includes you.

When you know a child in your neighborhood is in need of your help, do you say to yourself that's a problem for someone else?

Is a single teen or parent you know working two jobs just to make ends meet? And do you pray for the parent and the child before you go to sleep?

Are gangs and drugs making students want to stay home? And are you waiting on the system to correct this wrong?

If your answer to any of these questions is yes, then it's time your good efforts step up to being your best!

Ask youself the question, "What is it I can do?" And remember an important part of that village is you.

You are looking at the first president of the U.S. that happens to be black and I know given the racial tension today, it's hard to believe that.

I am going to be an expert robotics engineer, designing technology so advanced people will consult me from far and near.

I am the future ambassador to the island Haiti. My goal is to restore economic stability and destroy political frustration.

I am the one who will be credited with redirecting gang members to work towards peace, stopping them from killing babies, selling drugs, and cleaning our streets.

All these dreams sound great but none will come true, if we don't get a collective response from you.

Our parents, neighbors, teachers and friends help us make new beginnings and stop speeding up our end.

Ask us the question, "What do you want me to do?" And remember an important part of that village is you.

Our answer is that you question our leadership and make heard our voices; only then will we begin to increase our choices.

Involve yourselves in our schools and reassemble the extended family because what's happening to our community is nothing short of tragedy.

When Girl X was brutalized and Lenard Clark was beaten in Bridgeport, Jesse and WGCI were there to lend support.

But where are Jesse and GCI on an everyday basis, typically not in our neighborhood helping out familiar faces.

And though the million man march was great, it ended with only a speech. Let's create one million jobs and get our youth off the streets.

The only way this can happen is if you've paved the way, just as Malcolm, King, and Harold did in your day.

We want to get the chance to make you and all of America proud, and finally to be able to shout out loud.

That all of us in this graduating class are successful due to the effort that was amassed.

And though the challenge is hard, it is worth the wild, because it takes a whole village to raise a child.

Tamara Thompson Fair
Owner, Pill Hill Development Center and Near the Pier Nursery School
Chicago, Illinois

"Lo, children are a heritage of the Lord . . . and all your (spiritual) children shall be disciples (taught) by the Lord and obedient to his will, and great shall be the peace and undisturbed composure of your children."

Psalm 127:3 (KJV) and Isaiah 54:13 (Amp. KJV)

I consider it an honor and a privilege to be set aside, by God, as a teacher of children. They are a precious commodity to Him. Only God can give the anointing and the wisdom to teach what really needs to be imparted to them. Each teacher must decide to become an educator who recognizes the responsibility that God has given, and also recognize that we will be held accountable. Each child, individually, represents a total package of that which it takes to complete the plan of God for the earth! Each child has been genetically coded for a specific task upon the earth, "before they were placed in their mothers' wombs" and teachers are responsible for shaping and molding the character of these persons for their God ordained earthly assignments. I am convinced that this is my personal charge upon the earth and if it had not been for teachers who accepted this God given assignment, where would I be? Where would you be? Teaching must not be aimed towards the content of the curriculum but towards the character of the child!!

Reverend Valierie Y. Jordan-Brooks
Suitland, Maryland
High School Counselor and Teacher

A Parent's Thoughts . . .

27 February 1997

To Whom It May Concern:

My name is Denise Jefferson and I am the parent of two Backus Middle School graduates. This letter is to inform you of certain experiences at Backus which have been invaluable to the emotional, social as well as academic development of my chldren.

My first child, who is now attending Flint Hill, a private shcool in VA, came to Backus during a transitional period. I was very unimpressed by the environment and after several unsettling incidents that were not handled satisfactorily by the Administration, I began my search for a private school. It was only because of the efforts of three dedicated, committed teachers that my daughter not only remained that first year, but returned the next year to graduate. Ms. Sheffey, her French teacher, Ms. Ashton, her gym techer and Ms. Howard, her science teacher. It is Ms. Howard that I am writing about today.

During the first year at Backus, Ms. Howard showed such concern with her students that I almost felt guilty considering transferring Antonette (my daughter). Even with the management problems, I felt that what Ms. Howard and some of the other teachers had to offer was worth giving the school a second chance. I am glad I did. Antonette developed study habits that are carrying her successfully through high school, due in no small part to Ms. Howard's insistence on her working up to her potential. Although I was impressed by Ms. Howard's competence, credentials, and multiple degrees, it was her character and total involvement with her students that won me over. Antonette danced at the Lincoln Theater for the Martin Luther King Birthday celebration, because Ms. Howard who also studied dance, stayed after school, oranized a dance class and arranged for them to perform there as well as at several other places. My daughter went to California, with a trip arranged by Ms. Howard for some of her students. When my daughter needed transportation to the various extra curricular activities Ms. Howard was always inviting them to, the competitions she was always entering them in, the seminars she was always registering them for, Ms. Howard came and picked her up and brought her home, if that was necessary. I know this is probably long for a recommendation letter, but I am very grateful for the opportunity to show just a small bit of the gratitude I feel, having had not one, but two of my children's lives touched by such an extraordinary teacher. The kind that were abundant in my day, but I find pretty rare nowadays. I am certain that Ms. Howard's applied pressure in the classroom and creative outlets after school were central in shaping my daughter's success in academics and sports currently. She was recently inducted into the Honor Society, averaged about 7 pts per basketball game this season and did receive A's in math and science.

Two years later, Ms. Howard is putting in the same exra efforts with her students. I cannot tell you of all the activities my son has come home and asked me could he "go with Ms. Howard to?" So I will just relate this one incident:

One evening my son Tony was working late in the science lab at school. When I arrived at the school I asked him why he had not gotten my permission to stay so late. He explained to me that three students were working on a project that was to be entered into a science competition in the morning, but at the last minute the teacher dropped out and consequently two of the students. That left an unfinished project and one disappointed student who had done the bulk of the work. Ms. Howard stepped into the teacher's place who had dropped out, brought the unfinished project and materials to her classroom, recruited two other students (my son and another young lady) and worked at the school on the project until the janitors told them they had to leave. At this point they were not finished, but the competition was at Howard University at 7 am. The only thing to do, if you are Ms. Howard, is to have the children come to your house and finish the project, spend the night, then take them to the competition in the morning. Which is what she did. Although one of our students was quoted in the Washington Post Metro section, they did not place; but I cannot imagine all that they learned from this experience about responsibility, perseverance, going the extra mile, pride and dignity. Especially, since Ms. Howard herself will not tell you about the details of this experience, except from the viewpoint of the kids' being in another competition. She wasn't so concerned about having to take over at the last minute as she was upset because they probably could have placed if they'd had more time. I don't know what these projects and grants are all about, I just have a lay person's and a parent's understanding, but what I do know is that a teacher like Ms. Howard should be supported as fully as they possibly can. I also know if students are hungry she has fed them and if the school doesn't have the materials, she buys them. She and teachers like her are so needed today, not only by the children being shorted by budget cuts, but by single parents like myself, so glad that somebody cares enough about my child to go over and above the call of duty for the future of us all.

Sincerely,
Denise Jefferson

A Student's Thoughts . . .

Dear Ms. Howard,
  Thank you very much for paying for my ticket to Florida. That was very kind of you to do that for me. I will personally try to pay you back in any way I can. I would also like to thank you for all of the other things that you've done for me. Thank you for being there for me when I needed someone to talk to, for being my teacher, and just for being you.
  Thanks Alot! !!!!!

Sincerely,
Tameka L. Marshall

Why I think Ms. Howard should receive an award from the SECME Department

April 16, 1997

  I think Ms. Howard should receive an award from the SECME Department because she has showed and taught me and many others how to work well with our hands. She had also provided the SECME team with the finest instructors who have instructed us with building boats (canoes), mouse trap cars, bridges, and etc. Ms. Howard should receive an award because she has spent many days after school working with the people who participate in SECME with several projects and activities.
  Ms. Howard has encouraged me to join SECME. Once I joined in with the SECME team I thought it was going to be boring, but it has helped improve my grades, work with others, and taught me how to be competitive.

Wayne Stevenson

Why I think Ms. Howard should receive an award
for the SECME program at Betie Backus

I believe that Ms. Howard should receive this award because she has taught me, along with other students, how to be responsible and work well with others. Some teachers do not really care if their students do well or learn anything, but Ms. Howard really does care if you learn to the best of your ability. She always says that if your going to start something finish it. She has a very strong determination. Rain, snow, sleet or hail she will work on something concerning SECME or education. Even with third degree burns she'll keep working. If a teacher gives up hope on us you can always count on Ms. Howard to be there. Ms. Howard takes this program very seriously and the students. You would think that we were her own kids or her life depended upon it. In SECME she has provided for us with the best instructors working with us in building our boats, houses, bridges, etc. such as architects and engineers. The SECME Team have worked very hard and accomplished a lot of things thanks to Ms. V. Howard and her strong determination. No one can take her determination away from her no matter what it takes. That is the exact reason why she should receive this award.

Sincerely,
Antonio Jefferson
8th Grade Student

A Thought from the Community

July 23, 1997

Donald J Quigg Award
Office of Public Affairs
US Patent & Trademark Office
Washington, D.C. 20231

RE: **Nomination of Veryl Howard**

Dear Sir/Madame:

Enclosed please find the nomination of Ms. Veryl Howard for the Donald J Quigg Award.

Ms. Howard has worked with the Darrell Green Youth Life Foundation for more than a year. During that time we have come to know and admire her commitment and dedication to her students as well as the community at large. What impresses us most is her steadfastness to ensure, to the best of her ability, that anything she contributes to is completed in excellence.

As you will read, Ms. Howard is the epitome of an innovative, interesting and inspirational educator and academician. I have personally visited her classroom on different occasions, met her principle and worked with several of her students on various projects. She is highly respected and revered by her subordinates and superiors alike.

It is with great honor and pleasure that Ms. Howard is nominated. In an era when teachers are more concerned with their personal gain rather than the prosperity of their students and community, Ms. Howard is an icon of righteousness, selflessness and sacrifice.

The Donald J Quigg Award for Excellence would indeed reward a teacher of excellence if Ms. Howard is selected.

Best regards
Dawn Hicks
Adminstrator

September 10, 1997

To Whom It May Concern:

Veryl Howard has been both a professional and personal acquaintance of mine for over five years.

In this time, she has been an important resource for guests for many of the BET's shows . . . especially the network's popular talk show, 'Our Voices.' Our entire staff consistently counts on her dependability and eagerness to assist, not only in securing guests, but in any additional way we need.

Moreover, her strong dedication and commitment to bettering the lives of children is outstanding. She often brings her students to our production facility for tours . . . exposing them to professionals and environments that they may not be otherwise.

As a result of Ms. Howard's strong character and tremendous people skills, she has my enthusiastic recommendation and will be a valuable asset to any organization that will employ her.

Sincerely,
Stacey Ward
Producer, BET News

the purpose of scholarship as a deeper and "truer" understanding of literature, Thorpe signals the intrinsic thrust of the volume. One after another, seven "extraliterary" disciplines are brought *into* literature as tools to be exploited. The psychoanalytic critics Frederick Crews applauds absorbed Freudianism "into their literary sense." Leon Edel depicts biography as a "department of literature." While warning about the danger of a self-enclosed integration that cuts poetry off from defining circumstances, J. Hillis Miller cautions against studies of literature's contexts that move so far beyond the poem they became something else. The goal of literary study remains elucidation of intrinsic meanings of poems, plays, and novels that "show themselves forth as they are" (in Thorpe, *Relations*).

The 1982 *Interrelations of Literature* (Barricelli and Gibaldi) appears at first to differ, with nearly double the number of entries. History and biography do not reappear, but they were covered in a separate book. Myth, psychology, sociology, religion, and music are back, and the new entrants are linguistics, philosophy, folklore, politics, law, science, visual arts, and film. The rhetoric of interdisciplinarity abounds in talk of "interplay," "inherent" ties, "reciprocal process," "interpenetration," "interaction," "symmetries," "symbiotic" and "complementary" relations. Nonetheless, literature's extraliterary ties are brought into a world in which literature is "the hub of the wheel of knowledge" and the "logical locus" for integration of knowledge. Studying literature as an isolated aesthetic or national entity theoretically denies its centrifugal movement across borders. Yet, the editors announce that the interdisciplinary thrust of developments such as comparative literature has restored literature to its "pristine position as a central cognitive resource in society, as its most faithful and comprehensive interpreter."

Relations with sociology further illustrate the intrinsic thrust of the two volumes. In 1967, Leo Lowenthal called sociology one of literature's "first cousins." At the time, the major practices were sociology of literature and literary uses of sociological knowledge. Marxist explanation was limited and sociological studies of literature scarce. "Tentative communication" was occurring in studies of mass culture and media, and some bridge building was evident in the conceptualization of literature as a manifestation of social history. However, the rapprochement of social sciences and humanities was more promise than reality (in Thorpe *Relations*). When Priscilla Clark described the relationship in 1982, literature remained the unifying point of view. Representation, she wrote, came down to a choice of which category is the *explicans* and which is the *explicandum*. The concepts of writer, genre, literature, and public are defined by the contexts in which they occur, placing practices at points along a continuum of commitments to social factors and literary meaning. Even so Clark maintained, sociology of literature should clarify the *literary* significance of literature's social context. Sociology *extends* understanding of literature and is concerned with the production and effect of *meaning*. Consequently, the social relations of literature are "not extraliterary but are literature itself" (in Barricelli and Gibaldi).

Even with their intrinsic thrust, these volumes illustrate the challenge of mapping knowledge. The picture differs depending on whether the locus is a particular project or coordinate and whether activities are grouped in broad or narrow categories. Time is another factor. In the 1982 *Interrelations,* Steven Scher grounded relations with music in a notion "as old as the first stirrings of aesthetic consciousness." However, relations shift. Thomas McFarland reported that literature and philosophy sometimes come together in mutual fecundation, sometimes occlude one another, and other times move apart. Gunn traced ties with religion "to the very origins of literature." Yet, although literature and religious tradition had a complementary relationship from classical antiquity to the Renaissance, toward the end the relationship became more adversarial. By the late eighteenth century, literature was viewed as an alternative or substitute for religion. In modern studies, existentialism was initially the dominant focus. Critical studies developed in overlapping stages. The first, from the late 1920s to World War II, was pastoral or therapeutic. The second, dating to the mid-1960s, was broadly apologetic and correlative or essentially historicist. The third, beginning in the mid or late 1960s, focused on either generic or anthropological issues. Subsequently, structuralism, phenomenology, hermeneutics, and poststructuralism challenged traditional constructions.

Mapping Change

Guides to disciplinary practice are also valuable indicators of interdisciplinary change. The 1963 and 1970 editions of *The Aims and Methods of Scholarship in Modern Languages and Literatures* (Thorpe) depicted a fourfold division into Linguistics, Textual Criticism, Literary History, and Literary Criticism. The 1981 *Introduction to Scholarship in Modern Languages and Literatures* (Gibaldi) retained familiar categories but substituted Historical Scholarship for Literary History while adding Literary

Theory and The Scholar in Society. This addition signaled two diverging trends: one moving toward the speculative and abstruse, the other toward the complex relationship between scholarship and the "real world." Both trends are readily apparent in the 1992 update of the *Introduction* (Gibaldi). Linguistics has became Language and Composition, with subsections on linguistics; language, culture, and society; language acquisition and language learning; and rhetoric and composition. Literary Criticism is now Literary Studies, with subsections on textual scholarship, canonicity and textuality, interpretation, historical scholarship, and theory. Most significant, a new category appears. Cross-Disciplinary and Cultural Studies contains subsections on interdisciplinary studies, feminist and gender studies, ethnic and minority studies, border studies, and cultural studies. This addition reinforces the claim that literary studies is evolving in the direction of interdisciplinarity and cultural studies. Being accorded a separate essay, though, is only the most obvious measure of the first trend. Interdisciplinarity pervades the volume. It has become part of the rhetoric of mainstream practice.

The depiction of disciplinary relations changed in kind. In the 1982 *Interrelations,* Jonathan Culler characterized relations between linguistics and literature as a "fundamental and continuing separation." During the early 1980s, allegiance to the philological ideal of a comprehensive discipline remained alive in classical and medieval studies, but surveys of linguistic devices in literature were common practice. The scholars who were most enthusiastic about the relationship faulted linguists for concentrating on phonological and syntactic systems and making the sentence the largest unit of analysis. They pushed for a broader linguistics of discourse. When Dennis Baron described the relationship of language, culture, and society in the 1992 *Introduction,* he highlighted the impact of Theory, women's and gender studies, speculation on pedagogy and the role of computers, and new interdisciplinary interests in writing. Linguistics had moved from phonological and syntactic theory to a broader concern for language acquisition, second-language teaching, and language in its social setting. Heightened interest in the social context of language use had also stimulated new studies ranging from global theories of orality and national language policy to turn-taking in conversations.

Relations with psychology are another case in point. Traditionally, literary critics associated psychology with Sigmund Freud and often assigned unconscious meanings ahistorically and impersonally to literary works. By the 1982 *Interrelations,* psychoanalytic interpretations were placing greater emphasis on language and the role of transference and counter-transference. In a second MLA-published book of disciplinary representation, the 1992 *Redrawing the Boundaries,* Meredith Skura reported a split between followers of Freud and Jacques Lacan. The "psyche" group—composed of Freudians, Kleinians, object relations theorists, and Winnicottian interpreters—emphasizes reading as evidence of an individual mind. The "analysis" group—composed of Lacanians—directs attention away from an autonomous self that exists prior to language and an author's unconsciousness to the text in which it may be found or the inter-subjective process. Lacan claimed the subject is constituted by the intersubjective system of language and culture. The American psychoanalytic profession tended to ignore Lacan, but he was widely adopted by American critics because he offered the groundwork for a radical critique of essentialist assumptions about human nature. Nonetheless, he practiced a New Critical kind of reading by festishizing a rhetorical icon. Ultimately, Skura concluded, despite Lacan's distrust of consciousness and elevation of signification over psychology the literary critic was restored to the center of human activity in a new science of language.

The Measure of History

History is a recurring benchmark of disciplinary relations in humanities. Like art history and music, literature was anchored on the chronological order of periodization. The generalist model also regarded both literary studies and history as primary activities for cultivating gentlemen (Moran 114, 118). In the 1967 *Relations,* Rosalie Cole called history "everybody's sister." At the time, intellectual history and history of ideas were the major practices, though literature remained the primary object. In the 1981 *Introduction,* Barbara Kiefer Lewalski reported that the walls safeguarding the purity of criticism and interpretation were largely demolished. The territory was more extensive and less clearly demarcated. Nonetheless, contextual studies were still conducted in the interest of criticism and interpretation. Lewalski warned against imposing contemporary political perspectives, lest literature be rendered a document or transformed into sociology. She admonished scholars in the history of ideas and in social and cultural history to "honor the uniqueness of the literary work" (in Gibaldi). Looking back in the 1992 *Introduction,* Annabel Patterson underscored the dominance of literature at the time in biographies, studies of sources and contexts, the history of literary elements and forms, and social and cultural history. Scholars typically combined formalist techniques with self-contained histories of ideas, genres, and topics. Applied with a positivistic force to interpretation, history produced a wealth of facts. By and large, though, the past was kept to a reductive background (183–84).

Disciplinary relations underwent a dramatic shift with the rise of the new historicism during the early 1980s. The keywords "interplay," "negotiation," and "circulation" signaled a shifting conceptualization of history from "background" to "shared code," reformulating the relationship of the social and the aesthetic in a "network" of practices, beliefs, and institutions that constitute culture. Joe Moran recalls the impact of the movement in the U.S. It straddled the divide between history and literary criticism by exploring what Louis Montrose called "the historicity of texts" and "the textuality of history." Stephen Greenblatt described the new approach as a response to two traditional assumptions about literary studies: New Criticism's emphasis on the verbal icon, with an accompanying view of the literary text as a self-contained, formal, and thematic unity; and literary history's assumption that historical material constitutes a secondary background that is unified and consistent. New historical work also challenged the social scientific aspirations of the discipline of history and shared a semiotic view of the concept of culture with the anthropology of Clifford Geertz (137–41).

In her 1992 update on relations with history, Patterson speculated that recent scholarship might eventually be located in the domains of social and cultural history. It incorporates subjects that were previously classified as external contexts, especially contemporary politics and social milieu. Once autonomous literary texts are being placed within the conditions that produced them, and new topics have emerged such as women's education, incarceration, and hospitalization. The "road back to history," Patterson recalled, began with structuralism, social history, and the cultural archaeology of Michel Foucault. In blending philosophy with social history, Foucault crossed the boundaries of text and context. The earliest notable impact was in studies of the English Renaissance. New historicism had the "force of a polemic," propelling the conviction that texts are products of and must be resituated within historical, social, political, and economic environments. It was also indebted, Brook Thomas adds, to social historians who challenged consensus histories and sweeping intellectual histories in their own discipline (184–86).

Most anthologies of scholarship contain a mix of affiliations that mark differing assessments of the older historicism and other "isms," differing views of disciplinarity and interdisciplinarity, and individual agendas. The practices lumped under the label "new historicism" are decidedly plural. Yet, they exhibit a common shift from language- to history-based study that expanded cultural critique or cultural studies in English, art history, French, and sometimes German. Realignment of figure and ground in the shift from "background" to "circulation" has not made historians out of literary scholars. New historicism tends to produce a thick description that brackets together literary and ethnographic analysis. The interdisciplinarity of the movement, Thomas suggests, is indicated by the difference between the rhetorical figures of synecdoche and chiamus. Older organic models were dominated by synecdoche, viewing the whole in a part. Chiasmus places literature in a different relation to other cultural practices and disciplines. When established categories are defamiliarized, character, language, and theme are not apportioned exclusively to literary scholars, "primitive" customs to anthropologists, and demographic patterns to social historians. Disciplinary economies still operate, though, transforming chiasmus from difference to identity. Most specialists begin with and emphasize literature or assume the starting point is connected somehow with other literary works (9–12).

Historians, for their part, have been critical of new historicism. They fault it for eclectic nuggeting, anecdotalism, textual imperialism, and a superficial brand of association that links texts without considering their connections or differences. Dominick LaCapra criticized new historical practices for being a "pseudosolution of weak montage" and lacking a sense of interactions between levels of society and culture (*Soundings*, 193; qtd. in Moran 140–41). Despite these problems, Louis Montrose emphasized, some of the most complex and persistent problems literature faculty face inhabit the discursive spaces traversed by the term "new historicism," including the essential or historical bases on which literature is distinguished from other discourses; relations between cultural practices and social, political, and economic processes; and the consequences of poststructuralist theories of textuality for historical or materialist criticism (19). Moreover, Carolyn Porter contends we have reached a point at which antiformalist projects that emerged in literary studies—for example, new historicism and cultural criticism—and oppositional critical practices marginalized by formalism—for example, Marxist, feminist, African Americanist, and Third World studies—occupy a new common ground called "discourse" or "social text." Traditional boundaries between the literary and the extraliterary have faded, and scholars are no longer constrained by the canon. Calling this hybrid space a common ground, though, does not ignore the fact that it is also a battleground and in some practices the "extraliterary" are still retextualized as "literary" (26–27).

From Conjunctive Relation to the Double-Sided Question

New developments compound the task of mapping. In the 1992 *Introduction to Scholarship,* Gunn defined four approaches. The simplest is on disciplinary ground. In literary studies, the traditional critical coordinates are author, reader, material or linguistic components of a text, and the world. The map changes depending on which coordinate is the axis. If *text* is the axis, a number of developments appear—such as structuralist, formalist, and generic interests; hermeneutics or interpretation theory; and certain forms of Marxist criticism. If *reader* is the axis, others appear—such as audience-oriented criticism. The most conventional strategy is tracing the relationship of one discipline to another. Applying this conjunctive strategy, Gunn identified a wide range of examples associated with interdisciplinarity:

> *literature and philosophy:* phenomenological criticism, hermeneutics, deconstruction, neopragmaticism, ethical criticism, the new rhetorical criticism;
>
> *literature and anthropology:* structuralism, ethnography, or thick description, folklore and folklife studies, myth criticism;
>
> *literature and psychology:* psychoanalytic criticism, reader-response criticism, anxiety-of-influence criticism, cultural psychology;
>
> *literature and politics:* sociological criticism, cultural studies, ideological criticism, materialist studies;
>
> *literature and religion:* theological apologetics, recuperative hermeneutics, generic and historical criticism, rhetoric studies;
>
> *literature and linguistics:* Russian formalism, stylistics, narratology, semiotics.
>
> (Gunn, "Interdisciplinary Studies" 249)

The map changes, however, if another question is asked. What new subjects and topics have emerged? A host of other examples appears—such as the history of the book, the materialism of the body, psychoanalysis of the reader, the sociology of conventions, and the ideology of gender, race, and class. Intertextuality, power, and the status of "others" also belong on the list and each topic, in turn, projected further lines of investigation. Studies of representation such as Greenblatt's *Shakespearean Negotiations* crafted new combinations of historicist, reader-response, cultural materialist, hermeneutic, semiotic, and deconstructionist modes of inquiry. Studies of the body evolved into studies of representation. In *The Body in Pain,* Elaine Scarry interwove psychoanalytic, cultural, materialistic, neo-Marxist, and new-historicist approaches. New theoretical work, Catherine Gallagher adds, sometimes constituted an intervention that moved beyond elucidation of literature to investigate, for example, how conceptions of the body in the Renaissance supported the discourse of state power (168). This degree of complexity seems to defy mapping: "The threading of disciplinary principles and procedures," Gunn remarked, "is frequently doubled, tripled, and quadrupled in ways that are not only mixed but, from a conventional disciplinary perspective, somewhat off center." They do not develop in a linear fashion, and are not traceable in all their effects. They are characterized by overlapping, underlayered, interlaced, crosshatched affiliations, collations, and alliances that have ill-understood and unpredictable feedbacks ("Interdisciplinary Studies" 248–49).

Audience-oriented criticism is a prime example. Emerging from social, intellectual, and literary developments in Germany during the late 1960s, it fostered new ways of examining the established canon and once excluded works of mass media and popular literature. As the subfield evolved, it moved beyond German *Rezeptiongeschichte* into a general interweaving of categories and procedures from linguistics with literary theory while incorporating social and political histories of readership. Susan Suleiman identified six major approaches oriented to rhetorical, semiotic and structuralist, phenomenological, subjective and psychological, historical and sociological, and hermeneutic interests. Here too, though, early claims of interdisciplinarity were overstated. As audience-oriented criticism and reader-response theory took root in literary studies, art history, and sociology, the approach was often folded back into the primacy of word, image, and behavior (6–7).

The final and most difficult approach is rarely acknowledged. Correlate fields such as anthropology, philosophy, religious studies, and psychology have changed. The changes, Gunn emphasizes, challenge assumptions about the strength of boundaries while working to erode them: "The inevitable result of much interdisciplinary study, if not its ostensible purpose, is to dispute and disorder conventional understandings of relations between such things as origin and terminus, center and periphery, focus and margin, inside and outside." Ultimately, Gunn contends, interdisciplinarity is a double-sided question. Relational studies of the conjunctive kind proceed from the question of what literature has to do with other disciplines. Gunn and most proponents of critical interdisciplinarity stipulate that "genuine" interdisciplinarity alters the constitutive question that generates interdisciplinary inquiry in the first place. It asks how insights and methods of another field or structure can remodel understanding of literature and the ways literary conceptions and approaches remodel allied fields and subject materials ("Interdisciplinary Studies" 241–43, 249; *Thinking* 193–97).

Debating Interdisciplinarity

Debate on interdisciplinarity appears across all sectors of the discipline, though one of the most intense sites has been eighteenth-century studies. The defining rubrics of the Enlightenment framework were aesthetic autonomy, authorship, disinterestedness, and gendered sexuality. New historicism, cultural materialism, feminist literary history, and deconstruction transformed thinking about traditional rubrics by crossing the boundaries separating individual arts from each other and from historical, scientific, and social scientific discourses (J. Bender 79–80). In studies of Alexander Pope's poetry, for example, interest began shifting from intrinsic interests in language and literary techniques to investigations that reconstructed the worlds of the poet and the reader. Historical and interdisciplinary interests were not strongly aligned with Theory, though, stirring talk of a "return to history."

What began as a "movement," Phillip Harth recalls, escalated into a "stampede" (4). Change was not uniformly welcomed, however. In the Spring 1979 issue of *Eighteenth-Century Life*, Arthur Scouten maintained that the proper function of interdisciplinary work is to provide increased knowledge of authors and their works. He objected to the heralding of interdisciplinarity in the American Society for Eighteenth-Century Studies and new leanings toward sociology, psychology, medicine, and history of science. Quite rightly, Scouten exposed errors that result from shallow knowledge of other disciplines. Yet, he leaps to the opposite extreme, branding "tangents" in the direction of other disciplines as "whoring after strange gods." Writing in the same issue, Richard Schwartz also expressed a priority for "contextual" approaches that preserve the primacy of the text and criticized generalists for sprawling across the curriculum in a Leonardesque ambition. "True" interdisciplinary work, Schwartz contended, involves specialized learning and skills instead of universal knowledge. If the imported approach takes on greater importance, he warned, errors will result from shallow depth, and other disciplines will become tools for "literary ideologues."

David Sheehan's contribution to the debate differed. All teachers and students of the period, he argued, are of necessity involved in "cross-disciplinary" studies. In distinguishing between a "soft" and a "harder" approach, Sheehan emphasized that both kinds of work address the working problems all students of literature face. The soft approach turns to material in another discipline to illustrate something that is clear in the text but not in a context. For example, in his "Epistle to Burlington" Alexander Pope praised Burlington and the Palladian influence in architecture. The combination of beauty and use Pope recommended in art might be placed in the context of architecture by viewing illustrations of Palladian villas. A harder approach turns to another discipline out of necessity, using its materials and methods to solve a problem raised by a text. In the Preface to his novel *Joseph Andrews*, Henry Fielding compared his art of character to the caricatures of painter William Hogarth. Fielding defended Hogarth against charges of practicing the "monstrous and unnatural" extreme of burlesque, and a year later Hogarth affirmed that distinction. In this example, the problem of definition necessitated using material from one discipline in order to understand what is presented in another, raising questions about what each means by caricature, the accuracy of Fielding's observations, and their value in understanding his art. In the first case, Pope's praise of Burlington and the Palladian combination of use and beauty are clear. The interdisciplinary approach *invites* establishing context. In the second case, Fielding's Preface and Hogarth's print *require* interdisciplinarity to understand the questions they raise.

Many advocates of critical interdisciplinarity criticize small-scale problem solving such as Sheehan's "harder" approach, because it does not question the prevailing disciplinary order of knowledge. This kind of contextualizing and the quiet daily flow of influence that derives from borrowing are productive forms of interdisciplinary work that should not be dismissed outright. Yet, the new interdisciplinarity represents a more profound engagement of disciplinarity. John Bender prefers the label "transdisciplinary" for approaches that do not simply create new ways of thinking about traditional rubrics. "It is one thing," Bender explains, "to compare literature with the other arts or with—shall we say—philosophy, conceived as uniquely structured disciplines, and quite another to treat novels, paintings, buildings, logical treatises, legislation, and institutional regulations as texts participating in the complex and contestatory processes through which societies define and maintain the structure not only of their institutions but of human entities" (87–88). The latter move raises Gunn's double-sided question.

Roland Barthes also raised the double-sided question in an oft-cited definition. "Interdisciplinarity," Barthes wrote in 1977, "is not the calm of an easy security." It begins when the solidarity of existing disciplines breaks down. The break may occur suddenly, even "violently," through disruptions of fashion and new objects or languages that lack a place in the fields being brought together. The starting point is an "unease in classification." From there a "certain mutation" may be detected, although the change appears more often in the form of an epistemological slide than a sharp break. It is not enough, he added, to take a topic and surround it with two or three sciences: "Interdisciplinarity consists in creating a new object that belongs to no one." The combined action of Marxism, Freudianism, and structuralism demanded a relativization of relations of writer, reader, and critic that produced a new object—the "text." In contrast to the older notion of a "work" as a fragment of substance, Barthes defined the text as a wider methodological field invested with several meanings in a network of relations with other texts and influences.

The New Interdisciplinarity

E. Ann Kaplan and George Levine link the notion of a "new interdisciplinarity" with increased recognition of the arbitrary nature of disciplinary boundaries. Interdisciplinarity, they find, is no longer a luxury ("Introduction" 3–4). However, Stanley Fish challenged the underlying logic of new interdisciplinarity. As an agenda, Fish wrote, interdisciplinarity seems to flow naturally from the imperatives of left culturalist theory. Deconstruction, Marxism, feminism, radical neopragmatism, and new historicism were all critical of two kinds of boundary making: the social structures by which lines of political authority are maintained, and the institutional structures by which disciplines establish and extend territorial claims. Transgressing boundaries is a subversive process—a *revolution tout court.*

Yet, any strategy that calls into question the foundations of disciplines theoretically negates itself if it becomes institutionalized. The multitude of studies and projects, Fish maintained, are not radical. They center on straightforward tasks that require information and techniques from other disciplines. Or, they expand imperialistically into other territories. Or, they establish a new discipline composed of people who represent themselves as "antidisciplinary" but become a new breed of counterprofessionals ("Being Interdisciplinary").

Fish struck a chord. His position was widely embraced, but it was also countered. Arabella Lyon offered an alternative conception, likening knowledge practices to a river. They are not static. Knowledge practices have currents and flows, tributaries, eddies, and confluences (682). Gunn judged Fish's position to be a conservative and pessimistic political stance that perpetuates the dualism of disciplinarity and interdisciplinarity. Fish claims interdisciplinarity is impossible because one cannot inhabit more than a single territory at a time. Yet, Gunn answered, the question of interdisciplinarity is not framed by the stark poles of how to free or to fix the mind but how to subtitilize it. The radical claim that interdisciplinarity will open the mind is as misleading as the conservative claim that it will leave it closed (*Thinking* 188–91). Richard Turner likened the practitioner working within while also thinking reflexively about a discipline to twentieth-century physicists, who negotiated between competing claims and efforts to transcend them in theorizing about unified theory (114–15). Fish subsequently extended his critique by characterizing historicized and politicized criticism as a totalizing ambition that lies outside the framework of literary studies. Moran adds, though, that Fish's position is based on two oversimplifications: first, that disciplines are coherent or homogenous and, second, that interdisciplinarity is synonymous with the quest for an ultimate synthesis of knowledge. The projects of cultural materialism and new historicism, for instance, are more likely to denaturalize disciplinary divisions and challenge orthodoxies (145–47).

Indicative of the growing momentum for interdisciplinarity in the discipline, in 1996 the Modern Language Association published responses to a call for comments on whether its goals are being achieved. The profession's sense of the idea, Alan Rauch answered, has not changed much. The figure of the eclectic polymath remains predominant, validating disciplinary boundaries and suggesting that interdisciplinarity is about capacity and retention more than synthesis and analysis. The popular image of interdisciplinary programs disguises the more complex cultural matrix of inquiries, including Rauch's own field of science, technology, and society studies. A more sophisticated dissolution of disciplinary boundaries occurs in the field and the curriculum reforms it prompts. The field also moves beyond the dichotomy of instrumental versus critical interdisciplinarity in integrations of problem solving and critique. In his reply, Derek Attridge distinguished feminism, deconstruction, and cultural studies from the absorptive process. Attridge regards the creation of new disciplines, including metadisciplines and subdisciplines, as an "inherent" function of interdisciplinarity. He cautions, though, that interdisciplinarity still runs the risk of producing inhibiting codes and cultures ("Forum").

Other respondents reported problems of practice. Jacqueline Henkel questioned how much scholars and teachers are actually invested in interdisciplinary research. The surface evidence of publication suggests so, but models and modes of discourse in other fields are not regularly examined. Some activities bear fruit, such as borrowings, collaborations, and cross-departmental inquiries into questions that individuals cannot solve by themselves. Yet, finding collaborative partners and compatible projects can be difficult, let alone career rewards for co-authorships and jobs for graduate students. Dubbing interdisciplinarity a "vexed term," Sara Van den Berg called attention to the crossfire of legitimation. Some psychoanalysts smirk at literary critics' assumption that psychoanalytic theory stopped with Freud (or Jung, Winnicott, or Lacan). Literary critics smile back at their assumption that literary theory stopped with New Criticism. Sociologists criticize literary critics for pirating odd bits of sociological thinking but come under attack themselves for pirating pieces of literature without regard for interpretation or aesthetic qualities. Susan Balee cited additional examples. One French historian opposed literary critics' use of Foucault, claiming he is "out of favor," and dismissed Stephen Greenblatt's new historical work as anecdotal nuggeting. One anthropologist called literary critics' use of Clifford Geertz and Levi Strauss outmoded borrowings, and a psychology professor dismissed Carol Gilligan as a pop psychologist ("Forum").

The following year, Bruce Robbins expressed increasing dissatisfaction with two particular arguments: that commitment to a given discipline is a willful self-blinkering detracting from intellectuals' higher responsibility to truth and justice, and that politics cannot be separated from criticism or any discipline because "everything is political." Seeking a more satisfactory framework, Robbins returned to Kant's 1798 *Conflict of the Faculties.*

Kant conceded that politics could not be kept out of the university, but aligned it with law, medicine, and theology because they had greater proximity to government power and were subject to its control. By renouncing politics, Kant gave philosophy a unique right to autonomy and the freedom to evaluate everything. In the late twentieth century, the characteristic interdisciplinary counterstatement to Kant was Foucault's fusion of power and knowledge. Conflation of power and knowledge became a defining principle of Theory and cultural studies. This stance, though, has not stopped disciplines from claiming to offer an unspecialized and synthesizing vision. Something more is needed, Robbins exhorted, than an instinctive assertion of proprietary rights and oscillating back and forth between invocations of a utopic "de-disciplining" and the cynical view that everyone is looking out for disciplinary self-interests. The vocabulary of public significance in which claims are pressed, he added, must be "transdisciplinary" in the service of a common ethical or political language ("Less Disciplinary").

The End of Discipline?

Delivering the 1980 MLA presidential address, Helen Vendler warned against "a general interdisciplinary Polonius like religious-historical-philosophical-cultural overview" (qtd. in Graff 254). Two years later, Walter Jackson Bate urged a return to the Renaissance ideal of *literrae humaniores,* and the following decade Alvin Kernan lamented that literature was being "emptied out": "Deconstructive philosophical terrorist, intellectual revolutionary, and feminist freedom-fighter" might only be fashions of the moment, he wrote, but the assault on meaning threatened to dissipate the accumulated capital of discipline (*Death of Literature* 200–01, 211–12). Opposition continues. In his 1997 book *Literature Lost,* John Ellis attacked the new centrality of politics and power, the arcane language of Theory, and cultural studies. He blamed them for declining enrollment and charged feminism, in particular, with veering off course into "outlandish, wildly unrealistic ideas" and "hysteria" over patriarchal conspiracies. Ellis's inflammatory language undermines his case. Even less vehement critics, however, cast doubt on what goes in the name of interdisciplinarity today. While serving as MLA president in 1999, Edward Said remarked that all kinds of fragmented, jargonized subjects now flourish in ahistorical limbo. They are not completely anthropological, sociological, philosophical, or psychological, but they carry some of the marks of those disciplines.

A fundamental question underlies these critiques. Has literature been lost? "Literature as it was," John Carlos Rowe answers, "can't be saved." The term now encompasses older texts and "extraliterary" materials such as letters, diaries, films, paintings, manifestos, and philosophical, political, psychological, religious, and medical treatises (204). In the 1970s, Richard Ohmann recalls, poststructuralist Theory began to unsettle the premise of a coherent and stable text, de-aestheticizing literature and surrendering its difference from other forms of speech and writing. The success of Theory justified including "literally everything" from film, romances, and hip-hop to museums and sexuality. The expansionist move, though, put English in direct competition with other disciplines. This might have been an advance, if everyone agreed cultural studies was the work of the future; if faculty in other disciplines leapt at opportunities for collaboration; and if administrators, trustees, founders, journalists, and voters saw the change as an exciting revolution. None of this happened to an appreciable degree, however. Internal strife and resentment followed, along with mockery from the media and political Right. The curriculum lost whatever coherence it had, importing material and methods from outside and spilling into interdisciplinary and multicultural studies (216–18).

Expansion, though, does not mean "literature" has been abandoned. When criticism is accused of abandoning literature, Robbins replies, the objection is often not against outright rejection of the category so much as broadening it. Under the aegis of Theory and cultural studies, more subject matter has been claimed since the 1960s. This expansionist embrace, though, is also fraught with irony. It has not been conducted in the name of texts treated as organic wholes. Yet, it displays the operations of literariness in other senses. Social identities are placed in a wider field of texts and genres of discourse, while literary and literary-critical modalities are transferred into other disciplines. Theory and cultural studies were antitotalizing in intent, but they became totalizing in social or transdisciplinary form, enacting the same claim to "synthesizing" or "all-embracing" status that Kant made for philosophy and others make for their disciplines ("Less Disciplinary" 108–09).

As for the question of coherence, W. B. Carnochan contends that it never existed. The early split of North American literature and language departments into three areas—philology, literature as moral uplift, and rhetoric and composition—is still present in the guise of Theory, literature as political and ethical understanding, and rhetoric and composition (qtd. in Hutcheon, "Introduction" 1722). Molly Hite describes English in the United States as more like three disciplines with separate faculty, budgets, and value systems. The first and most prestigious variant—literature and Theory—now includes cultural, media, gender, and Third World studies. Composition is the second variant and creative writing the third (149). Many departments also include film studies and ESL. The current structural trend of the discipline, Ann Middleton finds, is moving toward topical and interest-group fragmentation, while "text," "Theory," and "discourse" are operating as boundary concepts across disciplines (23). Few dispute that transformations have redrawn the parameters of subfields, Greenblatt and Gunn add. Resistance to formalism and the extremes of specialism are widespread, new forms of texts are being studied, and the repertoire of explanatory tools and frameworks has expanded. What individuals are to make of these changes, however, is less clear ("Introduction" 1).

Classroom practices are one measure. When Francis Oakley examined the data in 1997, he found that change has occurred primarily through addition rather than substitution. Between 1965 and 1985, the basic configuration of the major changed only slightly. Most departments continued to require traditional historical coverage. The combined data from surveys of British and American literature, upper-division Renaissance literature (excluding Shakespeare), the nineteenth-century British novel, and American literature from 1800 to 1865 counters allegations that evidence of continuity masks radical change. The majority of respondents were teaching a consistent core of works, most by traditional authors. Of the nearly 65% who had added required readings, between 25 and 30% introduced traditional major authors, although between a third and a half chose less commonly taught writers. The MLA's 1995 report on introductory survey courses revealed a traditional list as well, and the majority of instructors appeared to be setting familiar goals such as gaining skills of close reading, understanding literary forms and genres, and learning the intellectual, historical, and biographical backgrounds necessary for understanding literature in a given period. Two-thirds and more also favored traditional approaches such as history of ideas and New Criticism. The only comparative innovation that came close, at 61%, was feminist perspectives. Like all instruments, Oakley notes, the survey raises questions of methodology. The question designed to elicit how many favor poststructuralist goals was worded in a manner that might have dissuaded large numbers from answering "yes." Averages based on aggregated figures may also conceal important trends. When figures are broken down, faculty who received PhDs since the 1980s and faculty of all ages at PhD-granting universities are more likely to emphasize less traditional goals ("Ignorant Armies" 71–76). Cultural studies is also more prominent among many younger faculty, underscoring a pattern of generational differences in all humanities disciplines (Miller, "Theory" 131–33; Miller, *Illustration* 145).

Future Forecasts

Jeffery Williams dubs the faculty who entered literary studies in the late 1980s through 1990s the "posttheory generation." They are paradoxically positioned. Intensely theoretical, they arrived after the theoretical debates and wars of the 1970s. The aggregate practices of cultural, lesbigay, and race studies and associated movements signal a new period in the history of the discipline. Yet, older practices have not been jettisoned. They are engaged in a dialogue with new approaches to traditional historical research, bibliographical work, and close readings of texts. Recent scholarship is also reworking older theoretical positions, resulting in less exclusionary, more eclectic, and flexible hybrids that document heightened multidisciplinarity. The deconstructive critique of center and margin, for example, is fundamental to the project of postcolonialism. Yet, the project also draws on Marxist critiques of power and imperialism, postcolonial studies are rooted in specific historical instances and place, and distinctions of sex and gender are combined with a poststructuralist anti-essentialism that evolved into gender studies and underwrites lesbigay studies. Big Theory, Williams adds, has trickled down to loosely allied foci affiliated with or defined by identity politics and the practice of identity studies along axes of sex, race, and place.

The elevated status of American literature in the discipline is also as significant as the shift from teaching texts as literature, not grammar. For much of the early history of the discipline, literature meant *British* texts. Courses in American literature proliferated during the 1950s on the heels of postwar patriotism. By mid-century, Americanists had attained influence in the curriculum, where Ralph Waldo Emerson was installed as the embodiment of a model of humanism that upheld higher spiritual values and the social and political status quo (Shumway, "Emerson" 101, 103). In reviewing more recent literary and cultural studies of the post–Civil War period, Philip Fisher found that scholarship since the 1970s has explored the complex relations between culture and writer or speaker. New authors have entered the canon, and traditional works are being reread through the lens of new approaches. The newness of scholarship, Fisher suggests, is summed up by a shift from myth to rhetorics and from a single fixed story to open questions of culture (232, 237). Reviewing the period to the Civil War, Cecelia Tichi found parallel reevaluations. The relationship of major and marginal or minor texts is being rethought, along with the thematics of individualism and American identity and the divide of elite and popular culture. Exemplary scholarship of a traditional kind should not be overlooked, though. It continues in studies of national character in Hawthorne and Melville, democratic ideals, and Thoreau's classical influences.

Inevitably, talk of transformation into cultural studies arose. Michael Ryan identified three crucial moments in this evolution:

1. Feminist, ethnic, and leftist criticism forced recognition that literary texts are fundamentally documents and social texts with sociohistorical referents;
2. Structuralism and semiotics demonstrated that texts are shaped by social codes, conventions, and representations, debunking the idea of literary autonomy;
3. The rising importance of mass media and popular culture compelled critics to admit the crucial formative and educational roles of these new discourses
   (qtd. in Leitch 403–04, Ryan "Cultural Studies")

The turn toward cultural studies is not without danger. Transdisciplinary methodology, Jo-Ann Wallace cautions, differs from a program or discipline. The first reason—methodology—holds potential for collaboration, more flexible exchanges and groupings, and new questions and knowledges. The second—institutional structure—can become a contested site of struggle for funding and affiliation. The "easy slippage" into cultural studies poses an especially serious threat to small disciplines such as art history, film studies, classics, and philosophy. Joining a modern languages department or a comparative cultural studies department might result in productive collaboration, but the integrity of subjects does not follow naturally when faculty are simply moved around. Even if faculty in English studies can "do" cultural studies, Wallace warns, they cannot necessarily teach art history, film, philosophy, or other disciplines. The utopic promise of new interdisciplinarity collapses in a superficial eclecticism promoted under the banner of a dubious fusion of literature, art, music, and other humanities. Renewal of the cultural function of literature also collapses. It is no longer waged on the ground of liberal humanism but polyglot specialization in a field crowded with competing subspecialities.

Talk of globalization abounds as well. It is not new, Gunn observed in the Introduction to a 2001 *PMLA* forum on the topic. From the medieval period forward, cultural migrations with literary consequences have occurred in Europe. Writing in Europe has been in continuous conversation with emergent literatures of the Americas from the early modern period forward, and literary studies has a history of engagements with studies of world history, the history of religions, language, and comparative literature. In recent decades, though, interest in the internationalization of literature and cultural studies has expanded. Gunn and Paul Jay highlight the increasingly postnational and transnational nature of literary writing in English. The nationalist ideal in American literary studies is no longer constrained within national borders either. It is unfolding in a transnational economic and cultural exchange characterized by the global flow of cultural products and commodities. Influence is neither linear nor one-directional, Jay adds. It is a reciprocal process that fosters more comparative approaches and wider contexts for studying literature and other media. This shift is signified by a new vocabulary of "hybridity," "diaspora" "transculturation," "subaltern," "hegemony," "deterritorialization," "rhizome," "mestizo," "Eurocentrism," and "othering." The pluralization, heterogeneity, and polyvocality of national traditions is not a simple broadening of disciplinary domain. It can only be fully assessed and understood Jay urges, by drawing on critical methods from the entire range of human sciences.

Literary studies demonstrates both the successes and the limits of interdisciplinarity. Proponents and opponents alike now speak of transformation from a discipline to an interdisciplinary field. However, Greenblatt and Gunn remind us, the domain of interdisciplinarity is not entered every time a border is crossed. The desire to see from different sides of the same border is often confused with sustained interactions ("Introduction" 4–5). Many faculty today, Linda Pratt commented in an MLA forum on the future of the discipline in 2002, consider English to be "very interdisciplinary." Yet, research still tends to be solitary, incorporating fragments of history, sociology, ethnography, and psychology as contexts for a broad definition of texts. Pratt urges more collaborative work with others in forums that nurture informed interdisciplinary work. Ultimately, Gunn advises, the intellectual future of interdisciplinary studies will depend on avoiding the temptations of reductionism—thinking methods of one field are sufficient to interpret the materials of many— and the appetite for metaphorical transfer—treating materials of one field as mere epiphenomena of the subjects of another. The future of interdisciplinarity will also depend on adequate economic capital and administrative support for new curriculum and graduate programs, centers and summer institutes, visiting and permanent professorships, publication outlets, interdepartmental colloquia, and scholarships ("Interdisciplinary Studies" 255; *Thinking* 210). The lesson of critical mass repeats.

Chapter 5

REFIGURING THE VISUAL

The other disciplines in this set of case studies—art and music—have several features in common. They inherited a humanistic identity vested in creativity and the values of liberal education. They occupy a presence beyond the academy in performance venues, museums, and other cultural institutions. They are nonverbal media whose data are more resistant to verbal explication than the data of other humanities (R. Parker 10). And, during the latter half of the twentieth century, they underwent a number of changes. The changes occurred in music later than in art history, but the canons of both disciplines expanded, interdisciplinary interests broadened, and new critical, theoretical, and sociohistorical approaches influenced the ways that both art and music are understood.

This chapter addresses a series of continuing questions about disciplines with particular regard to art history. What were the early warrants for interdisciplinarity in the discipline? What changes promoted a new art history, and what were its interdisciplinary dynamics? What similarities and differences appear in theory and in practice? How has the identity of the discipline changed? What are the key points of debate on interdisciplinarity, and how do they figure in discussions of the discipline's current status and future prospects?

From the Old to the New

Art did not enter the halls of higher learning until visual arts moved from the manual arts to the liberal arts. This shift was aided by a new system of education in the sixteenth century, when academies of art began to rival the traditional apprenticeship system. Giorgio Vasari's evolutionary approach to style history influenced the general outlines of art history in Europe for several centuries to come. In *Lives of the Most Eminent Painters, Sculptors, and Architects* (1550), Vasari extolled the High Renaissance as the pinnacle of excellence. Vasari's method was a series of aesthetic and moral value judgments interwoven with anecdotes and references to purported facts (Kraft 58–59, 61). Barbara Stafford dates the origin of art history to the eighteenth century. It was a borrower from the start, taking attitudes and vocabularies from prior or canonical disciplines and constructing a hybrid identity from mathematics, rhetoric and poetics, and philosophy (especially Neo-Platonism). The discipline's founders were mindful of an intellectual deficit. Artists were inclined to offer inductive and "artisanal" conjectures about visual and aesthetic matters, not deductive or exact knowledge about a fixed or stable mental territory with objects of intellection (7).

In a familiar historical pattern, the study of art as an empirical science began in the late nineteenth century. The founders of the modern discipline extended the canon to include post-Renaissance art and channeled the concept of style to formal characteristics such as the design elements of color, shape, line, texture, and space. Works, artists, styles, and national or ethnic groups could be compared and classified, explicated, and interpreted in a systematic fashion, making the critic an intermediary between the artist and the public (Kraft 59–60). Facts also became the basis for assessing contested philosophies of art using comparative methods adapted from philology. Art historical research could be separated ontologically from other fields, including aesthetics and attitudes and feelings. Interpretations could be legitimated with the status of eternal truths parallel to scientific laws, and the problematics of production and reception were placed beyond formalist science (Preziosi, "Question" 365–70).

The conventional story of the discipline's origin in this country begins in elite universities. The first regular professor of art history in the United States, Charles Eliot Norton, began lecturing at Harvard in 1874 on the "History of the Fine Arts as Connected with Literature" (Roberts and Turner 78). Even though art history was a latecomer, Thomas Reese recounts, a 1912 report revealed that ninety-five universities were teaching the subject and sixty-eight were offering courses by someone with a chair in the subject. Fewer than four-fifths of one percent of the teaching body, however, specialized in art and archaeology. The rest taught in departments of classics, Semitic languages, biblical literature, French and Romance languages, and history. Before 1920, art history was usually seated in the liberal arts college. It took on expanded and competing functions in the growing network of departments, although professional identity continued to be associated with a generalized notion of art education. Practical teaching of fine arts also had a strong legacy in American education. After 1917, though, annual professional meetings became sites for discussing technical courses, production or pedagogical tools, and courses for the lay public, museum workers, writers, and professionals in the history of fine arts (545–46).

Interdisciplinary Warrants

Periodization was the most powerful basis of interdisciplinary relation. Common motifs, themes, and genres suggested synchronic relations within chronological eras and stylistic categories. In reviewing theories of periodization, Alastair Fowler found that the concept of a *Zeitgeist* underlies many formulations. In German, the word means spirit of the times or a general trend or feeling. Praz's concept of *ductus* held that every epoch has a peculiar handwriting. The concept descended from Oswald Spengler's doctrine that it is possible to divine the constitution of a state from details of artistic form or to reconstruct the history of a century from details of ornaments, architecture, writings, or data of a political, economic, and religious nature. In the nineteenth century, interart comparison was typically formulated in terms of historical criteria, the *Zeitgeist,* or a *Formwille.* The theory of Goethian or romantic organicism also treated arts as a holistic unity, and, in the twentieth century, E. H. Gombrich's concept of norms, theories of social reflexes, and theories of technical achievement provided a basis for unity. True believers in *Zeitgeist,* Fowler observed, have little time for mundane processes of influence, imitation, or achievement. They prefer to intuit essences directly. Their discourse centers on the spirit of movements, periods, or cultural moments thought to convey a tight coherence among all cultural activities and a complete parallelism of arts (Fowler 489–90; Steiner 3, 186).

Just as literary studies had the polymaths Edmund Burke and Northrop Frye, art history had an individual who stood at the crux of disciplinarity and interdisciplinarity. European émigrés who came to this country during the 1920s and 1940s were a major stimulus for constructing art history as scientific research. The most prominent of them prior to and after World War II was Erwin Panofsky. In 1953, Panofsky reflected on the difference between German and American academic cultures. Extolling the European model of *universitas magistrorum et scholarium* and the German *Lehrfreiheit* and *Lernfreiheit,* he criticized the democratic educational mission of the American university, replacement of the collegial chair system with departments, and the penchant for completeness in a balanced curriculum. He also differed from John Dewey, who believed that art should be integrated into everyday life. The juxtaposition of Dewey's democratic ideals and Panofsky's hierarchical approach, Reese notes, exposes a major schism in American art history and humanities. The American educational mission promoted the value of arts in society. The European scholarly mission privileged acquisition of humanistic learning and knowledge (546–47).

Even as Panofsky upheld traditional ideals, however, he departed from formalist practices. He did not challenge the traditional canon, accepting High Renaissance art as the norm. Nor did he displace stylistic analysis as a primary methodology. Yet, he emphasized interpretation over observation of facts, urging other scholars to engage in hermeneutic decoding of the meaning and symbols of works. In considering the world surrounding stylistic change, Panofsky practiced a form of early contextualist critique, drawing insights from philosophy, religion, mythology, and other material beyond art (Kraft 62–63). Martin Herman calls Panofsky's 1951 book *Gothic Architecture and Scholasticism* a "dazzling display of interdisciplinary scholarship." Scholasticism was a more specific method of connecting subjects than *Zeitgeist* or shared chronology. A universal scholarly habit visible in music, theology, and architecture, scholasticism located order and unity within a system of distinguishable but related parts. *Manifestatio* was the first controlling principle. Its characteristic feature was systematic articulation and interrelation of homologous parts. In a High Gothic cathedral, for example, Romanesque and Gothic elements were juxtaposed in a systematic ordering of structural elements based on division and subdivision. *Concordia* provided the means for achieving synthesis through a process of accepting and reconciling contradictory possibilities within the methodological framework provided by *manifestatio* (35–38).

The New Art History

Donald Preziosi likens modern art history to an Ames Room or a Foucauldian heterotropic space of contradictory practices and theoretical positions. It has an illusory unity and coherence, projecting an ideological matrix from disparate sources onto a common screen (*Rethinking* 157–58). The changing nature of art was a factor in the evolution of a "new art history." New stylistic movements such as pure form, color field painting, and minimal art had little in common visually with earlier traditions. The notion of American art also expanded to include works by women and different cultural groups. The boundary between high and low or popular art eroded, legitimating the artistry of once-excluded objects such as furniture and quilts, cartoons and graffiti, commercial illustrations, and tattooing. The field of works expanded on a global scale with large exhibits on Chinese painting and excavations, African art, and the art of the Mamluks and the Mughals. New hybrid genres emerged, such as performance art with its combinations of music, visual art, literary expression, and theatrical performance (Kraft 64–65). Interart forms crafted from new media and digital technology began appearing as well, and multigenre forms emanating from cultural movements for identity and equality such as the Black Arts movement and the Chicano Performing and Graphic Arts.

Scholarship changed in kind. In the late 1980s, historical empiricism and traditional style analysis still dominated the mainstream. Talk of new art history was growing, though. Selma Kraft identified two general directions. One—coming from social sciences—accentuated production and use. It focused on the political, cultural, social, and economic conditions under which art is made and on subjects such as patronage, the art public, and workshop practices. The other—closer to humanities—drew on critical, semiotic, and deconstructionist approaches, especially from literary theory and philosophy. Both strains differed from the interdisciplinarity of Panofsky, who was interested in the inherent meaning of works regarded as exact reflectors of attitudes and values. The new art history critiqued assumptions about self-evident meaning and uniformities of interpretation that ignore differences of ethnicity, race, gender, and class. Scholars began treating artworks as texts and as structures of signification whose meaning depends on the interpretation that is applied. They weighed the relative merits of disciplinary methods and protocols, examined historical origins of the discipline, and explored processes of professionalization. They expanded art history's relationship with art criticism, aesthetic philosophy, markets, exhibitions, and museology. They used insights from Marxism to understand social and economic determinations, and they borrowed explanations of repressed instincts from psychoanalysis, power relationships from political theory, institutions from sociology, and structures from anthropology (65–66).

The new art history is not focused solely on the present, even though the status of twentieth-century art rose dramatically. Scholars are returning to earlier historical periods to understand, for example, Paleolithic imagery and marking and palimpsesting through the lenses of new critical approaches. They are also bringing new insights to bear on iconography, attribution of works, genre definition and development (Preziosi, *Rethinking* 155). The new art history is not solely the product of art historians either. Many of the most stimulating writers on art history matters, Richard Brilliant points out, are philosophers, psychologists, historians of English and French literature, semioticians, anthropologists, social psychologists and critics (204). Art history, David Lubin adds, lost its exclusive franchise on visual images as rival disciplines—anthropology, comparative literature, English, and sociology—and interdisciplinary fields—American studies, film studies, material culture studies, and visual culture studies—claimed their own stakes in analyzing and interpreting visual materials (175).

Two developments—sociology of art and feminist art history—illustrate the shifting terms of interdisciplinarity. In the late 1960s and early 1970s, social history focused primarily on the *things* of modern social iconography such as peasants, dance halls, and other objects. From the early 1980s forward, modes of analysis derived from literary criticism inspired art historians to examine visual artifacts as if they were *words*, capable of performing tropes and exhibiting mechanisms of signification (Herbert 537). New scholarship in general, Janet Woolf recalls, exhibited a more interactive understanding of the relationship between cultural forms and social process. T. J. Clark's 1973 and 1974 essays on the social history of art were catalysts for moving beyond aesthetic autonomy and treating society as a background. Even in the 1990s, though, limits persisted. As sociology of art developed in the U.S., sociologists tended to apply existing tools and methods to new areas and did not engage in aesthetics or deep discussion of the content of works. Humanists, in turn, tended to prioritize intertextuality, emphasizing discursive over "extratextual" dimensions. The sociology brought to bear on texts was often shallow and mechanistic. A mutually constitutive relationship, Woolf admonishes, requires integrating textual analysis with sociological investigation of institutions of cultural production and the social and political processes in which it occurs (708–09).

In a 1992 anthology of new scholarship, Norma Broude and Mary Garrard remembered how feminist art history was associated initially with rediscovering forgotten women artists. Feminism, though, also raised more fundamental questions. Feminist scholars challenged the defining values, categories, and conceptual structures of the discipline while developing a feminist theory and discourse for understanding art. In doing so, they drew on Theory and other critical perspectives. They did not borrow them wholesale, however. Theory had generally ignored issues of gender, and the death-of-the-author stance ran counter to feminist efforts to assert a place for women in the canon. Critical theory also privileged texts over images. Adapting borrowings to their purposes, feminist critics shifted the focus from formalist analysis of the narrow spheres of artist or art object to cultural systems and attendant sociopolitical forces. They operated with a pragmatic "foot in both camps," working the faultlines of Enlightenment and postmodern agendas. Laura Mulvey's groundbreaking work in 1973 contributed one of the most influential conceptual tools, an understanding of power through the viewpoint of males looking at females portrayed as passive objects of a controlling "gaze." In exploring practices of representation and spectatorship in films, Mulvey drew on the psychoanalytic theories of Freud and Lacan. Her work stimulated widespread investigations of the female body's objectification and sociocultural uses as a signifier in art.

Rethinking the Discipline

As always, change provoked debate. During the 1980s and 1990s, sessions on new approaches and on interdisciplinarity dotted the programs of the College Art Association's annual meetings and publications, including the Winter 1982 issue of *Art Journal* on "The Crisis in the Discipline" and books entitled *The New Art History, Rethinking Art History,* and *The End of the History of Art?* (Bal, *Reading "Rembrandt"* 25). Stephen Melville posed a number of questions raised by the emergence of new art history. Is it really new or a renewed social history of arts? Or a new semiotic ground? A call for a poststructuralist art history or a postmodern discipline? Or an art history that returns to its historical roots while renewing or transforming them? Some scholars see themselves as interventionists working from outside the traditional discipline, some as integrationists striving to create a larger field, and others as agents of a critical return to the original conceptual foundation. More questions follow. Are new practices inside or outside the discipline proper? And, what relationship do their proponents have with founding figures of the discipline—loyalty or betrayal? (31).

Addressing the last issue, Preziosi asks further related questions. Are the founders of a discipline the source of error or of precedent? Do new developments eclipse older interests? Or do present-day practitioners forget their predecessors' depth and insight? Panofsky may be read as anticipating contemporary semiology and Alois Riegel as prefiguring the concerns of structuralism. The disputatious nature of the present may also be over-stated. Over time, art history has steered through numerous rhetorical bat-tles between formalism and contextualism, social history and connoisseur-ship, and modernist and poststructuralist semiologies. The salient issues in debates on the discipline, Preziosi finds, hinge on several factors:

- boundaries and the proper domain or object of study;
- the manner in which artworks and visual artifacts produce signification or re-flect meaning or contents or generate certain effects for and among viewers and users;
- relations between art history and art criticism;
- relations between interpretation in art criticism and creation in artistic practice.
                                            (*Rethinking* xiii, 2, 7, 18, 157–58)

Opponents of new practices made their objections clear in print and at a walkout in the College Art Association. Donald Kuspit identified four rea-sons for negative reactions to structuralist and poststructuralist theories. Many art historians assume an artwork has a sacral quality that distin-guishes it from ordinary objects. They believe that the visual has a greater proximity to the "madness of inner life" that cannot be captured by lin-guistic gestures and, correspondingly, that the visual is more closely linked with a "bodiliness" that cannot be described by words. They also grant the artist primacy over the critic (346; qtd. in Gabbard, "Introduction" 18). Even among advocates, new practices raised concern. William Hood re-ported in 1987 that many American art historians seemed at times indiffer-ent or even hostile to older rigors of style criticism, textual analysis, and other foundations. Yet, they were concerned about losing what made art history unique, along with their personal identity (185). In introducing the 1982 "Crisis" issue, Preziosi suggested that changes might already have precipitated "the end of art history" and previous understandings of "art." Historical theories and practices were being reconstructed and the outlines of a new discipline being sketched ("Origins" 325). The following year, Stafford asked whether art history is even a "discipline"—with a discrete method and precise subject. Or, is it a "field"—with a heterogeneous reper-toire of varied and unified interests? (8)

On close inspection, Mieke Bal reflects, symptoms of crisis are decep-tive. They actually highlight an "astonishing vitality." The willingness of art historians to challenge their discipline, its expanding boundaries, and the creation of new fields does not mean that art history is "giving up the ghost." Opponents who lament that it may not survive new challenges and may lose self-determination might have a point. But the question is not whether art history is "sick" or "in the pink," or both. It is engaged in intensive challenging, addressing, and overcoming the threat of foreclosure. Art history may even, Bal asserts, have become predominant in humanities. In the 1970s and early 1980s, linguistics laid claim to the status of a central discipline. In the 1980s, anthropology enjoyed wide influence. In the 1990s, scholars from other fields drew increasingly on art history (*Reading "Rembrandt"* 25–26). The current array of tools and perspectives, Griselda Pollock adds, underscores the problematic of what is admissible as argument, evidence, or concept in a discipline. If curatorial and connoisseurial functions of art are no longer the basis of humanism, what is? A variety of theories now interrelate visual arts with cultural sign systems or discursive formations and ideological apparatuses (38–39).

From Interart Comparison to Word and Image Studies

When the topic of "Inter/disciplinarity" was the special focus in a 1995 issue of *Art Bulletin,* a range of views appeared. Whether the exchange of information and analytic tools should occur, James Herbert reported, is no longer a source of conflict. The questions now are with whom, in what form, and how much. Herbert regards interrogation of disciplinarity as the most promising function (537, 539). Making the case for a more modest role, Carlos Ginzberg defended "interdisciplinarity from within" conventional practices over an "interdisciplinarity from without" that illustrates general, preexisting formulations in an overtly theoretical approach. Ginzberg also disputed the current promotion of interdisciplinarity as a remedy for the narrow-mindedness and conservatism of a discipline or as a weapon against it. Both attitudes, he maintains, are based on misperceptions. The prevailing formulation rejects a narrowly positivistic attitude in favor of a broader and theoretically oriented approach exemplified by Régis Michel's call for a "nonhistory of art" arising from dialogue with semioticians, philosophers, and anthropologists. Yet, Ginzburg challenged Michel's assertion that the traditional practice of connoisseurship has undergone a "full metamorphosis."

The problem of determining who created a specific watercolor demonstrates the value of interdisciplinarity from within. When a drawing of peonies was auctioned at Christie's, it was identified as a work of Northern Italian origin in the sixteenth century. In 1991, Fritz Koreny attributed the drawing to Martin Schongauer, dating it to roughly 1473 and classifying it as a study for a well-known painting by Schongauer known as "Madonna of the Rose Garden." However, Ginzburg asks, could the drawing be a later copy by another artist who was familiar with Schongauer? Koreny presented a detailed analysis of the paper on which the study was painted, with the watermark of a gothic "p" with flower as evidence. If research starts with analysis of the watermark instead, the attribution in sixteenth-century Northern Italy and the search for origin in Basel or the surrounding area during the 1470s might be dismissed. A massive number of watermarks show a gothic "p" with flower, and art historians differ widely on the number of Schongauer's drawings. Attribution might be achieved by relying on stylistic evidence alone. Yet, a different answer emerged from a "largely unintentional convergence" of botanists, archivists, paleographers, experts in watermarks, and art historians who provided data that were not necessarily compatible. Different datings had to be sorted out. Good connoisseurship such as Koreny's, Ginzburg concludes, has a cognitive richness that is characterized by a productive "interplay of vetoes and compatibilities, doubts and suggestions."

Interart comparison is a more generic example of the limited form of interdisciplinary relation. The practice goes by many names, including sister arts, comparative or interdisciplinary arts, interart studies or the inter-arts borderland, and the study of analogies, interrelationships, and mutual illumination. The tradition was shaped by the doctrine of mimesis, which holds that a work is a faithful imitation of reality. Art, in effect, mirrors nature. The most famous formulation was Horace's concept of *ut pictura poesis*. Poetry was said to paint the world on the mind's eye, and painting to present mute objects in a framework that makes them speak. *Ut musica poesis* compares literature to music, and *ut musica pictura* compares music and painting. More recently, a new form posited a relationship between painting and critical prose. In *ut pictura theoria,* the reference may not be literature or poetry but criticism, philosophy, and metaphysics. The word "theory," W. J. T. Mitchell suggests, stands in the same relation to abstract art as traditional literary forms did to representational paintings. Literature and visual arts became the most prominent pairing in interart comparison, because they were both regarded as mimetic arts and were both studied in the context of the history of ideas. Literary painting, which depicts subject matters and images of the human body, was also privileged over nonliterary forms such as landscape painting, abstract art, still life, and other genre painting (Weisstein 256; Melville and Readings, "Introduction" 8; Mitchell, *Picture Theory* 27, 220–22; Mitchell "Against Comparison 34).

Interart relations are neither simple nor linear. They constitute a complex dialectic in an intricate pattern of coincidences and divergences (Kleiner 31). Some genres of painting and drawing invoke literary antecedents or historical contexts. Some artists incorporate words or letters into paintings, and some paintings represent the act of writing, as the artist Paul Klee did when he incorporated handwritten titles. Other works recreate or literally constitute the things they delineate. Calligrams, for example, arrange words as visual representations of subjects, such as George Herbert's "The Altar," William Carlos Williams's "The Yellow Smokestack," the pattern poems of John Hollander, and the genre of concrete poetry. A literary work, in turn, might have an outward appearance that depends on design or graphic elements, such as hieroglyphs or Chinese characters. Or, it might stimulate the visual sense through images, metaphors, or similes. Some writers reproduce visual styles, such as impressionist syntax in prose. Others borrow certain techniques or models, such as the grotesque, collage, and camera-eye techniques. Others focus on art and artists as their subjects or borrow particular themes or motifs. The illuminated books of William Blake illustrate the range of combinations in composite texts, from "disjunctive" illustrations with no textual references to the complete "synthetic" collapse of the distinction between writing and drawing (Weisstein 259; Miller, *Illustration* 73–74; Mitchell, *Picture Theory* 91–92).

Scholarship, in turn, varies. Interart comparison focused traditionally on similarities and differences, demonstrating the superiority of one art over others, polemicizing against fusion or separation, and reducing all arts to the same principles. Jon Green identified three major approaches in scholarship and teaching about literature and other arts: investigations of common origins in a search for an ancient unity comparable to stem languages, experiential-psychological studies that depict arts as extensions of the senses in time and space, and structural-semiotic analyses that view arts as alternative language systems. Robert K. Wallace has explored the widest range of parallels and influences in comparisons of works by Jane Austen and Wolfgang Amadeus Mozart, Emily Bronte and Beethoven, Herman Melville and J. M. W. Turner, and Herman Melville and Frank Stella (8).

The Limits of Interart Comparison

Rosamond Tuve observed that every interart comparison involves a metaphor. Yet, Fowler asks, what makes a metaphor sound? Vague impressions, free associations, subjective responses, mere coincidences, and selective or fanciful details may outweigh hard evidence. A feature literally present in one art may be only figuratively present in another. Proof of relationship may depend on exaggerated generalizations. Or, different subjects may demand different treatments, and the arts are not precisely symmetrical. Heinrich Wölfflin maintained that a serious approach to comparison must rest on strictly stylistic analogy, pointing the way toward isomorphism. Yet, some of Wölfflin's analogies have been questioned, such as the rise of baroque style in visual art during the seventeenth century and a parallel loosening of grammatical forms in language. Sculpture, Mitchell adds, has a physical materiality and worldly presentness that forces the word and image problem into a relationship of word and object. Photography, especially the photographic essay, entails a different relationship between image and language (Fowler 498–99; Green 11; Mitchell, *Picture Theory* 281–322).

When Wendy Steiner explored the relationship between modern literature and painting in *The Colors of Rhetoric,* she found multiple bases for comparison and historical shifts in priority. Architecture was privileged in the Middle Ages, painting in the Renaissance and post-Renaissance, sculpture in the eighteenth century, and music in the early nineteenth century. Priority shifted again with structuralism and semiotics. The new science of discovering similarities compared and contrasted minimal units with the hope of revealing semantic and pragmatic conventions in each art along with combinatory rules. Structural correspondence, however, runs into difficulties. Literature does not present the same problem of minimal units that painting does, with its variances of colors, geometrical shapes, brush strokes, and figures. Different genres also support different notions of correspondence. Rules do not carry the same authority for each art in a pair, and some equivalencies such as tone of voice in painting may not exist. Steiner cites differing philosophical views as well. Universalists believe that similarities mark preexisting substantive resemblances between two systems of phenomena. Relativists treat them as social correspondences to particular conventions, rules, forms, and structures.

Even the mainstay of comparison—periodization—is problematic. While Impressionists were creating new visions on canvas, a similar revolt against tradition was occurring in poetry. The French Symbolist poets used words to create atmosphere and moods. Yet, impressionism did not occur in all art forms at the same time. The same is true of minimalism. It appeared in painting as early as 1913, in Malevich's experiment in reduction to the fewest possible elements. It did not appear in music until the 1980s, in, for example, the compositions of Phillip Glass (Scholl 9). All qualities of art are not necessarily equal in every period either, exposing the diachronic limits of analogy. Comparison of two disciplines within the Victorian period is complicated by changing conceptions of the artifact that raise doubts about generalizations over time. Periodization also has a normative tendency, leading Gombrich to doubt the possibility of any purely morphological description of style. One style—especially classical—may be privileged. Others—especially gothic or rococo—are reduced to inferior status. Furthermore, the question of what fits within a particular period may be disputed. We might agree on broad attributions of Renaissance style, but classify a particular set of objects as either baroque or mannerist (Fowler 501–02, 506, 509).

These problems do not render interart comparison invalid. Scholarship has deepened our understanding of the variety of relations. Ultimately, though, Mitchell likens interart comparison to rearranging the deck chairs on a ship. Interart comparison historically encountered three limitations. It was based on the presumption of a unifying, homogenous concept such as meaning or representation and on a science of comparing and differentiating propositions. The strategy of systematic comparison and contrast ignored other forms of relation. It was also a ritualistic and highly generalized historicism that affirmed the dominant sequence of historical periods and a canonical master-narrative leading to the present. Alternative histories, countermemories, or resistant practices were neglected. In its most ambitious forms, interart comparison argued for the existence of extended formal analogies across the arts capable of revealing structural homologies between texts and images united by dominant historical styles. In more cautious versions, scholars traced particular comparisons and their consequences in literary and artistic practice. At its best, interart comparison resisted compartmentalization of media into particular disciplines and the academic administration of knowledge. At its worst, it collaborated in preserving the insularity of disciplines and the amateurishness of interdisciplinary efforts (*Picture Theory* 87, "Against Comparison" 31).

The Fault Line of Word and Image

When French scholars were pioneering structuralist art history, their Anglo-American counterparts were avoiding Theory and focusing on sociological issues such as patronage. Yet, Bal recalls, within a relatively short time new interdisciplinary investigations emerged. The work of three scholars illustrates the shift that occurred. A quick succession of books by Norman Bryson—*Word and Image* in 1981, *Vision and Painting* in 1983, and *Tradition and Desire* in 1984—stimulated expanded word-and-image studies. In showing how texts interfere with painting and its perception and how textuality determines the rhetorical effect of paintings, Bryson engaged in a new "visual poetics." His distinction between discursivity and figurality as modes of representation in painting became widely recognized. Bryson used figurality in the etymological sense of formness and materiality. He defined discursivity as propositional content. The figural aspect of an image is composed of features belonging to a visual experience independent of language—its "being-as-image." Yet, the two modes interact. The East Window of Christchurch Cathedral illustrates their interaction. Discursive aspects invoke prior biblical texts on which the image depends, inscriptions that signal how to perceive the panels, and the overall meaning generated by internal juxtapositions (*Reading "Rembrandt"* 31–33).

The work of Svetlana Alpers and Michael Fried also indicated the shifting terms of disciplinary relation. In her 1985 book *The Art of Describing: Dutch Art in the Seventeenth Century,* Alpers challenged the privileging of narrative art in the Italian mode by drawing on visual and verbal documents pertaining to visual culture in the Netherlands, including ideas about vision and scientific reliability, the invention of instruments for perfecting vision, and the impulse to document structures visually in forms such as map making. In her 1988 book *Rembrandt's Enterprise,* Alpers challenged her own prior view of the artist, treating him as both the product and an instrument of change by analyzing the materiality of painting, his economic activities and the economic organization of the art business, Rembrandt's place in the business, and his use of theatricality. In his 1980 *Absorption and Beholder in the Age of Diderot,* Michael Fried treated Diderot's writing on painting as an inherent part of artistic production. Fried explored the interaction between critic and artist as a dialectic, not a hierarchical order, and examined theatricality as a mode of looking, composition, and representation that unites word and image into one composite sign. In his

1987 book *Realism, Writing, Disfiguration,* Fried explored analogous issues and compositional affinities in the painting of Thomas Eakins and the
writing of Stephen Crane (*Reading "Rembrandt"* 28–30, 50, 57).

Reflecting widening interest in new approaches, Bal continues, learned
journals began publishing articles treating visual arts as sign systems and
demonstrating how paintings, photographs, sculptures, and architecture are
imbued with textuality and discourse. The premise that images may be read
as texts became widely accepted, even a lingua franca in the discipline. In a
survey of new developments in 1991, Bal and Bryson argued that semiotics
had moved beyond a linguistic turn to a semiotic turn capable of producing
a transdisciplinary theory. Semiotics challenged the positivist view of knowledge by presenting an antirealist theory of the sign and a political assertion
of questions of gender and power. The interdisciplinary animus for a new
understanding of the relationship between visuality and verbality, though,
was greater in art history than in literary studies. Reading texts for imagery
was still regarded as an relic of psychologistic approaches to literary experience and methods such as motif-hunting, image-counting, and figurative and
formal analysis. Generally speaking, literary studies has not been changed by
new discoveries in studies of visuality to the degree art history was affected
by semiotics and literary theory (*Reading "Rembrandt"* 13–15).

Cultural Analysis and Visual Culture

Bal's own work exemplifies the move beyond older modes of interart comparison. In her 1991 book *Reading "Rembrandt,"* she drew on methods
from art history, gender analysis, and reader-response theory to explore
theoretical and interpretive problems in relations between verbal and visual art. Bal situates the book in critical studies of culture. "Rembrandt" is
not a set of discrete works attributed solely to one artist. It is a cultural text
that engages the relationship between a work as a thing and its reception as
an event. The question of reception engages both the narrativity and visuality of works as well as the social context in which they emerge. Context
becomes a text that can be read using a multidisciplinary semiotic methodology that treats medium-bound terms such as spectatorship, storytelling,
rhetoric, reading, discursivity, and visuality as aspects rather than essences.
Shifting attention away from intrinsic properties of discrete visual and verbal domains opens up larger questions of representation and interpretation

that facilitate a systematic interrogation of the ways arts emerge, circulate, and are intertwined within a culture.

Each chapter confronts one or more artworks with texts that are related in a number of ways: as sources or pre-texts, responses, thematic companions or counterparts, theoretical subtexts, surrounding contexts, and critical rewritings. In a chapter on the semiotics of rape, Bal employs the tool of rhetoric to read the story of Lucretia and intertextual references to images and stories in parallel traditions. In a chapter juxtaposing semiotics, psychoanalysis, and art criticism and interpretation, she demonstrates the importance of making each contribution explicit. Disciplinary relationships are not one-sided. In the process of making the meaning of a work more complex, psychoanalytic discourse gains a new dimension. Melancholia becomes a motivation in artistic creation as well as a mode of representation. The case for textuality does not sacrifice visual specificity or impose a new unity. The dilemma of two mutually exclusive positions, Bal counsels, can only be resolved by relinquishing a unified concept of meaning. The result is neither a harmonization of the conflict nor a dialectical resolution but radicalization of the poles of opposition, leaving room for more than two kinds of meaning. Juxtaposition and transfer play key roles in interdisciplinary analysis. Approaches traditionally limited to visual or verbal domains and to high or popular culture are placed in a new relationship.

In two subsequent books, Bal made the case for cultural analysis as a central interdisciplinary practice for humanities and cultural studies. Introducing a 1999 collection of essays on *The Practice of Cultural Analysis,* Bal took a graffito on a wall as the starting point. Translated from Dutch, it means "Note/I hold you dear/ I have not/ thought you up." Adopted as an emblem for the Amsterdam School for Cultural Analysis, this short, uncanonical, and transgressive text-image embodies a concept at the heart of cultural analysis. Its presence on a wall is a public exhibit that even in its simplicity engages the complex interdiscursivity of visual performance and verbal argument. Cultural analysis of objects is neither abstract nor utopic. Bal calls it an "interdiscipline" with a specific object and a set of collaborating disciplines that includes social sciences. Nor is it nondisciplinary, methodologically eclectic, or indifferent. It is primarily analytic and representative of much of the interdisciplinary work that goes on in humanities and in cultural studies today.

In *Travelling Concepts in Humanities,* Bal highlighted the methodological potential of concepts as the backbone of interdisciplinary study of culture. Boundary concepts have long played a role in facilitating connections (Klein, *Crossing Boundaries* 50–52). Bal's major exemplars are image, mise en scène, framing, performance, tradition, intention, and critical intimacy. Concepts exhibit both specificity and intersubjectivity. They do not mean the same thing for everyone, but they foster common discussion as they travel between disciplines, between individuals, between periods, and between academic communities. In the process of travel, their meaning and use change. Their changeability becomes part of their usefulness. Concepts have an analytical and theoretical force with the potential to go beyond merely using a fashionable name, a common form of multidisciplinary diffusion. They stimulate productive propagation, prompting a new articulation with an emphasis on and ordering of phenomena within the cultural field that does not impose transdisciplinary universalism. The basis of interdisciplinary work, Bal maintains, is selecting one path while bracketing others.

In a case study on the Dutch Zwaerte Piet (Black Peter), she shows how the tradition of masqueraded black-faced fools traveled between high and popular art in an intertextual discourse of race that is embedded in not only seventeenth-century Dutch portraiture but contemporary reworkings of questions of race. Cultural analysis is not medium bound. It does not exist without connections to other disciplines, and it recognizes that fields such as postcolonial studies have been catalysts for disciplinary change. At the same time, interdisciplinary analysis has a specificity that is not lost in superficial generalisms. Informed borrowing, Bal stresses, is crucial. An image must not be used for a priori theoretical or political points without asking what it has to say. "Surfing and "zapping" only produce "muddled multidisciplinarity," not the productive interdisciplinarity that results from paying a "good quality of attention" to the subjects and objects that make up a particular culture.

The Pictorial Turn and Expanding Visual Culture

The emergent field of visual culture moves further beyond interart comparison and word-and-image studies. The best prospect for describing representations in art or any other medium, Mitchell argues, lies in the immanent vernaculars of representational practices. Sometimes the language of semiotics intersected with those vernaculars, as in the notion of an "icon." Yet, semiotics was often promoted as a neutral scientific metalanguage that, in the end, did not produce a "transdisciplinary" theory lacking biased vocabulary. The languages of visuality, Beate Allert emphasizes, are pluralistic ("Introduction" 1). In 1994, Mitchell proposed the concept of a "pictorial turn" to name the challenge that visuality presents to the dominant textual model of the world in humanities. Vision is a mode of cultural expression and communication as fundamental and widespread as language. Spectatorship in turn may be as deep a problem as reading. Spectatorship is concerned with the look, the gaze, the glance, and practices of observation, surveillance, and visual pleasure. The pictorial turn in contemporary life and some disciplines of the human sciences is changing the way that visual culture is produced and consumed while raising new questions and new versions of old questions about the place of visuality in language and other modes of representation ("Interdisciplinarity" 540; *Picture Theory* 14–15n10, 87n8).

Nicholas Mirzoeff has traced the rise of "visual culture." The label evolved from a phrase used in several fields, including art history, film and media studies, semiotics, history of science, interart comparison, and philosophical inquiries into art and representation. Conversations about visuality also occur in cultural studies, queer theory, and African-American studies, and among psychoanalysts, anthropologists, phenomenologists, theorists, and optical technologists. The term gained currency because the contemporary era is saturated with images, from art to technologies of computer-aided design, magnetic resonance imaging, and multispectral sensors. The rise of new hybrid textualities from digitizing visual, audio, and alphabetic information also heightened interest. Because visual culture is not created from a single medium or located in a single place, the field directs attention away from structure and formal settings, such as an art gallery, to the centrality of visual experience in everyday life. Moreover, visuality is not simply a medium of information and mass culture. It offers a kind of pleasure and sensual immediacy unrivaled by print, making the sublime qualities of images of as much interest as their sociopolitical power to persuade (*Introduction* 1–31; "What is?").

The academic field of visual culture has been stylized in several ways, from a new scientism based in linguistics or semiotics to the "visual front" of cultural studies or a new aestheticism that moves cultural studies away from signs and meaning towards sensation and feeling, perception and effect. Irit Rogoff likens its "transdisciplinary" and "cross-methodological" character to the complexities of cultural studies. To say that visual culture is the study of images, Rogoff cautions, is not enough. Vision and the visual world are the locus for a complex interplay of aesthetic values, gender stereotypes, power relations, and audio, spatial, and psychic dynamics of spectatorship. Images do not stay put within discrete disciplinary fields such as documentary film or Renaissance painting. The object is constantly reproduced and older ascriptions of meaning to an author are supplanted by the conditions and historical specificities of image making (16).

The challenge in redescribing the entire image/text problematic, Mitchell stresses, is to identify critical practices that facilitate connectedness while working against the homogenizing tendencies of older comparative strategies and semiotic science. If the only accomplishment is the "dedisciplinary exercise" of making disciplinary segregation more difficult, Mitchell speculates, that would be enough. He warns against rapid professionalizing or disciplining. The term visual culture names a problematic, not a well-defined theoretical object. An easy pluralism is not the answer either, if it denies a general force to the concept of vision. Yet, the hybrid concept of imagetext is not a transdisciplinary theory or metalanguage in the sense of a Hegelian stable synthesis. It embodies Salter and Hearn's notion of "the churn in the system."

Mitchell considers visual culture to be primarily an "inside-out" phenomenon. It appears outside art history while opening up the larger field of vernacular images, media, and the everyday practice of visual art. At the same time, it may appear to be deep inside the discipline's traditional focus on the sensuous and the semiotic particularity of visual images. Art history has always been more than a history of works. It has drawn on theorized models of spectatorship, visual pleasure, and social, intersubjective relations in the scopic field. The relationship with literary studies is more ambiguous. Textual scholars have tended to privilege textual theory and verbal notions of culture. Hence, visual culture is both an outer boundary and an inner "black hole" in the heart of verbal culture. Literary studies encounters the problematic of visuality as an inside-out form of interdisciplinarity. The visual comes to language as a figure of semiotic otherness, as the "other" medium and "sister" art or rival. Art history traditionally inserted visual objects *into* explanatory and interpretive discourse. Semiotic and literary theory broke that pattern. The premise of an "iconology of the text" prompted rereading or reviewing texts in light of visual culture, propelled by advances in film, mass culture, and larger efforts in art history (*Picture Theory* 7, 210; "Interdisciplinarity" 541–43).

The current complexity of interdisciplinarity is demonstrated by visual culture's relations with other fields. Mitchell distinguishes visual culture from feminism, gender studies, and race and ethnicity studies. It is not political or an academic movement in the mode of cultural studies. Unlike race, gender, and class, it has no innate politics. Like language, though, visuality is a medium in which politics are conducted. The field is also indebted to feminism, gender and ethnic studies, critical theory, and cultural studies. The objects studied in cultural studies often combine visual and verbal materials in media such as film and television, advertising, and illustrated texts. Film and media studies constitute another major intersection. Most academic programs in visual culture took their starting point in film programs, where there was a tradition of theorizing about spectatorship, visuality, mass circulation of images, and acoustic and linguistic dimensions of film. Media studies deals directly with images, sounds, and spectacles that circulate in radio, television, film, print media, and other products of the culture industry. They are not identical, however (Mitchell, *Picture Theory* 542–43; J. H. Miller, *Illustration* 9).

If visual culture is to avoid being conflated with film and media studies, Mitchell advises, it must pose the same questions that produce the "indisciplinary" and "inside-out" effect in other areas. To what extent can models of visuality constructed for film be transferred to other media? How do film and television fit within varieties of visual media? Should visual culture start by postulating the imbrication of vision with other senses, insisting on the "audiovisual" and "imagetext" in order to portray visual media and everyday visual experience as a mixed construct? Visual culture's most important contribution to cinema and media studies may be its resistance to exclusive emphasis on modern and contemporary culture. Visuality did not begin with photography, cinema, or television. Moreover, it flourishes in non-Western and nontechnological societies ("Interdisciplinarity" 542–43).

David Scholle's reflection on the interdisciplinary character of media studies offers an insightful parallel. Scholle calls mass communication a "boundary discipline" situated between professional schools and the liberal arts. The field was initially constructed as a practical enterprise in schools of mass communications and speech departments. A "postdiscipline" construction would not create new degrees centered on vocational goals or the liberal arts canon. Scholle invokes G. J. Shepherd's catalogue of choices: the "undisciplinary" response (continuing to service disciplines), the "antidisciplinary" response (rejecting foundations), and the "disciplinary" response (establishing ontological grounding). Scholle himself rejects the "undisciplinary" and "disciplinary," advocating a solution that lies between antidisciplinarity and a plurality of activities. The "antidisciplinary" impetus of a democratic curriculum must be incorporated, but a "radically interdisciplinary" field would counteract the dispersal of interests by remaining a locus of experiment and a field of action that critically interrogates older definitions and patterns of interdisciplinarity. Like Mirzoeff's and Mitchell's visions of visual culture, Sholle's vision of media studies would not reside comfortably within existing structures. It is part of a larger body of postdisciplinary endeavors that includes cultural studies, gay and lesbian studies, African American studies, visual culture, and other fields whose viability relies on challenging their host institutions (Mirzoeff, "What is" 11).

The academic landscape of visuality has changed profoundly. Yet, Barbara Stafford's assessment in 1988 still applies. Asymmetry in the transference of interpretative skills "haunts" interdisciplinarity. Practices often impose one specialized *techne* on another, applying a priori techniques in a form of agonistic intellectual management that ignores the specificity of an individual case. Readings of images have become more sophisticated, aided by investigations of *mentalités*, structuralism, deconstructionism, phenomenology, Lacanian psychology, reception theory, a broadened notion of hermeneutics, and now new forms of cultural study. However, mutual critical reflection on the strengths and weaknesses of the various interactive fields and methods is often missing. *Geistesgeschichte* and iconography have been unseated, but art history still lacks a commonly agreed-upon language for analyzing images (6–7). Throughout the history of relations between visual and verbal arts, Giles Gunn adds, there has been little recognition of each in the image of the other, despite fruitful exchanges and programs organized to examine the relationship and exemplary interdisciplinary scholarship. "If art historians routinely eschew criticism for cataloguing, evaluation for description," Gunn reports, "literary historians and critics have typically treated all the fine arts as mere complements, adjuncts, illustrations of the verbal arts." New interdisciplinary scholarship holds the promise of a more constitutive relation. More interactive research and an adequate corps of reviewers, however, will be crucial to shaping and to encouraging joint projects ("Interdisciplinary Studies" 250–51 and *Thinking* 205–06). The lesson of critical mass repeats, yet again.

Chapter 6

RETUNING THE AURAL

Someone once said that writing about music is as meaningless as dancing about architecture. Musical data resist verbal explication more than the data of other humanities, especially in the case of historical works that were never recorded (R. Parker 10). Music is not routinely included in national reports on the state of humanities either. When the journal *Interdisciplinary Humanities* devoted two issues to the subject, they bore the subtitle "The 'Lost Dimension' in the Humanities." Music tends to be segregated from other humanities because it is participatory, and greater emphasis is placed on performative aspects and technical skills (Gray 13). It also has a low priority in K–12 and college education, "extra-" or "nonmusical" phenomena have not been featured at undergraduate and graduate levels, and the discipline was slower to respond to new developments in humanities. In the mid-1990s, there was scant talk of new historicism, no parallel to the revisionism promoted by Marxism and feminism in literary studies and art history, and a continuing separation from social and political worlds. Even in the late 1990s, the self-critical historical scholarship that began to dominate other disciplines in the 1970s and 1980s was only slowly emerging (Treitler 210–12, 225–26; Kassabian 1, 3).

This chapter completes the first set of case studies by exploring similar questions about music. What were the early warrants for interdisciplinarity in the discipline? What changes in the nature of music and music scholarship led to the rise of a new musicology in the 1980s? What were the impacts in musicology, ethnomusicology, music theory, popular music studies, and studies of American music? How is the traditional boundary separating musicality and sociality shifting and the relationship between intrinsic and extrinsic properties of music changing? How do interdisciplinary practices differ? And, what implications do new interdisciplinary practices have for the current state of the discipline?

From Mousiké to the New Musicology

Like literature, music originally was originally a broader concept than our current definition. The ancient Greek *mousiké* encompassed poetry and dance and was more of an ethical, political, and religious concept. In shaping Greek traditions to the needs of the orator, Romans advocated music as a tool for public speaking and the professions. The medieval university treated *musica* in philosophical and verbalistic terms and, in keeping with the rest of the *quadrivium* of the seven liberal arts, emphasized measurement, proportion, and harmonious relationships. The first bachelor's degree in the subject was conferred in 1463, but music did not figure in general education until the fifteenth century and was not recognized as a separate faculty at Oxford until 1636. During the Renaissance and eighteenth centuries, expressive power received greater attention than abstract numerical ratio, though a tension between speculative and practical theory was apparent. The Renaissance musician ideally mastered both theoretical and practical musical knowledge. However, *musica theorica* was divided from *musica practica*. *Theorica* was a scholarly activity based on a traditional body of knowledge about tuning systems and their mathematical bases. *Practica* was the business of musicians, usually singers in chapel choirs.

In this country, music was the only one of the seven liberal arts that was not included in the curriculum when Harvard College was founded in 1636. The dominance of verbalistic studies meant that music developed in other venues, primarily in the church and the community. Applied music was not regarded as a subject worthy of academic credit, and Harvard did not grant credit for courses in form, harmony, and counterpart until 1873. During the eighteenth century, a distinct body of writings on historical, stylistic, critical, and theoretical matters emerged in Europe. The nineteenth century, though, was a turning point. The Romantics, who regarded music as the paradigmatic art, studied creative-poetic dimensions that had been ignored in previous eras. The doctrine of *musica poetica* held that music says something in the manner of a rhetorical oration. The conceptual shift to *poetica* reconstituted an idea associated with vocal music in the sixteenth and seventeenth centuries and in the eighteenth century with instrumental music. A number of other forces also coalesced, including the shift from a mimetic to an expressive aesthetic, the concept of creative genius, the idea of detached contemplation of art, the notion that a work of art is autonomous from other cultural forces, and cultivation of a Romantic subjectivity. (The opening summary draws on Wager and McGrath 19, 21–21, 27; Bohlman, "Epilogue" 199; D. Greene 55; McCreless 24, 27–28; Kerman 65).

The disciplined study of music is only about two centuries old (Kassabian 1). Like art history, music was a borrower from the start. Leo Treitler calls music a "parasitic discipline of sorts." Musicology was the first major branch of the discipline to develop. It depended on art history for the paradigm of style history and literary studies for paleographic and philological principles. Medieval music, for example, was studied with principles of text criticism and stemmatics borrowed from classical philology (210, 216). Synoptic theorizing and the generalist tradition also fostered connections. Albert William Levi proposed that music involves a "radiating theory" of overlapping value-concerns in arts and humanities. The radiating center of intention, Levi argued, was the defining property of any discipline (Sibbald 19). The generalist model of culture furnished a holistic view of moral, social, and religious development. In studying the cultural meaning of music in antebellum America, Richard Hooker found that proponents of musical appreciation regarded listening to music as a physical exercise in moral character and social skills. Cultivation of taste in music was considered both "literary" and "literate," in the sense of elocution and a language of feeling with social purpose. Performance standards and criticism juxtaposed the "illiteracy" of oral tradition to precise reading of musical texts following rules of practice. The act of performance, in turn, promoted social habits of order, obedience, and union. Taste was equivalent to character and had the capacity to aid in reforming society. Listening to Beethoven, John Sullivan Dwight remarked, would make better Americans (qtd. in Levy and Tischler 70).

The Disciplining of Music

The modern discipline has three primary branches: musicology, ethnomusicology, and music theory. Along with ethnomusicology, musicology was regarded as a "humanistic" discipline rather than an "art" of composition or performance (McCreless 14, 35). American musicology descended directly from the German *Musikwissenschaft* that developed in the late nineteenth century (Kerman 11). The new science of music was intended to be an all-inclusive discipline of Western music moving from antiquity to the present. American musicology inherited the German emphasis on positivist historiography and stylistic evolution, downplaying criticism and theory to the point that until recently music was regarded as almost exclusively a historical discipline. The repertoire of performance also favored Western European works spanning the years 1750 to 1900, with pride of place going to composers such as Bach, Beethoven, and Mozart (McCreless 15, Treitler 213).

Canon formation played a central role in disciplining music. Katherine Bergeron defines a canon as an ideal of order made material, physical, and visible. The music canon is not just a body of works, Robert Morgan adds. It is constituted by a performance repertory, a publication apparatus, and a compositional "language" based on shared assumptions. A composition, Treitler explains, was regarded as a closed, fixed product that displayed attributes of organic unity and originality by virtue of its origin in the creative impulse. The object of study was an autonomous work conceptualized as a structure inferable from a score or analytical notation that served in turn as a blueprint for performance. The textual notation of a score denoted presumably essential, unambiguous, and unified details. The concept of tonality was equally crucial. "To play in tune," as Bergeron put it," is to uphold the canon." Playing out of tune broke the coherence and unity of the traditional canonical "grammar" of music and hierarchies of compositional value. In the musical scale, order was audible in a finite set of intervals tuned by mathematical calculation and ratio. Nonmusical content such as unpitched "noise" was placed historically outside the discipline proper (Bergeron, "Prologue" 2–3; Morgan 44; Treitler 213, 215, 220–21).

The dominant tonal system was challenged as early as the nineteenth century, although Arnold Schoenberg's first nontriadic, nontonal compositions in 1907 were a symbolic benchmark of change. Schoenberg's twelve-tone system was the starting point for contemporary avant-garde compositional theory (Kerman 69). Over the course of the century, the nature of music continued to change. Artists such as John Cage sought a unique sound corpus for each composition and allowed the indeterminacy of chance and randomness to determine musical materials and order. Noise and even silence gained a place in the canon and the definition of music. In the 1960s borrowing also became a major compositional practice, initially in quotations of established Western tonal forms then early historical styles and popular, folk, and non-Western music. New hybrid genres such as performance art further challenged the traditional boundaries of discipline, and orchestras and opera houses began to combine recent and older music and play secondary composers. New directions are especially visible in mass media, which disseminate a full range of art music from Western and other cultures plus folk and popular music. The current pluralism, Morgan concludes, has rendered music a "melange of conflicting subcultures" that interact in complex ways, challenging the notion of a dominant musical mainstream (57).

Scholarship expanded in kind. Initially, Levy and Tischler report, aesthetic and antiquarian interests dominated. Three approaches prevailed well into the twentieth century: biographies, sentimental local studies, and compendia of orchestras, choruses, soloists, composers, educational institutions, and churches. Concert or art traditions were privileged, although some early twentieth-century composers drew on vernacular sources such as familiar folk tunes and popular melodies. Virgil Thomson was instrumental in shifting the terms of debate from a European standard to an American style marked by greater use of folk and popular sources in composition. Music histories followed suit. W. S. B. Mathews's 1889 *A Hundred Years of Music in America* was one of the first to explore historical and cultural contexts. Louis Elson's 1925 *History of American Music* described everyday life as a "primitive" prologue to the "real culture" of European art music but included a chapter on American women. John Tasker Howard's 1930 *Our American Music* retained a high culture bias, but he was open to historical perspective and included some women composers, Native and African American music, and oral traditions. In *America's Music,* first published in 1955, Gilbert Chase considered the social and political role of music and analyzed jazz, folk, and rock. By the 1970s, collections were becoming more inclusive and the elitism of high versus low genres was being rethought. By the 1990s, more varieties of popular music were being studied, and African Americans, women, Latinos and Asian Americans, and regional traditions were being formally recognized.

In the positivistic paradigm of the late 1950s and early 1960s, empirically grounded facts and historicism were prioritized (J. Shepherd 190). New scholarship, though, redefined meaning as an interplay of musical texts, their cultural contexts, the dynamics of performance, and the experience of listeners. Marxists critiqued essentialist binaries, especially separations of serious and popular music and the individual and the social. Poststructuralist criticism influenced by Michel Foucault called into question the master narrative of tonality. Postmodernist questions about the validity of global universalizing stimulated interest in local, everyday, variable, and contingent aspects of music-making. Deconstructive analysis unveiled operations of power related to gender, race, and class and the ways that music constructs social identities and spaces. Feminist, gay, lesbian, and Black scholars uncovered historical details about lesser-known composers. Heightened interest in popular and folk cultures stimulated studies of contemporary genres, and revisionist historiographers turned to new kinds of archival documents of material and popular cultures. Communication-centered folklorists began examining the social organization of community music-making, and musicologists began using ethnomusicological methods to study the distant past (Ray Allen 185). Cognitive science studies of how music functions in the brain and feminist studies of how music affects the body also extended understanding of why tonality retained its hold on musical style for 150 years (Pasler 18).

The "Historico-Critico-Musicological Broadside"

Positivistic musicology came under scrutiny in the mid-1960s, but the 1980s was a turning point propelled by the work of Leo Treitler and Joseph Kerman. In a 1980 essay on music theory, Kerman extended his earlier call for more contextual studies of music events and social history. He argued for historical and culturally thick descriptions of works that take into account the life and intent of composers and audiences as well as cultural and aesthetic norms and semiotic traditions for communicating meaning in a given time and place. In his 1985 book, *Contemplating Music,* Kerman went on to examine the histories of major subdisciplines. He did not cite critical theorists in other disciplines and fields explicitly, but, in pointing to new approaches, Kerman prefigured many current interests. He imagined an implicitly interdisciplinary music criticism that would cross musicological, theoretical, and textual boundaries while embracing affective responses in a critical-aesthetic synthesis. He also foresaw a new history of meaning that would bring together political, social, economic, intellectual, and artistic insights (see also McCreless 21, Kassabian 1, Schwarz 181–83).

To borrow the words of Patrick McCreless, what followed was a "historico-critico-musicological broadside." As a child of the 1980s, McCreless reflected, new musicology exhibits several traits of postmodern thought. It rejects the structural autonomy and immanent meaning of artworks, questions the received canon, looks at surfaces rather than deep structures, and views a work as a complex product of signifying practices and social norms (42–43). In a review of key books in the new scholarship, David Schwarz said they give the impression of a discipline responding to critical theory. In musicology and ethnomusicology, critical theory "quickened" an aspect of the discipline already in place. Connections between works and their environment were being theorized in a wide range of practices, from biographical histories of composers and their social contexts to modes of production to conditions in the mind of the listener that produce and encode meaning (180). In her 1991 book *Feminist Endings,* for example, Susan McClary theorized the ways that music produces, represents, and problematizes gender (180). The 1993 anthology *Queering the Pitch* explored the ways music, gender, and difference are structured. These and other works opened up theoretical and musical spaces that subtended the 1997 book *Keeping Score.* Subtitled *Music, Disciplinarity, and Culture,* it is part of a growing body of studies of disciplinary formations that includes the 1992 anthology *Disciplining Music* (Kassabian 8–9).

Resistance ran high in the oldest branch of the discipline. Musicologists faulted poststructuralist work for undue emphasis on power relations and universalist notions of meaning, the experience of music, and the analyst's role. Overstated claims of newness also came under attack and, reminiscent of art history, the borrowing of literary theory. Roger Parker identified three major strands in music's relationship with language and literature: philology, structuralism, and the cluster of feminism, deconstruction, new historicism and other approaches often grouped under the "postmodern" label. Both structuralism and postmodernism were imported more or less wholesale, though Parker deems structuralism to be more of a "paint-job" than "a sea-change." Evocations of literary theory were attacked for mirroring what literary critics were saying about verbal language, the arbitrary nature of linguistic signs, and the subjective and unstable character of verbal meaning. Nonetheless, music theorists began subjecting the language of common-practice tonality to deconstruction. By 1997, analytical models derived from linguistics and offshoots such as narrative theory were becoming more mainstream in musical analysis and ethnomusicology (11–13). Tension between competing approaches is not new. Yet, Godwin and Woolf find, the current battle over humanism is bringing the dichotomy of internality and externality to the fore. The defense of the aesthetic is typically mounted on a total refusal of critical approaches. The greater challenge is defending the aesthetic from the perspective of a practice that is concerned with an essentially sound, if overstated, project such as critique of the notion of transcendence in art or the social-historical-ideological coordinates of culture (134).

Provoked by new scholarship on Beethoven's *Ninth Symphony*, Pieter van den Toorn rebutted attacks on traditional methods. On one side of a looming dichotomy, he charged, new musicologists fault theory and analysis for being conservative and elitist, specialist and insular, formalist and positivistic, objective and scientific, as well as masculinist. On the other side, they promote approaches that are multifaceted and multicultural, literary and poetic, expressive and subjective, liberal and democratic, populist and feminist. Van den Toorn indicted the imposition of Marxist-economic, sociopolitical, and psychological agendas and models of "officially sponsored ideologies of inter-, cross-, and multi-everything" that collapse under the weight of musical particularity. Countering Susan McClary's work in particular, he argued that tension-and-release patterns of tonal music may be understood in ways unrelated to sexual conflict and a male-defined tonality. Responding to Treitler's attack on style history for emphasizing general abstractions, he acknowledged the value of new understandings of the musically sensing subject and the social aspects of music. Yet, he criticized accentuating external forces and extramusical properties at the expense of technical and intrinsic properties. Schenker's technical terms, Van den Toorn contended, are actually more democratic than Treitler's poetic and "sympathetically interdisciplinary" model that emphasizes immediate and personal impact on the listener.

Comparable to literary studies and art history, the foregrounding of newness in music should not obscure continuation of traditional practices. Archival work has been crucial to establishing accurate editions, taxonomies, bibliographies, discographies, and authentic performances. Older skills of textual analysis, narratology, iconography, and musicology are also being redeployed (Goodwin and Woolf 135). Some scholars are using analytical and critical readings of scores to question prior understandings. Others, including historians who embrace the theory of *mentalités* or *Zeitgeist,* are examining music's relations to other arts and to society (Pasler 17). The new dialogue about musicology, Bohlman adds, takes the form of both inter- and intradisciplinary exchange (208). At the subdisciplinary level, scholars carry questions from one specialty to another, and cross-fertilizations produce hybrid methodologies. Some who study the traditional canon, Jann Pasler reports, are asking whether instrumental music embodies social narratives in the same way as opera and vocal music. Others are asking the same question about improvised music. Questions normally raised in art music about issues such as the abstract complexity and structural integrity of a work are being asked of popular and indigenous music. And, the reverse. Questions that arose in studying popular music, its listeners, and mass media are being posed about classical music. Postmodernist efforts to level hierarchies and to acknowledge the interpenetration of music in the world have also lessened the bias against studying art music apart from other traditions in segregated markets. Jazz is being taught as art music and a wider range of non-Western musics and hybrid forms resulting from cultural exchanges between East and West, Africa and the Caribbean, and North and South America (20).

Expanding Trajectories of Change

Change has occurred in the other major branches of the discipline as well. Theory is concerned with the structure of music or, as Kerman calls it, "what makes music 'work.'" Scholars engage in a variety of studies, from the formation of scales and chords to procedures for distributing pitch and principles of form. Kerman likens these aspects to vocabulary, grammar, syntax, and rhetoric in language and the technical procedures of musical analysis to parsing, linguistic reduction, and *explication du texte* (13). Interest of a speculative-theoretical nature dates from the ancient Greeks, but the roots of modern theory lie in an aesthetic ideology that arose around the turn of the nineteenth century. The metaphor of a work as rhetoric—emphasizing phrase structure, melodic succession, theme, materials, and tonal plan—shifted to the metaphor of structure. Interest in structural autonomy was accompanied by interest in form, teleological motivic development, and musical logic. In an era that valued originality, change also took on greater importance, raising new questions. Should theory preserve traditional theoretical virtues? Explain stability by developing theories to clarify how practice operates? Concentrate on the pedagogy of originality by teaching original composition? Or, explain originality by analyzing a work once it was created? Nineteenth-century theorists attempted all these goals, but there was no original American theory at the time. Even in the first half of the twentieth century, American theory was essentially coterminous with pedagogy (McCreless 26–30).

Modern music theory is a product of the 1950s and 1960s. In contrast to musicology, it is American in origin. Around 1960, music theory began assuming a distinct identity. The first specialist journal appeared in 1957, although the Society for Music Theory did not form until 1978. The goal was to deal systematically with music "itself," not as categories of style, historical evolution, positivistic facts, or pedagogy. Like structural linguists, the founders of music theory believed that texts enact a generalized musical language and that their basic material lies beneath the surface. The initial focus was Western tradition and the dominant mode of analysis the science of Schenkerian theory, which sought the essence of tonal music in an invariable abstract formula of pitch-class set theory. Schenker was a Viennese theorist who immigrated to the United States (U.S.). He sought a deep structure of interpretations that made it possible to move beyond theory in a pedagogical sense to an intellectually coherent and empirically validated system. Schenker and his followers believed that a composition expresses intrinsic properties such as linear progressions, neighboring and chromatic tones, and modulations. Scholars also investigated twelve-tone theory for atonal and twelve-tone music and conducted research on the history of theory, its pedagogy, and perception and cognition. Both theory and positivist musicology claimed explication of musical works as their disciplinary turf, and they shared a common philosophical basis and aesthetic ideology. In aiming to develop explicit and testable bases for analysis, though, theory leaned toward a model of essences (McCreless 15, 18, 20–21, 34, 41; Kerman 84).

When positivist musicology began to wane, music theory was still committed to a formalist ideology. That left the space of interpretation and criticism open for the new musicology. The tension between theory and new musicology. McCreless suggests, may be viewed in terms of modernism and postmodernism. Theory regarded explanation as the primary function of scholarship. Postmodernism favored interpretation. By 1987, theory was coming under fire (20, 42–43). Music theory's horizons expanded as scholars developed greater historical awareness, moved beyond abstraction and value-free analysis, became more reflexive and self-critical of the discipline, explored sociocultural associations, and paid greater attention to matters of expression and taste that engage creators, patrons, and listeners. Interest in perception and cognition also expanded (Kassabian 19). And, preliminary connections were made to literary and critical theory as well as the history and philosophy of science. As Schenker's fundamental structure was rethought, the composition was understood in a new way—as a network of factors moving between surface and underlying compositional parameters, rather than a strict hierarchy (Bergeron 7).

Comparable to literary studies and art history, new scholarship is not focused solely on contemporary works, despite heightened interest in the period after 1900. Researchers are examining previously ignored compositions by figures such as Bach and Beethoven, and they are combining internationalist and externalist approaches in new syntheses that undermine the strict dichotomy of the intrinsic and the extrinsic. Peter Burkholder highlights Leonard Ratner's research on the classic era in particular. Ratner examined how Europeans in the second half of the eighteenth century thought about music and illuminated the diverse styles that Mozart blended. Each style had an association with a certain social class, activity, or event. This kind of analysis exhibits an internalist interest in harmonic, melodic, thematic, rhythmic, metric, and phrase structures. Yet, it also recognizes that stylistic allusions and the meanings they carry require historical understanding. They have strong national, class, emotional, and other cultural associations. Burkholder urges theorists and historians of style or meaning not to duck questions of value in considering how music was used and performed, how styles and practices changed, and how pieces were constructed and unified. Even period generalizations are being called into question. Eighteenth-century music, for example, has a heterogeneity born of blending elements of various styles, a tool of musical construction that dates from at least the alternation of solo polyphony with choral chant in medieval liturgical music (21–23).

Ethnomusiciology, American Music, and Popular Music Studies

Ethnomusicology is conventionally defined as the study of non-Western musics. Like musicology it is German in origin. *Vergleischende Musikwissenschaft* was a form of comparative study that branched off from musicology in the late nineteenth and early twentieth centuries (McCreless 15). Music historians usually date the origin of a formal subdiscipline to the 1950s and 1960s, portraying it as a revolt against historical musicology. Philip Bohlman, though, describes its emergence as an effort to transform the study of non-Western music and culture by broadening ethnomusicology's own canons and writing about music in the mode of ethnography. The role of anthropology was catalytic, contributing new methodologies and capacities for fieldwork. Moreover, both anthropologists and music scholars realized that the musics being "discovered" did not necessarily bear a relationship to Western musical vocabularies or have the same cultural function and technical criteria. African music, for instance, differs from the musical language and harmonic properties of functional tonality that dominated European art music from roughly 1600 to 1880. Much of the interest derives from the interplay between cross-rhythms or polyrhythms and melodic inflections or "bending" notes. John Shepherd suggests it is inherently interdisciplinary in form. In many African cultures, a single word means both music and dance. In many oral cultures, the historian is also a poet, and the poet is a singer, musician, and dancer. A new language and discourse were needed for representing the uniqueness of "other" music (Bohlman, "Ethnomusicology's Challenge" 120–22, 128–32).

The mission of ethnomusicology implied boundary crossing from the beginning, but the 1977 Congress of the International Musicological Society focused explicitly on the theme of "Interdisciplinary Horizons in the Study of Musical Traditions, East and West" (Kerman 172). In the 1980s and 1990s, Lornell and Rasmussen recount, ethnomusicologists expanded their purview to include not only practices characterized by age and place but practices imbued with the complexities of contemporary, mediated, transnational, and postmodern developments. The New World also became a field of study, not just the music of the distant "other." The study of American music underscores the current plurality of American cultural studies. Lornell and Rasmussen locate it within and across a family of allied fields of American studies, ethnomusicology, folklore, and multicultural studies. The literature, in turn, is a composite of scholarship on American music, world music, cultural geography, ethnicity, and identity. Interest in American music is not new. Precedents date to the 1920s. Since the 1970s, however, the number of books about vernacular music has increased and new series have been established devoted to music in American life (9–11, 13, 15). New scholarship, Gena Caponi-Tabery adds, highlights a series of shifts that have occurred since the 1960s: from product- to process-oriented study, from composition to performance, and from music as text to social practice. The third shift in particular is a paradigmatic move that both draws from and contributes to the interdisciplinary methodology of American studies (164).

The changing demographics of the United States also fostered new cultural hybrids that became the subject of folk-music studies. Syncretism has long been a source of hybridity, exemplified by exchanges between

African American and Southern American religious music, exchanges between white and black musicians in minstrelsy, and Louis Gottschalk's blending of European and African elements (Caponi-Tabery 165–66). However, in the past individual groups were usually studied in isolation. Today, Ray Allen reports, scholars are focusing on the interaction of contiguous music cultures in a new syncretism of mixed styles that mark patterns of historical migration and transplantation across regional, rural and urban, cultural, and national boundaries. Studies of hybrid forms examine both the sound of the music and its multicultural provenance and social and economic dynamics. Older community-based styles of folk music have been transformed via mass media into popular styles of swing, country, rock, and soul that cycle back, reinvigorating community-based performance with the dialectic forces of folk versus popular, community versus mass culture, and aural versus mediated communication (185). The new demographics, George Lipsitz adds, have produced global cities that are living laboratories of hybrid genres. The blending of Latino and African American genres produced a distinctive bass-oriented sound in the music of 2 Live Crew, a group that combined hip-hop elements with immigrant music from the Caribbean. Likewise, the popular music heard in Miami combines forms from around the country and the world, giving Latin rap in Miami an intercultural dynamic (*American Studies* 141–42, 146–47).

Like ethnomethodology, popular music studies cross the boundaries of the aesthetic and the social. In a widely read essay on "American Musicology and the European Tradition" written in 1961, Frank Harrison called for a closer alliance of musicology with contemporary musical life. This alliance is manifested most intensely in popular music and, Harrison emphasized, it must be understood in terms of social use and value (7–9; qtd. in Kerman 37). Like ethnomethodology, popular music studies also call into question the analytical paradigm developed for studying European art music. Many scholars dispute the suitability of that paradigm. John Covach, though, proposes rock music as a testing ground for the appropriateness of traditional methods in understanding the style, aesthetic effect, and other musicological issues in popular music. As proof, he cites a modified Schenkerian approach to works of the Beatles, Paul Simon, and Jimi Hendrix (81–85, 89n25). John Shepherd joins Covach in calling for a more complex understanding of the relationship between sociality and musicality. Popular and art music should not be dichotomized, aligning popular music with the social and "serious" music with the asocial. "Creativity and sociality are not antithetical," Shepherd wrote, "but mutually necessary" (87).

Indicative of widening interest, courses on ethnomethodology, popular music, and the sociology of music have increased. Yet, they often remain peripheral to the mainstream and in some cases only carry elective credit. When American popular music is taught in music departments in the U.S., it is usually presented as part of ethnomusicology or, more often, left for American Studies or sociology departments. Historical musicology remains the dominant approach to studying music as historical and cultural process. Simon Frith proposed that popular music be studied in programs operating with the underlying assumptions of interdisciplinarity, such as American studies and cultural studies, not in the confines of established disciplines or disciplines that focus on one aspect of social and cultural realities. However, Shepherd cautions, these contexts are often isolated, and their teachers are influenced by the problematics of their own disciplines and fields. Janet Woolf's caveat in chapter 5 about bridging aesthetics and sociality in art history returns to mind. Neither of the two principal disciplines that have contributed to popular music studies—sociology and musicology—has adequate theoretical protocols for understanding the meaning of popular music. Sociologists tend to believe that answers to the question of meaning are found in contextual processes—in social, historical, cultural, economic, political, psychological, and biographical properties—that are extrinsic to an event but imbue it with meaning and significance. Musicologists tend to believe that answers lie in textual processes—in sonic, motional, verbal, and visual properties (Shepherd 197, 204–08).

Interdisciplinary Practices

Here, too, interdisciplinary practices differ. One of the mainstays of practice is as visible in music as it was in literary studies and art history. Interart comparison has been conducted in a variety of ways, from comparing specific elements in music and other arts—such as rhythm, tone, balance, repetition, and counterpoint—to identifying historical ties between particular genres—such as the rondeau, the symphony, and the verse forms of writers such Algernon Swinburne and Thomas Mann. Music and architecture have been linked in Western art theory, with architecture characterized as "frozen music" and music as "liquid architecture" (Cassidy 21). The musicality of literature and the narrative element of music have also been studied, writers have attempted to translate musical technique into literature, and music is allied with literature in hybrid genres such as sung lyrics. However, the problem of equivalence occurs in music as much as it did in art history. The search for a governing concept is not straightforward. Analysis centered on rhythm, as Fowler suggests, would be better than analysis centered on harmony. Rhythm is a shared stylistic technique in architecture, painting, poetry, and sculpture. Yet, it is not identical in each domain. One of poetry's many rhythms might prove metaphorically equivalent in function to the rhythm of a colonnade. In examining a poem by Pope, though, which aspect should be selected? Spoken or metrical rhythm? Rhythm within a line, the larger narrative pattern of verse paragraphs, or the entire work? (501). Even the widely accepted premise of a musical "text" is problematic, failing to account fully for the dynamics of composition, transmission, notation, and performance in music (Treitler 210).

Music also exhibits the same limits of practice observed in literary studies and art history. In the past, few studies redrew boundaries in a "cross-or-transdisciplinary" manner, though Giles Gunn applauds work being done in the fields of ethnomusicology, the aesthetics of music, and opera studies ("Interdisciplinary Studies" 250–51). Opera in particular is an interdisciplinary performance art produced by the collaboration of librettists, composers, and other artists such as directors, conductors, designers, singers, and musicians. It is a complex mix of musical, dramatic, poetic, and visual elements. Musicological analysis is not enough, or a dramatic perspective on staging, or literary interests in language, genre, narrative, and source texts. All these dimensions plus social and cultural history must be considered if opera is to be understood fully in its contexts of production and reception (Hutcheon and Hutcheon, "Convenience" 1366). As scholars grew increasingly discontent with the limits of both traditional disciplinary practices and interart comparison, some musicologists sought new approaches that viewed music in cultural and social contexts. All outcomes are not the same, however. Two exemplars—interdiscursivity in opera studies and the emergent field of jazz studies—illustrate differences of scale and goals.

Interdiscursivity

Extended reflections on interdisciplinary process are rare, especially in music. However, Linda and Michael Hutcheon's studies of opera, literature, and medicine offer an in-depth demonstration (Hutcheon and Hutcheon "A Convenience"; Hutcheon "Disciplinary Formation"). They began when Linda, a professor of English and comparative literature, and Michael, a professor of medicine, puzzled over an event in Richard Wagner's opera *Parsifal*—the death of the character Amfortas. The comparative literature expert suspected a spear wound inflicted as Amfortas laid in the arms of a seductress. Recalling widespread concern in the nineteenth century about venereal disease, the medical expert suspected syphilis.

The verbs in Linda Hutcheon's description of what followed provide a rare glimpse into the actual process of interdisciplinary analysis. Intrigued but skeptical, she began to "mull over" standard interpretations of the opera. "Once the seeds of the ideas of syphilis had been planted," other parts of the opera "started to take on different meanings." Recalling literary parallels, she "began to see" the dangerous Flower Maidens of the opera in a "different light." When she told her research partner, "another piece of the puzzle fell into place," suggesting a reason why *Blumenmädchen* were considered dangerous to Grail Knights. Her speculation "brought to his mind" the extent of syphilis in military campaigns from the sixteenth century onward, leading her in turn to suggest a Christianized reading of syphilis over the last 500 years that "might have something to do with" racial and sexual issues. Amfortas was wounded during a dalliance with a woman dressed in Arab style. Connections among sex, disease, and race were familiar in nineteenth-century discourse on social decline, in campaigns against prostitutes and venereal disease, and in anti-Semitic writings, including those of Wagner. "As more and more of these pieces cohered," the authors became "hooked." They attributed the lack of previous writing on their speculation to a disinclination to discuss syphilis and the likelihood that it would escape a monodisciplinary examination. Yet, the combined forces of historical, social, political, literary, musical, and dramatic complexities "demand multidisciplinary perspectives."

In contemplating their next step, the Hutcheons knew their medical and literary backgrounds would not be enough. Reminiscent of the discussion of practices in chapter 3, they did not presume that they could learn to think or to write like musicologists or historians. Yet, they could learn the discourse of musicology and history enough to formulate each discipline's issues in its own terms, including the rules of evidence and standards of evaluation each would bring to bear on the immediate research question. They would keep the core of analysis fixed on the literary and medical historical perspectives that constituted their expertise while accepting the burden of comprehension. The literary scholar had to recognize that the body is not transparent and the physician recognize that language is not transparent. In agreeing that bodies and texts must be interpreted within a cultural context, the two of them established a structuring principle for collaboration. The result was not a simple sum of the literary and medical parts. They were working on cultural and social issues that transcend disciplinary boundaries such as representations of disease and sexuality, death and dying. It was a "synthetic, synoptic convergence of perspectives."

The *Parsifal* inquiry also sheds light on the nature of collaboration. The conversation or dialogue model is a dominant scheme. In face-to-face relations, interaction potentially occurs on all levels, from brainstorming and planning to drafting and revising. Talk is a way of "composing aloud." The only way to produce a single-voiced text, the Hutcheons found, is to keep talking. Feedback and exchange are keys to creating shared standards and expectations. Their collaboration did not resemble the model used in scientific laboratories so much as the model of mutual support described by feminist scholars Sandra Gilbert and Susan Gubar. Mindful of gender-laden assumptions about women being more successful collaborators, on the premise that they use group maintenance strategies, the Hutcheons describe effective collaborators as "psychologically androgynous." Participants must shift roles constantly to achieve "jointness," listening indefinitely and surrendering anything from general ideas to specific words.

When they began to study Wagner's opera *Tristan und Isolde,* the Hutcheons expanded their team. Over the years, this opera has generated a multidisciplinary range of commentary. Erika Reiman, who was writing a dissertation on Robert Schumann, and Jean Paul, brought musicological expertise and sensitivity to the interactions of literature and music. Russell Kilbourn, a doctoral candidate in comparative literature working on related areas of nineteenth- and twentieth-century European philosophy and literature, brought philosophical expertise, interest in film, and prior experience working with the Hutcheons. Jill Scott, a comparative literature student researching representations of the figure of Electra in literature and opera, contributed extensive knowledge of German Romantic literature and Freudian theory. Helmut Reichenbächer, a German born- and trained-student who had a first degree in music literature and was completing a dissertation on Canadian literature, brought knowledge of music and proficiency in German language. The expanded team embodied a dialogic model, although the Hutcheons still served in the role of project directors. Everyone was an intellectual equal in the research phase, but the Hutcheons wrote jointly and the others produced individual outcomes.

The Hutcheons's initial hypotheses formed the basis for collective brainstorming about individual research paths. The process was complementary and cooperative, not strictly collaborative. Each student wrote a separate conference paper on the theme of death and dying. Yet, they pooled their findings and results. The collaborative and complementary dynamics came together as individuals "workshopped" their drafts with the entire team, revising and editing each other's work. The first iteration almost always had specific disciplinary audiences in mind—some literary, others medical, some cultural studies, and others operatic. Nevertheless, presentations often had an interdisciplinary dimension by incorporating visual images, video and audio clips, and alternating speaking voices. The complexity of the project would have been greater if everyone had written together. Each individual, though, began to think differently, to listen carefully and to look for new ways to integrate insights. Roles also changed as team members questioned each other critically, countering the view that collaborative work minimizes contention and substantive critique to achieve harmony and unity. The group developed a collective respect for their personal and disciplinary differences in a "rhetoric of dissensus." Acting as each other's audiences, individuals were also able to assess the impact and accessibility of their work across disciplinary boundaries.

The Hutcheons classify their activities as "interdiscursivity," not "interdisciplinarity." Interdiscursivity makes more modest claims, it is associated more with borrowing, and it does not entail or depend on a full or formal disciplinary formation. If "true interdisciplinarity" means equal and plural preparation of the kind that Norma Bryson and Mieke Bal acquired, it is rare. Linda Hutcheon learned the discourse of musicology by taking courses and reading extensively in music theory and history. However, even interdiscursivity is not superficial. Breadth of knowledge requires more than knowing how to cull a supportive quotation from a different field. Learning another discipline's discourse means learning to formulate and articulate the issues in a field. If not, parts of another discourse that are not considered central or current may be used. Blind faith may be placed in experts or the reverse, a romanticized amateurism result. Giles Gunn's warning comes to mind: "To bring together two or more disciplines into significant interaction with one another requires considerable mastery of the subtleties and particularities of each, together with sufficient imagination and tact, ingenuity and persuasiveness to convince others of the utility of linkages ("Interdisciplinary Studies" 239). To do "truly interdisciplinary work," Linda Hutcheon concluded, means being able to "walk the walk" not just talk it—to contextualize, historicize, and interpret with credibility.

Jazz Studies

The emergent field of jazz studies differs from interdiscursivity in several ways. It is present across multiple genres, it encounters the institutional challenges of interdisciplinary fields, and, like popular music, it is inextricably embedded within a sociopolitical framework. Certain art forms, Robert O'Meally asserted, "cry out for an interdisciplinary approach." In the process of American artistic exchange, jazz became a recurring element across humanistic forms, giving it a "cross-disciplinary beat or *cadence*" in expressions as diverse as Muhammad Ali's rhythmical rhymes and boxing-dancing, the tonal colors and visual equivalents of harmonic intervals in Romare Bearden's painting, and the blues idiom in African American literature. The most commonly cited elements of a black aesthetic are present in the jazz sensibility, including the call-and-response pattern, repetitions within difference, rhythms oriented to Afro dance beats, solo breaks and other improvisations, and interchanges with the blues and other genres ("Preface" xiv, "Introduction" 3). Jazz is also a theme and a cultural style. In dance, for example, it is both the subject and the musical basis of productions as well as a quality in instrumentation and performance, from rhythms and melodic phrases to second liners in a New Orleans funeral march (O'Meally, "Introduction" 273). Jazz is all the more compelling an example because, Donna Cassidy emphasizes, it has never been a fixed form. It was historically a product of hybridization, and intermixing has remained a distinct feature since it moved out of the South (71).

Like literature and art, jazz music has interart affiliations. Musicians such as Charles Mingus and Sun Ra were poets and lyricists, and jazz musicians had a presence in interdisciplinary arts communities such as Black Mountain and the Harlem Renaissance. And vice versa. Many authors have incorporated the subject and the sound of jazz into literature. Toni Morrison's novel *Jazz* and Wray Douglas's *Man Orchid* emulated the spontaneity of improvisatory music in language, and writer Amiri Baraka once patterned his style of recitation after the sounds of Albert Ayler's saxophone (Mackey

614; L. Thomas 260–62, 267). For their part, visual artists have made jazz both a subject and an expressive technique. This linkage is illustrated beautifully in the collection *Seeing Jazz* (Folley-Cooper, Macanic, and McNeil). Cassidy's study of jazz and cultural identity in American art between 1910 and 1940 explores the interplay of art and music as an aesthetic model for a modern tempo. Others, too, have called attention to the work of Romare Bearden and Aaron Douglas. Albert Murray equates the high-affect colors, improvisational patterns, and perspectival distortions of Bearden's collage and painting style with blues timbres, down-home onomatopoeia, urban dissonance, and cacophony (18). In his easel paintings, murals, and book illustrations, Douglas developed a geometric style akin to African American rhythms and concurrent elements of Art Deco design. The color changes suggest gestures and bodily movements of black dance and the sound and vocal patterns of black song (Powell 184–88). Arthur Jafa has also traced black visual intonation in the genre of film, manifested in irregular camera rates and frame replications that approximate vocal intonations of a "polyventiality" of tones, rhythms, perspectives (267).

Jazz was long ignored and even outright dismissed in studies of American culture. Few writers on jazz had training in historiography. A mixed group of journalists, musicologists, and enthusiasts, they tended to recirculate commonplace vernacular formulae, creating a shorthand historicism picked up by early jazz chroniclers. Until the 1930s, the small number of jazz critics in the United States were influenced largely by the social and cultural mores of their own society. Their primary concern was appreciation, not cultural understanding (Rasula 137–40). Jazz also suffered from the privileging of European art music and the divide of high and low genres that aligned "culture" with "refinement." High art music embodied tradition, harmony and hierarchy, and a segmented relationship between performer and audience. Jazz was cast in opposition as the embodiment of the new, the raucous and discordant, accessibility and spontaneity, and an interactive relationship between artist and audience (L. Levine 432–33).

Increased scholarly interest is reversing the long-standing neglect. Canonization has been a major activity in this process (Gabbard, "Intro" 10). The standard narrative moves from African origins and ragtime through a succession of styles or periods from New Orleans origins into the 1920s, swing in the 1930s, bebop in the 1940s, cool jazz and hard bop in the 1950s, and free jazz and fusion in the 1960s. Widely accepted as it is, Scott Deveaux cautions, this official history is an oversimplification. Jazz is enmeshed in a canon debate about which era and style constitute the essence of the form. At present, a "neoclassicist" movement led by performer Wynton Marsalis has prioritized the historical past over an avant garde and the commercial genre mixing of jazz and popular music (483–85).

New aesthetic discourses were also laced with idioms of commerce, politics, gender, and race. They must be treated, Bernard Gendron emphasizes, as integral to the emerging jazz aesthetic rather than intrusions or add-ons to a "pure" jazz aesthetic (34). A different definition appears, Deveaux proposes, if two major boundaries within which historians, critics, and musicians have situated the music are recognized—ethnicity and economics. Ethnicity acknowledges the centrality of *African* American culture. Economics exposes the relationship of jazz to capitalism and its separation from the popular music industry (483, 485–87). Like popular music studies, jazz also fronts the question of sociality. Any attempt to arrive at a definition, Gabbard affirms, must be based on sociocultural analysis. Jazz cannot be understood strictly on the basis of internal aesthetics and formalist criteria. It is a product of the cultural sphere and, of necessity, issues of race must be acknowledged ("Introduction" 17, 22n1). Heightened consciousness of the social and the political does not rule out aesthetic and sonic qualities. Yet, strict musicological analysis came into favor only recently in jazz criticism. As the musicological canon expanded, Don Randel recalls, older methodological tools were still used and concepts such as "the work itself" and "creative genius" were employed. Consequently, jazz scholarship often turned out to resemble other musicological scholarship, strong on archival and source-critical work but weak on biography and with little in between. Like popular music and ethnomusicology, jazz forces issues that have been minimized or ignored to the surface. "The work itself" is not easily defined, either. Notation was not central to what is considered perhaps the most important element in jazz—improvisation. Rhythm, timbre, and performance styles may also overwhelm harmony and counterpart (14).

In jazz studies, too, the role of critical theory is disputed. Adapting Donald Kuspit's explanation of the four beliefs that led art historians to resist structuralist and poststructuralist theories, Gabbard explains that disciples of jazz tend to respond to sensual, libidinous dimensions of the music. The "bodiliness" of the visual has an equivalent in the gut feelings of jazz, and jazz writers have a corresponding discomfort with words, privileging the experience of musicians ("Introduction" 18). Despite skepticism, though, a number of poststructuralist approaches informed jazz scholarship as scholars worked toward an indigenous black theory. This move is evident in Houston Baker's assimilation of metatheoretical strategies of tropology and archaeology in studying the blues and his treatment of rap as a postmodern deconstructive hybridity. Henry Louis Gates's theory of the signifying monkey also addresses issues at the heart of postmodern theorizing. In exploring the relationship between African and African American vernacular traditions and black literature, Gates drew on ancient poetry and myths of African, Latin American, and Caribbean culture. Black "signifyin'" is a mediating strategy of interaction with things, working through irony, parody, needling, and trickery to create a cultural space of expression and survival. Gary Tomlinson drew on Gates's theory in analyzing trumpeter Miles Davis's fusion period, John Murphy in discussing dialogue among jazz improvisers, and Samuel Floyd in analysis of Jelly Roll Morton's "Black Bottom Stomp" (Tomlinson 64–96; Kellner, *Media Culture* 187).

Here too, comparison with other interdisciplinary fields is instructive. Gabbard compares cinema studies and jazz studies. Until the early 1960s, cinema was outside the classroom, although universities had long hosted film societies, "hot" record societies, and student jazz bands. In the 1960s, some faculty in language and history departments used films, and in a few institutions students could take a cinema course. By and large, however, such courses were usually ghettoized in departments of English or theater. At present, jazz studies is at roughly the same point of development. A number of colleges and universities train musicians in the genre. But, in most of them, jazz is usually taught by musicologists more familiar with Eurocentric forms or by a lone jazz musician, despite noteworthy exceptions. In contrast, film studies has gained academic acceptance. The first doctorate was conferred in 1971 and by 1990 more than 300 institutions were offering degrees in film and film–related areas. At the time, only about 100 colleges and universities were offering mostly undergraduate degrees in jazz.

Cinema's academic success, Gabbard continues, is explained in part by the importation from France of *la politique des auteurs* in the 1960s. The theory authorized reading a film artist's work in terms of order, thematic unity, and transcendent artistic vision. In the 1970s and 1980s, new theories prompted rethinking auteurism. Film theoreticians now rely on Marxist, psychoanalytic, semiotic, and poststructuralist methodologies to connect forces outside the filmic text with meaning beneath a narrative surface. Once excluded groups are also demystifying and deconstructing the traditional canon, and scholars have adopted a specialized language. Gabbard compares jazz studies today to the era of auteurism. He speculates that it will follow a similar path by becoming a more stable fixture in universities. Scholars may become more self-conscious about the problematic of canon formation and will likely develop a professional discourse that draws on vocabularies of musicology, sociology, critical theory, and other disciplines. Yet, echoing J. T. Mitchell's view of the emergent field of visual culture in the previous chapter, jazz studies will still need to grapple with boundary questions (4–7).

The current flux of music, Pasler suggests, raises several questions that resonate across all three disciplinary case studies. Are new developments to be feared? Or, are they the result of a younger generation trying to create a place for themselves? Is caution in order? Or, would it stifle crossing boundaries and scrutinizing assumptions? Does music have a meaning independent of the contexts in which it is created, performed, and heard? Or, is it socially embedded? And, what effect do contexts have on musicians, the organization of musical life, and institutional support for music? (16). The lessons of literary studies and art history repeat; it is harder to talk in the singular anymore. Musics are proliferating and multiplying, along with their meanings (Bohlman, "Epilogue" 197). Meanwhile, the blurring of subdisciplinary boundaries continues to undermine the validity of older codifications, the notion of a center, and the binary exclusivity of being either inside or outside of an aesthetic work. In a pluralistic conception of discipline, Pasler suggests, the question is not so much what is new or old or what needs to be replaced or superseded, but instead how each perspective can enrich the other (21). Kassabian describes the discipline as a web of critiques that illuminate each other. Illumination is not simply a matter of correcting or altering the existing canon and practices. It means giving up the project of defining disciplines wholly according to the object of study. Music is reimagined as a "hetereogeneous intersection" of its traditional branches—theory, musicology, and ethnomusiciology—with cultural studies—ethnic studies, postcolonial studies, Marxism, and feminist anthropology (8, 9).

Part III

INTERDISCIPLINING "AMERICA"

Chapter 7

RECONSTRUCTING AMERICAN STUDIES

American studies is one of the oldest and, many argue, the most successful interdisciplinary fields in the United States. With the exception of isolated references, the term "American studies" did not appear much before 1920. The terms "American civilization" and "Americanist" were used more often. The institutional roots of the field lie in the 1920s and 1930s, when the first courses in American Civilization were offered at Yale, Harvard, Smith, the University of Pennsylvania, and George Washington University (Kerber 417). The first discernable degrees, conferences, and publications bearing the name date from the mid-1930s, although it took another twenty years for a full academic infrastructure to develop and the label to become widely used (Horwitz, "American Studies" 112). After World War II, the field expanded on the wave of a postwar demographic boom, the broadening of American higher education, and an increasing number of academic jobs. In tallying its current institutional presence, Michael Cowan reported undergraduate and graduate programs in over 400 colleges and universities worldwide; numerous curricula in high schools; academic journals in a dozen countries; dedicated lists in academic publishing houses; offices in a variety of governmental agencies, private foundations, museums, and research libraries; and professional associations in Europe, Asia, Africa, the Middle East, Latin America, the South Pacific, Canada, and the United States (105).

The recent appearance of a four-volume *Encyclopedia of American Studies* marks a point of maturity for the field. Programs are said to be "holding their own" and the membership of the American Studies Association is growing (Orvell, Butler, and Mechling vii–viii). Since interdisciplinarity has been part of the field's rhetoric of theory and practice from the beginning, this chapter addresses a series of related questions. What were the early warrants for and forms of interdisciplinarity? How has the balance of power between humanities and social science shifted over time? What new theory and practices resulted from the critical and cultural turns that began in the 1960s and 1970s? What is the basis for a field of "American cultural studies"? What role do changing conceptions of place and the text/context relation play in recent work? What lessons about interdisciplinarity derive from this exemplar?

The Search for an American Holism

American studies was developed primarily by humanists in English, history, and art departments (Mechling, "Axioms" 15). Many accounts of its origin highlight a nationalist impulse. However, a more complex set of interests planted the seed for expanded studies of American experience. The academic field and democratic social movements in the New Deal era shared conditions of possibility with class-conscious interethnic coalitions and mass movements that opened new cultural and intellectual space for the working class and ethnic and racial diversity. The founding of American studies may also be viewed as a continuation of the popular "discovery" and "invention" of American culture during the New Deal and World War II eras. In addition to focusing on literature and arts, New Deal cultural projects explored local histories, folkways, and the lives of ordinary people. New work in ethnography and folklore furthered interest in American culture, as well as the idea of American exceptionalism and the "cult of the common man" advocated by Popular Front Marxism and circulated in artistic and media projects (Orvell, Butler, and Mechling viii; Cowan 106–107; Lipsitz, "Shining City" 56–57; Lipsitz "Listening," 317; Lipsitz, *American Studies* xiv, 34–45; Denning, *Cultural Front* 69–70).

Mobilization for World War II co-opted the radicalism of the 1930s. A nationalist vision, interwoven with the language of idealism, dominated initial development of the field during the late 1940s and 1950s (Giles 526). Even then, however, not everyone was drawn to American studies for the same reason. For some, Paul Lauter recounts, it offered an academic framework for carrying out a left-liberal program associated with the wartime Office of Strategic Services and anticommunist tendencies in the early CIA as well as antifascist and pro-democratic liberal values. For others, it offered a form of intellectual work based in social and cultural analysis. In the context of the Cold War, American Studies may be viewed as an oppositional field where critical studies of American social and cultural institutions were possible ("Reconfiguring" 32; *Walden Pond* 23–24). Part of the intent was also to develop an alternative to formalist approaches. In literature, the challenge was directed at New Criticism's intrinsic focus on poetic texts. In history, the targets were the intellectual history synthesis, the history of ideas, and the consensus school's search for a singular "American mind."

The first generation of scholars tended to focus on the New England tradition. Efforts to build a broader study of national character and consciousness led to the first recognized interdisciplinary paradigm—the "myth-and-symbol" school. Scholars sought connections across imaginative works and popular culture, politics, anthropology, sociology, and economics. Led by individuals such as Henry Nash Smith, Leo Marx, and R. W. B. Lewis, the myth-and-symbol movement held sway during the 1950s and 1960s. Stories and images were treated as mythic and symbolic reflections of the dominant ideas in a given time, including the ideas of virgin land, the pastoral ideal, and the American Adam. Beyond these objectives, Daryl Umberger adds, one of the effects of the myth-and-symbol school was to push interdisciplinary studies closer to being an accepted academic practice (181). The word "interdisciplinary" became a mantra of curriculum reform and the banner for a rapprochement of humanities and social sciences (Horwitz, "American Studies" 116; Marx 46).

When the American Studies Association was founded in 1951, it adopted the explicit goal of studying American culture and history "as a whole," with the aim of unifying the plural and harmonizing differences (Wise, "Axioms" 517; Brantlinger 27). Literature and history, though, were the dominant disciplines, and the actual practice of teaching and scholarship was more multidisciplinary than interdisciplinary. A survey of undergraduate and graduate programs in 1948 revealed heavy dependence on courses in established departments, with only a small core of multidisciplinary and interdisciplinary courses sponsored by American studies programs. Faculty also tended to retain their locations in departmental homes or hold dual appointments. Over time, increasing focus on themes and on case-study problems fostered greater integration. Even then, however, methods were not necessarily fused or a new holism, interdisciplinary synthesis, or metadiscipline created. The promised bridging of humanities and social sciences did not occur either. Scholars and teachers did not delve deeply into the complex interactions between economic institutions and collective mentalities, arts, and expressions. Nor did they formulate a theoretical basis for analyzing them (Cowan 107; Orvell, Butler, and Mechling viii).

Appraising the Beginning

From the mid-1960s forward, the myth-and-symbol paradigm came under attack. Critics faulted it for a transcendental language of "literary power," a platonic view of intellectual history and consensualist ideology, methodological naiveté, reductive use of interdisciplinary and comparative analysis, and a gendered reinscription of the dominant culture. Gunther Lenz, though, advises a more measured appraisal. Henry Nash Smith was charged with propagating an "organicist holism." Yet, in aiming to study American culture and thought as a whole, Smith sought a systematic understanding of interactions between the unitary myth and utopian vision of American culture and the complexity and heterogeneity of that culture ("Periodization" 293). Linda Kerber also credits the myth-and-symbol school with broadening the definition of what counts as art, including "second-rate" literature (424). The myth-and-symbol paradigm is often depicted as hostile to social science as well, but some scholars did seek to understand how value-laden images influence social life. Allen Tate, for example, brought knowledge of regional cultures to bear on particular areas (Marx 40–42). The early development of the field, George Lipsitz adds, anticipated many cross-disciplinary epistemological and hermeneutic concerns of European Theory. The consensus myth served conservative political ends, but it did not prevent scholars from asking critical questions about the social construction of cultural categories and power relations within American society. A variety of social movements, cultural practitioners, and intellectuals preserved oppositional thought ("Listening" 317–18).

The inaugural issue of *American Quarterly* was also comparative on an international scale, and many articles did not deal with national character or myths and symbols. The issue contained investigations of language and religion, sports journalism, Yankee painters, the Yinglish music of Mickey Katz, and essays contesting the myth-and-symbol approach (Farrell, "American Studies" 185–86). In a review of forty-one articles appearing in *American Quarterly* between 1949 and 1965, Kuhn and Moskop found that even though social scientists played a minority role, it was a significant one. The articles were written by social scientists or exhibited a social science perspective on topics in popular culture, regional studies, institutional analysis, biography's intersection with history, methods and concepts, and power relations. James Farrell and Christopher Hoskins highlight one book in particular as a lesson in the danger of a rigid stage model of the field's history. Alan Trachtenberg's *Brooklyn Bridge* is often cited as an exemplar of the myth-and-symbol paradigm, but it anticipated interests at the heart of cultural studies. Trachtenberg looked at the bridge as history and as myth, crafting a synthesis of idealist epistemology—in the abstraction and transcendence of myth—and of materialist epistemology—in locating content in time, space, and social context. He also incorporated a critique of capitalist ideology and hegemony while questioning whether American society was unified. "Our culture," Trachtenberg concluded, was "majority culture."

Hopes for synthesis ran high in the first era of American studies. In 1968, Robert Meredith proclaimed that the field had come of age, having moved beyond initial "stirrings of discontent" in English and history departments to an extensive body of inquiry (xi). Five years later, however, Jay Mechling joined Meredith and David Wilson in characterizing the field as a "parcel of noble strivings tied loosely together by individual will and efforts." They found coherence lacking at all three levels—theory, method, and technique. Programs were also hampered by their marginal status and ad hoc curricula. Smith's 1957 vision indicated both the possibilities and limits of interdisciplinarity at the time. When Smith called for a method of analysis that was at once literary and sociological, he imagined students of literature taking account of sociological, historical, and anthropological data and methods while their counterparts drew on the data and methods of the arts. Smith predicted that an appropriate method would evolve in piecemeal fashion through "a kind of principled opportunism" in the course of daily struggles with various tasks and criticism of practices. The sociological mode of myth criticism did spawn studies of archetypal American characters, themes, plots, images, genres, and settings. Yet, Robert Sklar recalls, efforts to link texts and their cultural contexts stopped short of full-scale theorizing of the relationship between—on the one hand—values, beliefs, attitudes, and imaginative constructs and—on the other hand—social structure and forms. Sociologists tended to extract data and content from the arts without regard for expressive dimensions of culture. For their part, literary scholars treated America as a textualized universe (258).

If American studies were to achieve intellectual coherence, Mechling, Meredith, and Wilson implored, the concept of culture must occupy the center of the "discipline." Achieving disciplinary status became the hallmark of legitimacy and social scientific methods the means of achieving it.

They were not alone in this view. Robert Sykes argued that disciplinary integrity lie in the claim to being a social science, Mechling urged moving from a humanistic to an anthropological preoccupation, John Caughey promoted a new ethnosemantics, and Bruce Kuklick called for more empirical research and a more anthropological understanding of culture defined in terms of behavior ["Myth and Symbol"]. In 1970, Murray Murphey made what Barry Shank calls the "first overt statement of this disciplinary philosophy" when describing the American Civilization program at the University of Pennsylvania. At Pennsylvania, the problem of interdisciplinarity focused traditionally on the literature/history nexus. This approach failed because of irreconcilable differences between two understandings of culture: an orientation to social sciences that abandoned the use of literature and an orientation to literature grounded in the myth-image school and the criterion of aesthetic worth. In the 1960s, the department made an aggressive effort to move toward a disciplinary approach grounded in applying social sciences to contemporary and historical data. In addition to borrowing from social psychology, scholars took an anthropological orientation to culture that fostered an ethnographic method and attention to material objects (Murphey, "Pennsylvania" 496–97; Shank, "Embarrassment" 100–01).

The year 1974 was a time of reckoning. When Stanley Bailis assessed the state of interdisciplinarity in the field, he found it wanting. Ad hoc use of different disciplines, he charged, had led American studies to the point of incoherency. Efforts to build a holism out of multiple perspectives had resulted in a tower of Babel. Bailis characterized the field as an arena for disciplinary encounters and a staging ground for fresh topical pursuits in an incorporative élan that excluded nothing and was always beginning. The field was eclectic and pluralistic in using other theories and highly responsive to the flux of its historical surroundings. For the most part, though, its members continued to be trained in disciplines they continued to practice (203–04). The same year R. Gordon Kelly admitted that the marriage of literary criticism and history was not made in heaven. The aesthetic side of the relationship was still vested in a small canon of high-aesthetic achievements regarded as autonomous and generalizable, and the doctrine of literary power provided no clear principle for specifying the character or boundaries of a work's "social domain." Even so, glimpses of what was to come were apparent. Kelly's article on "Literature and the Historian" cites Richard Hoggart's 1969 publication *Contemporary Cultural Studies,* and his studies of children's literature bore commonality with the emergent framework of British cultural studies (Shank, "Embarrassment" 102–03).

The Critical and Cultural Turns

The period of the mid- to late 1960s and 1970s was a turning point, fueled by the cultural revolutions of the period and new scholarly approaches. Over the latter half of the century, scholarship opened to a fuller range of artistic expressions and intellectual, social, political, economic, and psychological forms of American life. American studies expanded to include ecological studies and environmental history; critiques of corporate capitalism and the global political economy; new area studies and African American studies, ethnic studies, women's studies, and urban studies; plus expanding research on popular, mass, and folk culture. In 1978, Gene Wise counted no less than seventy-four separate categories of specialization. During the 1980s, European cultural theory became an important component of scholarship and, in the 1980s and 1990s, increased attention was paid to gender, race, and ethnicity as well as region and class. Theory was not uniformly welcomed, and most work initially focused on validated literary and historical texts. Nonetheless, Lacanian psychoanalysis, Althusserian structuralist-Marxism, British cultural studies, deconstruction, poststructuralism, postmodernism, and other approaches generated new conceptualizations of the problematics of representation, power, and identity. The continuing dominance of literature and history was also challenged by a new generation of scholars, many of whom came from wider class, ethnic, and gender backgrounds than their predecessors (Wise, "Axioms" 519; Wise, "Paradigm Dramas" 519; Orvell, Butler, and Mechling viii; Lipsitz, *American Studies* xv–xvi, 23, 73, 95, 98–99, 105, 109; Umberger 182–83; Cowan 109–10).

Wise dubbed the 1960s and 1970s the "coming apart stage" of the field's history. Periodic identity crises have occurred in a number of older interdisciplinary fields, usually around the question of conceptual coherence (R. Miller 13). In American studies, new interests strained the intellectual history synthesis and accompanying assumption that America is an integrated whole. Indicative of this shift, the word "interdisciplinarity" was coupled increasingly with the words "innovation," "experiment," and "radicalism" (Shumway, "Interdisciplinarity" 14). David Marcell's 1977 call for "critical interdisciplinarity" and Giroux, Shumway, and Sosnoski's 1984 call for a "counterdisciplinary praxis" of cultural studies asserted a new intellectual and political vision of America defined by pluralism, relationality, and an expanded concept of culture.

Toward an American Cultural Studies

In introducing the *Encyclopedia,* Orvell, Butler, and Mechling identified culture as the core concept that generally unites the disparate work of American studies. The anthropological definition of culture has become widely accepted in recent years. Debate continues, though, on whether the framework is singular or plural. Orvell, Butler, and Mechling acknowledge the simultaneity of difference and universal, or near universal, elements that become part of everyone's knowledge by virtue of living in the midst of U.S. politics, social and religious values, and mass and popular culture. Some elements of American identity are distinct to particular subgroups. Others are shared in common (viii–ix). During the 1960s and 1970s, Shank recalls, two conceptualizations of culture were apparent in the field: as a separate realm of artistic and intellectual activity and as a causal agent underlying social process. The tension between the two divided American studies, although the new social history, new ethnography, and anthropological turn of the 1970s combined to produce a less value-directed sense of culture. Hopes rose for a new synthesis of a social-materialist bent. Studies of nonprint societies and popular and vernacular culture, along with the materialist orientation and focus on social structural determinants in social science methods, contributed to new histories "from the bottom up." Social history tended to focus on smaller groups and particular populations, but it gave rise to subfields of labor, women's, and black history ("Embarrassment" 97, 104).

The cultural studies approach that emerged in the 1980s and 1990s differed. It was not, Lipsitz emphasizes, a rebuke of the myth-and-symbol school or of the anthropology and social history of the 1970s. It was a response to new conditions and connections between culture and social structure. The New Deal version of social democracy largely ignored injustices based on race, gender, or sexual preference that were central to social movements and participatory democracy in the civil rights era. The defeats of the social movements of the 1960s and conservative countermobilizations in the 1970s and 1980s heightened academic interest in culture as a political force (*American Studies* 73, 110, 113). Winfried Fluck also distinguishes the new "cultural radicalism" from older forms of political radicalism. The most striking aspect of recent developments in humanities and American studies is not their theoretical bent. Approaches differ, but they are united by a realization that the central source of political domination is no longer attributed to political and economic structures but to culture (216).

As cultural studies developed in the United States, Lipsitz recalled, it needed to create its own academic home or to find one in which it could flourish. At the time, venues for popular culture studies were too narrow and fragmented, and history departments were largely unreceptive. English departments were more welcoming, but they were grappling with post-structuralist theory, and the concept of historicizing still had a shadowy existence in the discipline. American studies was a logical home. It had focused on cultural issues since the beginning, it had strong historicizing tendencies, and it was more open to socially inflected categories of analysis. Furthermore, there were significant connections between some of its members and the British cultural studies movement ("Shining City" 57–58). By the early twentieth-first century, Lauter adds, the ASA and *American Quarterly* were venues of choice for many scholars who identified themselves as doing cultural studies and having related interests in mass culture, media and its institutions, the politics of communications, and investigations of academic conventions and discourses (*Walden Pond* 14).

Lenz locates the premise of an "American cultural studies" in the vision of an inherently heterogeneous culture that reconstructs the idea of America and the nature of American studies on an intercultural and transnational scale. The 1980s and 1990s were a productive time in building this vision. Scholars drew on insights into multicultural dimensions of difference developed in women's studies, gender studies, and minority discourses. They conducted refined analyses of the meanings and interrelations of cultural texts and contexts. They responded to the challenges of postmodern, postcolonial, and multicultural theory. And, they created new ways of understanding cultural mediation and assimilation, new media and modes of communications, and the challenges presented by new sciences and an expanding technoculture ("Periodization" 294–95).

Despite the current cache of the term "American cultural studies," this is not the first time the notion has been proposed. In 1978, Gene Wise called for a new rhetoric of interdisciplinarity rooted in a set of elementary axioms for "American culture studies." When Mechling revisited the axioms and Wise's history of the "paradigm dramas" in 1999, he was struck by how prescient Wise was in predicting that American studies would adopt a pluralistic approach to American culture, rediscover the particular, repudiate exceptionalism, and move to a more comparative, cross-cultural approach ("Commentary" 213). In reality, Wise wrote, people do not live "wholly" in a larger culture. It is filtered to them through intermediary influences. The distinctive task of American studies becomes tracing the connections in a search for "dense facts" that reveal deeper meanings and point to other facts, ideas, and meanings. The metaphor of knowledge shifts in kind from building blocks in a pyramid to a series of dialogues that are inherently unfinishable.

Lauter's comparison of introductory graduate courses in American studies and their counterparts in English and history departments illustrates key tenets of the reconceptualization of culture. A course in American studies typically includes work by people located in English and history, but it also includes work in anthropology, art, music, political science, sociology, and cultural theory and practice. Core texts tend to exhibit five methodological principles. The first principle is *Frederic Jameson's injunction to "Always historicize."* Instead of focusing attention on formal qualities and structures of a text or a material object, attention is paid to why they emerge at a particular time and place and how the forms of their production, distribution, and consumption materialize. The historical imperative also encourages reflexive self-scrutiny among practitioners.

The second principle is *a broadened sense of textuality* that encompasses nonwritten forms while considering the ways that texts express relations of power and how they shape and are shaped by the material conditions of everyday life. Americanists and literary scholars share an interest in how language and form reveal the nature of argument and the ways that imagery and details reinforce or contradict a writer's ideas. They both treat texts as discourse in a larger network of texts and documents, social practices, laws, policies, and institutional forms of organization. They both engage in close readings of texts, including contracts, ads, and legislation. Yet, many Americanists, especially younger ones, are leaning toward a more ethnographic kind of investigation in order to root contemporary cultural speculations in material evidence. Scholars today, T. V. Reed adds, are looking at specific aesthetic and cultural forms as factors in mediating and helping to form class structure, such as musical theater, blackface minstrelsy, and productions of Shakespeare's plays in nineteenth-century America (359). Even as they do, though, Lauter reports that they still tend to emphasize reading of cultural texts over tracking the economic or political work texts perform or the concentration of material factors that shape particular cultural moments and material objects.

Lauter's third methodological principle is *an increased comparative and global outlook*. It has fostered the notion of a "postnational American studies" and a more comparative approach to race, gender, class, sexuality, and disability. The ways that multicultural identities are constituted have also become the focus of study. The fourth, though perhaps less widely shared, principle is *Antonio Gramsci's ideas about hegemony*. Gramsci offered a framework for understanding how particular groups gain authority over political and cultural life, how they respond to challenges from subordinated groups, how those groups generate their own cultural and social authority, and how power is contested, shifting, and protean. The fifth principle is *gaining a "certain purchase" by seeking areas of intersection between objects of study in the disciplines on which American Studies draws*. The field shares a focus on context with the discipline of history, an orientation to texts with literary studies, and a functional way of reading texts and objects with cultural anthropology. The cumulative effect is a new relational treatment of objects. Literary texts such as *Uncle Tom's Cabin* are studied for their interplay with sociological ideas about color and miscegenation, historical and legal debates informing policy and legislation such as the Fugitive Slave Act, tensions in the doctrine of evangelical Christianity, and questions of citizenship and race embedded in American constitutional jurisprudence and manifested in Supreme Court decisions such as *Dred Scott* (*Walden Pond* 14–18, "Reconfiguring" 26–30).

The current relationship of American studies and popular culture studies illustrates the complexity of American cultural studies. In 1969, Ray Browne launched what would become the Popular Culture Association at an ASA meeting. Prior to that point, American studies departments and programs were teaching popular, mass-mediated culture (Mechling, "Axioms" 10). The first issues of *American Quarterly* even contained discussions of popular music, film, and subcultural practices. Yet, tensions developed between the two movements, largely centered on status of the populace, low art, popular music and literature, film and television, and sports (Lipsitz, "Listening" 323). The expansion of cultural studies during the 1980s and 1990s encouraged wider interest in popular culture topics, paving the way for a renewed relationship. As a subfield of American studies, Tom Lansford reported in *The Encyclopedia*, popular culture has been a central component of the "discipline." Four broad approaches have emerged within American studies oriented to audience, historical, production, and textual analysis. Even with the new incentive cultural studies provides for expanded study of popular culture, though, debate continues on a

number of issues, including whether popular culture reflects the way people live and think or is a means by which to influence their behaviors and
values, the relationship between elite and low/popular culture, the importance of Western versus non-Western forms of culture in the United States,
and the importance of the various types of media that convey culture, including new electronic technologies (369–71).

Some contend that American studies and cultural studies have become
the same field. Others disagree. In a 1997 issue of the journal *American
Studies* focusing on the culture concept, Mechling faulted cultural studies
for undertheorized understandings of the key concepts of culture, history,
discourse, and class. Mechling called for a more specific conceptualization
of culture, greater familiarity with American history, movement beyond
print discourse, and a fuller understanding of oral cultures ("Axioms").
Writing in the same issue, Richard Horwitz faulted cultural studies for
overemphasizing the analogy between culture and text to the expense of
other analogues such as performance and game; overgeneralizations of
longing for anchors in social identity across space and time; and underem-
phasis on nonhierarchical principles of social differentiation and organization. The fiction of cultural studies providing the long-sought interdisciplinary method, Horwitz concluded, is dubious ("To Kvetch" 65–66).
Nonetheless, James Farrell wrote in that issue, the central questions and
concepts of cultural studies have expanded the repertoire of tools while
helping scholars see how people make meaning, the structures of meaning,
and the interactions of everyday life ("American Cultural Studies" 42–43).

The Question of Place

Paralleling the changing nature of culture, place has taken on a new complexity in American studies. Lipsitz identified two traditions. The institutional form canonized in paradigms such as myth-symbol-image, the
anthropology of uses-and-effects, new social history, and cultural studies
offers important ways of understanding American culture. Yet, they are
tied to connections between culture and place that may no longer be operating. A second American studies has emerged from grass-roots theorizing
about culture and power. Much of this work was created by exiles, migrants, and members of displaced groups. It is the American studies of C.
L. R. James, Duke Ellington, and America Paredes ("Shining City" 65–66;
American Studies 5, 27–28).

New understandings of place are apparent in scholarship on regionalism. Comparable to anthropology, Kris Fresonke reports, research on geographical regions has moved to a less grandiose scale than nationhood. In the 1970s, the effort to reorient American culture around environment and nature fostered the concept of bioregionalism, drawing on environmental science and new studies of communities. This concept is being adopted in feminist criticism and Latino and Native American studies, where the monolithic idea of national identity is resisted (12–13, 17). In studies of the West, the linear view of "progress" is also being supplanted by a more complex picture of interactions among cultural groups and geographical regions, the multiple sites and meanings of the core concept of "frontier," and cultural icons and narratives that shaped popular and academic conceptions of the West. The older West of Anglo settlers is being reconceptualized within a broader framework that incorporates the work of Indian, Chicano/a, African American, Asian American, and feminist and gender historians. New West historiography draws as well on art history, photography and film, rhetoric and semiotics, religious studies, technology, environmental studies, public health, and biomedicine.

Broadly speaking, Philip Fisher found, the claim of pluralism has prompted several episodes of regionalism. Cultural life in America, Fisher explains, swings like a pendulum between diverse sectional voices and the project of unity. Each swing to regionalism split the country along different faultlines, and each rewon unity brought a new plane of association. In the early twentieth century, massive immigration prompted a new kind of regionalism. Its ethnic base was evident in the diversity of languages, folk customs, humor, music, and beliefs set against the pull of uniformity in the Americanization movement, the core culture of public education and economic advancement, and a mobility that placed immigrants within the general American condition. The new regionalism accentuated gender and race over common identity. As a result, during the 1960s and 1970s, older American Studies departments found themselves regionalized into departments of black or African American, Jewish, women's, Native American, Chicano, Asian American, and sometimes gay studies. New identity claims fostered a new fundamentalism in the project of unmasking hegemony, essentialism, and operations of power framed by oppositions of black/white, female/male, Native American/settler, and gay/heterosexual. Alongside it, though, yet another American studies has evolved as an alternative or aftermath. It locates a set of underlying but permanently open national facts and cultural questions around which all identities are shaped, including democratic culture, the culture of freedom, and creation of a national life that is economic in orientation rather than religious or cultural (240–43).

In the new dynamics of place, borders have taken on greater importance. A border, Mae Henderson commented, is both a dividing line and a crossing zone where alternatives are being forged. Within interstitial spaces, new questions blur and merge older distinctions, contributing to the larger project of rethinking culture, canon, and disciplinarity (2, 5, 27). Correspondingly, the notion of biculturality is being challenged by new conditions of multiculturality, multilinguality, and the crossing of class lines (P. Allen 305). Global cities with sizable multilingual populations, from Miami and New York to Los Angeles, illustrate the role of immigration in forging a new hybridity of American culture and identity (Lipsitz, *American Studies* 10–12). Along the U.S./Mexico border in particular, New Mixtec identities have emerged, as well as new cross-cultural, multi-linguistic, and vernacular forms of art, media, and popular culture, and scholarly discourse (DeSoto 304). The concept of *mestiza* consciousness has had a particularly powerful impact on border theory and the parameters of American studies, sociological studies of immigration, and scholarship on gender (Elliott, "Chicano Literature" 307–08; Elliott, "Mestiza Consciousness" 106–07).

Michael Kearney draws an insightful parallel between the border and the disciplines that study it. Both are riddled with holes and contradictions in zones of contested space, capital, and meanings. Classical constructions of anthropology and history have been challenged and reordered by new studies of the border area and its cultural politics. Many of these studies are "antidisciplinary." They work to transcend the domains of standard disciplines and have formed outside the official institutional body of the state. They are not without risk, however. The rise and institutionalization of border studies may create an academic counterpart of the border patrol, controlling transnational ethnic minorities as objects of study (61–62). Interdisciplinarity, Lauter suggests, does double duty. Boundaries of genre, audience, and discipline intersect in borderlands scholarship, art, and everyday culture, challenging the processes by which differences are naturalized, installed, and maintained (*Walden Pond* 127–28, 133–34).

Ultimately, place is also a transnational question. Internationalism is not new. After World War II, international politics stimulated the growth of American studies programs, libraries, research institutions, associations, and publications abroad. Americanists traveled overseas to teach and lecture, while foreign scholars received funds to study in the United States. By the mid-1960s, Cowan notes, most leaders of the first and second generation of U.S. Americanists had spent time abroad on Fulbright scholarships, private foundation grants, and consulting work for the U.S. Information Agency. Their experiences heightened possibilities for cross-national comparative studies, although governmental and corporate support carried the pressure and temptation to serve as goodwill ambassadors (107). Robert Gross views the current heightened interest in transnational perspective as the latest move to alter an interdisciplinary field that was radically remade over two decades under the multicultural challenge. The effects of globalization, including the imperialism of American popular culture, have created a different climate for international perspective in which scholars from diverse ethnic communities are now playing a greater role. The effect is akin to looking through the reverse lens of a telescope, delivering a final blow to the concept of American exceptionalism, and carrying the multicultural impulse to an international plane (377, 380–81, 385, 387–89).

Reflecting on a career at home and abroad, Lauter concluded that the globalization of American culture always requires localization, whether in Houston or Kathmandu. American studies is no longer a one-way proposition. A transnational notion of America is changing the dominant culture back home through a new internationalization of knowledge and cross-border mingling of scholars who recode American images and narratives. Furthermore, interdisciplinarity does not mean the same thing from country to country. In Singapore and other parts of Asia, it appears to be a way of helping students understand social practice in the United States. It addresses questions of why people who work in U.S. business do what they do and how they do it, not how business is organized or financed. It examines the connections that link Sonny and Cher to Sonny and Newt Gingrich, not the constitutional parameters of American political decision-making. In Russia, it operates in part as a lever prying the self-interest of faculties attempting to sustain themselves by building up the walls of their disciplines. In Japan, it appears to be associated with generational change (*Walden Pond* 27–28, 122, 146–47, 150–52). Outside the United States, Horwitz adds, American Studies has consistently supported exchanges with a range of fields, including business, policy, social sciences, and humanities. Any set of topics, however, might dominate in a particular school, region, or nation. In Spain, American studies has emphasized the history, literature, and culture of its former colonies, especially Mexico. In China, recent diplomatic strategies and trade relations with the United States have been stressed. In many secondary schools outside the United States, the name also connotes instruction in English as a second language enriched by popular culture texts ("American Studies" 113).

Interdisciplinarity Redivivus

Given the multitude of changes, it is not surprising to find the name of the field a matter of debate. In 1998, Janice Radway contemplated options in her presidential address to ASA. "American studies" has been the most conventional and long-standing term, both inside and outside the academy. Indicative of the time, ASA's founders considered naming it the "American Civilization Society." Now that the elision of American culture with the United States is no longer a neutral issue, Radway speculated, the field might be called "United States Studies" and the ASA the "International Association for the Study of the United States" or the "Inter-American Studies Association." Or, current intersections with cultural studies might warrant "American Cultural Studies" and a "Society for Intercultural Studies." Each option has advantages and drawbacks. In the end, Radway concluded, the name American studies may well be retained, but the debate on naming has cast the new conditions of theory and practice into sharp focus.

A spirited response followed on the American Studies listserv, H-AMSTDY. In a posting on 7 December 1998, David Nye agreed that the inclusion of ethnic, gender, and racial minorities over the past fifteen years has been a positive development. Yet, he objected that Radway eliminated or removed everything else to the periphery, including interdisciplinary linkages of literature, the arts, history, business, technology, formal politics, environmental issues, media studies and popular culture. On 10 December 1998, Horwitz remarked that members of the old-guard leadership were the most alienated listeners in the audience. The published version of the speech, Robert Gross commented elsewhere, seems less alarming than reports on the spoken version. Radway's contention that the field has moved from an exceptionalist position to a more contested pluralistic terrain is hardly new, and the premise of homogeneous national identity was discredited long ago. Radway attempted to revitalize it via ethnic studies, embracing recent work on difference and the interdependencies of everyday life that shape images of dominant and subordinate classes (389–90).

As for interdisciplinarity, Lenz's assessment in 1982 still rings true. The quest for an "'inter- and supradisciplinary' *Einheitswissenschaft*"—based on an all-inclusive synthetic method, harmonious unity of knowledge, and totalizing science of culture—has been abandoned ("American Studies" 60). In weighing future prospects, Horwitz identified three options that roughly resemble stages of development in influential programs. The simplest and oldest is a loose "multidisciplinary" confederation of students and scholars working in a variety of humanities and social sciences. Cooperation is occasional and instrumental to a particular purpose, such as setting up a conference. The curriculum is the simple sum of everything available, and disciplinary courses are typically repackaged. When new approaches began appearing in the 1960s, the undergraduate structure of American studies was still characterized primarily by cross-departmental programs. Even today, most programs tend to mix existing approaches and subject matters.

A second conception is "cross-disciplinary" existence as an adjunct or semiautonomous region. The locus of cooperation would be an organized situation such as English courses taken by students in history departments. Cooperation would be institutionalized as a set of cross- or co-listed courses, and hiring decisions would be affected by curricular commitments that are not strictly department-based. Staff would gather irregularly to design a menu of courses from which students select options. Program administration would require one or two meetings a year and, if students have electives, a designated advisor. The third option is "inter" or "transdisciplinary" identity as an autonomous field. American studies would become more than the sum of its disciplinary parts or their repackaging. It would be a field of its own. Purposeful cooperation would be an explicit goal and a recognized means for improving teaching and research about American culture. Responsibility for curriculum, space, staff, and budget would be shared, and programs would have committed cores of instructors.

The other part of the name—"studies"—has encompassed significant variations over the history of the field. In general use, it signals a vaguely interdisciplinary approach without specifying which disciplines are broached or how they are bridged. People and interpretive structures from disciplines and other fields are engaged, but American studies remains in some ways smaller—in one location—and larger—in methodological eclecticism—than any one of them. The most common relationship to affiliated disciplines is *bricolage*. Candidates for American studies degrees are typically required to take America-oriented courses in several departments. Americanists are also expected to be comfortable with more than one medium of expertise, such as novels, artifacts, archival records, paintings, music, or polls. Scholars who augment sources in their disciplines may consider themselves "interdisciplinary" without necessarily leaving their departmental homes. Or, they may be "transdisciplinary" in their quest for methods and materials that complement each other. More often, though, they borrow insights from here or there, grabbing and mixing whatever works. They risk charges of dilettantism in exchange for gaining insights that both sectarianism and metatheory would impede. The oldest line of methodological discussion revolves around integration. For most of its history, American Studies has not developed its own method. Many believe that improvisation is the key to continued vitality, mixing diverse ingredients and cobbling together strategies to fit a particular need. Yet, Horwitz finds, in hindsight it has been relatively easy to detect regimens that were not particularly "transdisciplinary" or "not disciplinary" ("Kvetch" 65–66, "American Studies" 114–16).

The text/context relation continues to be a measure of interdisciplinarity. The earliest form of "context," Robert Berkhofer reported in a 1989 assessment of American studies, was a vague but polysemic definition of culture in disciplines as varied as music, art, literature, and the practice of intellectual history. In exposing patterns underlying American culture, scholars constituted a common framework for moving beyond special interests and methods. The dominance of textuality was challenged by the emergence of history as a perspective and a defined subject; new understandings of the oral, the visual, and the aural; and new understandings of aesthetic, social, political, economic, and psychological forces that produce meaning. Definitions still differ, though. At one end of a spectrum, the quest for one meaning is strong, anchored by a presupposition of contextual fundamentalism. Documents, artifacts, and texts are self-interpreting. Facts are "discovered," not "constituted," and in documentary and artifactual analysis historical narrative is verified in an essential structure by parallels within a past represented in a single (hi)story told by a single voice from a single point of view. At the other pole of definition, documentary and artifactual fundamentalism are denied and the premise of a single Great Story rejected. Much of new historical work in humanities, especially in the name of cultural studies, is devoted to demystifying abstract terms, subjects, and categories once considered basic to culture and the criteria sustaining canons.

Berkhofer identified three definitional patterns in reformulations of the text/context relationship. In *Context 1*, contextual understanding is derived solely from a text by a reader, whether inscribed by an author, as in the intentional model of communication, or constructed by a reader, as in the reader-response model. In *Context 2*, context is derived from other texts in an inter-textuality that remains, like Context 1, rooted in a closed conceptual realm. Both Contexts 1 and 2 are textualist in their problematics and methodology. Social reality is constituted and understood through broadly conceived forms of signifying practices. *Context 3* is premised on an extratextual world that breaks out of the circularity of textualist definitions. Competing views of the proper framework for American studies rest on contradictory approaches to not only context but the field itself. There are mutually incompatible positions on such basic issues as text and context, politics and paradigms, constructionism and historical representation, authority and objectivity. Less clear, Berkhofer reflected, is whether changing vocabularies and perspectives represent a new phase in American studies or a new form rooted in a postmodern engagement of poststructuralist, post-Marxist, postfeminist, and posthistoricist theory and practice. The new historicization in American studies sought a more reflexive perspective for contextualization without problems of narrow textuality, the older historicism of background context, and the new "posts." Yet, opposing methodologies remain the medium for contests over control of meaning within, between, and beyond disciplines.

The Lesson of American Studies

Interdisciplinarity is an evolving project in American studies. It has been a source of strength. Yet, Lauter laments, in teaching the strategy is honored more in the breach than in actual practice. A department, a project, and the field at large may be interdisciplinary, but practitioners may not be or one discipline may dominate over another. Used uncritically as a mantra, the term may also hide the disciplinary premises on which individuals work (*Walden Pond* 19–20, 151). Despite antidisciplinary sentiments in the field, the ASA also holds fast to disciplinary legitimacy. The organization's collection of classic articles published in *American Quarterly* over five decades is subtitled *The Evolution of a Discipline*. Commentators situate seventeen essays within the evolution of the field, including early anticipations of current scholarship. R. Gordon Kelly's 1974 "Literature and the Historian," Linda Kerber's 1976 "The Republican Mother: Women and the Enlightenment," Janice Radway's 1981 "The Utopian Impulse in Popular Literature: Gothic Romances and 'Feminist' Protest," and Houston Baker's 1987 "Modernism and the Harlem Renaissance" were early interventions in readership and popular culture, women's history and political history, reader-response criticism, the history of the book, and a cultural studies approach to African American literature (Maddox). Any representation, of course, is always a selection. In reviewing the collection, Farrell noted that essays on theory and method outnumber applications, and few pieces appear on business and economics, politics, religion, middle-class culture, American lifestyles, teaching and pedagogy, public cultural work, or practical dimensions ("American Studies").

ASA's stance on disciplinarity raises an old question. Is the purpose of an interdisciplinary field to be a forum outside the disciplines or to become one of them? Rejecting the notion of becoming a "discipline" that surveys a particular historical and cultural territory, Lauter proposes a "framework" within which people conduct a variety of intellectual ventures. In the future, he predicts, the constitution of programs will likely differ, becoming "cultural studies," "communications and society," "media theory," or "America in the world" (*Walden Pond* 25, 65). Mark Hulsether calls American studies a decentralized "movement" or "network" of institutional spaces. Some nodes function as centers because of their historical weight or current popularity, but there is little in the way of boundaries marking inside from outside (118–19). In her 1997 presidential address to ASA, Mary Helen Washington characterized emergent scholarship as a set of layers and intersections in a new interplay of formerly "marginal" and "mainstream" topics. Categories of race, class, gender, sexuality, and language are cross-cutting, intersecting, and impacting one another, making it impossible to keep them separate (7). Describing the field in the *Encyclopedia*, Cowan suggested it would be more accurate to speak of a variety of movements embedded within a wide range of practices, positions, and groups ("American Studies" 106). Ultimately, Murray Murphey contends, the problem is not to be "interdisciplinary" in the older notion of existing between established disciplines but to synthesize relevant disciplines so that a coherent understanding of a subject results ("Discipline" 19).

There are roughly two types of scholars in ASA today: those who migrated from a traditional discipline toward a more integrated approach to problems, themes, and issues that cut across disciplinary lines; and those trained in graduate programs that emphasize interdisciplinary thinking, often through synthesis of two or more disciplines. The "migrants" come from traditional disciplines and a range of fields, from labor studies and identity fields to environmental studies and media studies (Orvell, Butler, and Mechling viii). Their practices document the trend toward critical interdisciplinarity. New approaches, though, are still disputed. Resistance to cultural theory, Paul Giles points out, cannot be dismissed as the ideological position of a single group. Resistance ranges from a folksy style of progressivism among some members of the Popular Culture Association to a radical distrust of the "linguistic Left" among nativists who continue to object that texts and intertextuality do not constitute "real human beings" (526–27). Opponents also consider the conceptual radicalism of social constructionism and poststructural critical theory an unwelcome takeover. Leo Marx indicts multiculturalism in particular as the main enemy of holistic study, distracting from macroscopic developments by celebrating individual groups (qtd. in Lipsitz, *American Studies* 71)

The collective identity of the field, Lipsitz suggests, derives from local incarnations across hundreds of dispersed sites. The uneven activities and plural practices conducted under the name of American studies cohere around a common set of questions about national culture, identity, and the congruence of place and culture in the United States. New conditions and circumstances will continue to demand new ways of knowing and studying social relations and subjects that have emerged from dramatic changes in American society since the end of the Cold War. The field at large has become a home for original, insightful, and generative research. The ASA's annual convention and publications are venues of choice for young scholars from both traditional disciplines and allied fields, including cultural studies. The institutional identity of the field provides a "protective cover" for paradigm-breaking innovators, offering support and fostering social connections among individuals who would otherwise be isolated and disconnected (*American Studies* 32–33).

Surveying outcomes, Cowan highlights enlarged content, diversified theories and methods, strengthened institutional arrangements, and greater social diversity (106). Conventional historical and literary methods are giving way to cultural anthropology, ethnography, oral history, material culture, reader-response criticism, and sociology of literature (Fox-Genovese 8). Conference papers, dissertations, and publications are also exhibiting greater interest in music, visual culture, and media studies. The ultimate success of the field, Gunn suggests, derives from the number of undergraduate programs and majors throughout the United States and the world, the kinds and quality of graduate programs, and, more significantly, the creativity, integrity, and resilience of scholarship. Judged by these criteria, American studies has been an "efficacious" interdisciplinary initiative

("Interdisciplinary Studies" 243). Limits persist, however. For all the talk about crossing boundaries of the academy and the public, the institutional base of the field remains primarily academic and, Steven Watts warns, perilously irrelevant to most Americans (89). For all the talk of transnationalism, Hulsether adds, the central interest remains North American culture and society (118–19). Shortfalls of integration also persist. Delivering the 1990 presidential address to ASA, Martha Banta observed that interdisciplinarity too often consists of topic-oriented sessions attended by segmented audiences. Disagreements about the proper orientation of ASA tend to center on which subjects are worthier, privileging verbal arts and "new" minorities over visual forms and other ethnic literatures and pitting sciences and formalist practices against arts, imaginative literature, and politicized issues (379–81). The problem of segmentation persists, even as new interdisciplinary subgroups take root in ASA.

Introducing published remarks from a panel on the purpose of American studies at ASA's 2004 annual meeting, Simon J. Bronner reflected on the historical prevalence of the keyword "interdisciplinary." As the search for a signature method, theory, and purpose unfolded over the course of the twentieth century, the driving question shifted from asking how to integrate disciplines or approaches for humanistic studies of America as a "whole" to identifying problems or issues the field distinctively addresses. Interdisciplinarity remained constant in program descriptions and as a unifying statement. Toward the end of the century, though, new goals were being formulated that engaged issues of globalization and transnationalism, representational and semiotic communication, public heritage and applied work, ethnography and fieldwork, material and visual evidence, popular and folk material, and identity and cultural diversity. Bronner exhorts moving "beyond interdisciplinarity" now to secure increased resources and priority in the academy. The panelists, in turn, defined priorities for a new "post-interdisciplinary" praxis rooted in greater public engagement with the community, the crossroads of ethnic and American studies, a wider transitional and multidisciplinary scholarship and teaching that is neither anti- nor non-disciplinary, and repositioning and recontextualizing in the global arena.

Two themes, Campbell and Kean sum up, have preoccupied American studies since its inception: the question of American identity and an impatience with disciplinary boundaries that was accompanied by openness to experimentation. In recent years, the conversation about Americanness has been marked by division and opposition. Boundary consciousness runs high, and the starting point for viewing American culture is often the margin rather than the center. The metaphors of disorientation and disturbance have replaced the older metaphors of unity and harmony, and the either/or dichotomy has been supplanted by multicultural, multiperspectival, and critical ways of seeing. Within this framework, Campbell and Kean find, interdisciplinary studies both interconnect and transgress boundaries, providing a method for engaging the heterogeneity of culture and epistemology. An interdisciplinary American studies is a meeting place of many cultures and knowledges where identity, language, and space are constantly interchanged, contested, and crossed over (1–3, 10–11).

The fervor of newness is always shadowed by anxiety about identity. Recalling her own awkward beginning in an American studies graduate program, former ASA president Patricia Limerick remembered feeling "homeless," even though American studies has been a place of refuge for those who cannot find a home in more conventional neighborhoods. One of the charms of the field is its permeable borders, but expansive borders require adaptation to disorientation. The tensions of insiders and outsiders in ASA are writ large in the changing character of American culture, then written back again into American studies (451–54). "The broad rubric of American studies," George Lipsitz concludes, "now conceals more from us than it reveals." The vitality of contemporary cultural criticism and academic inquiry is not in doubt. Yet, being inclusive, open minded, and interdisciplinary carries a responsibility to define the conditions that bring members of a field together, the historical trajectories they inherit, and the forces that connect their work as researchers and teachers to broader social formations ("Yesterday" 441).

This effort is all the more important because the individuals who study American culture are not isolated to American studies. They call themselves Americanists, literary critics, historians, art historians, musicologists, and film and media critics, as well as feminists, African Americanists, and members of other ethnic and national groups. Many also see themselves as members of the field of cultural studies or "doing cultural studies" in some way. Creating space for their work will continue to require negotiating the boundary politics of inclusion and exclusion. European projections of a "discovered" America, Curzan and Wald remind us, were laced with a utopic promise of opportunity sanctioned by divine birthright. The rise of ethnic and women's studies in the 1960s and 1970s was a direct response to the discrepancy between the promise of America and compromised opportunities (118–20). Their work, as we will see in the next chapter, challenged and extended the nature of America and the nature of America studies.

Chapter 8

DEFINING OTHER AMERICAS

Douglas Bennett calls identity fields a kind of "sacred edge" in the re-opened battle over inclusion and exclusion (144). American studies was a staging ground for interests in race and gender. However, former President Mary Ellen Washington recalls, when the Radical Caucus of the American Studies Association (ASA) formed in 1969, African Americans were relatively invisible. The loosening of disciplinary boundaries was part of a new synthesis that should have made African American and American studies natural collaborators. That did not happen (3). By the mid-1970s, members of the former Radical Caucus were being elected to the ASA Council. They were subsequently joined by members of the Women's Committee. The general community of American studies was also becoming more diverse, and new programs finding support (Horwitz, "American Studies" 115; Mechling," Axioms" 10–11). In order to develop their interests fully, though, the "others" had to create their own fields.

Identity fields represented another "America" on the edge of the traditional frame (Campbell and Kean 30). They provided homes for studying previously neglected topics, imparting new personal and sociopolitical relevance, fostering collaborative work, and establishing interdisciplinary approaches capable of refiguring existing concepts, ideas, and frameworks (Garcia and Ratcliff 119, Olguin and Schmitz 439). In forging new pathways in the study of American culture, they also created a counterpressure on both the disciplines and American studies. In the case of American studies, the pressure was compounded by changes in departments of English and of history where studies of American literature and social history were securing a place (Mechling, "Axioms" 10). This chapter compares the trajectories of two major exemplars—African American and women's studies. The objective is not a full account of each field, but an understanding of how they forged new pathways for the study of American culture. Several related questions follow. How do these fields differ from other interdisciplinary fields? What parallels appear in the early period? What were the major gains and impediments in that period? What role have the concepts of unity and disciplinarity played in their evolution? How has interdisciplinarity been defined and practiced? What is their current status in the academy? What lessons about the academic home of interdisciplinarity emerge from these and other identity fields?

Interdisciplinary Prospects

Identity fields are qualitatively different from other interdisciplinary fields because they emerged from external historical events. They were the academic arm of movements that began in the social and political arena: in challenges to the political, social, and economic order; in struggles for ethnic, racial, and gender equality; in cultural and educational projects anchored in self-definition and pride; and in efforts to create curricular parity and build transdisciplinary paradigms. "Ethnic studies" is an umbrella term for fields that focus specifically on the ways that race and racism have shaped ethnic reality in America. The most frequent approach has been ethnic-specific studies located in separate programs, centers, and departments. Ethnic studies also became a component of American studies programs and departments, though far less often (Butler 96–97, DeSoto 302). Identity fields emerged at roughly the same time. The civil rights movements of the 1950s and 1960s and student activism in the mid- to late 1960s stirred widening protests on campuses. In 1968, San Francisco State College became the first predominantly white institution to establish a black studies program, and demands from coalitions of women and other groups followed. In 1968 and 1969, Asian American studies began at San Francisco State University and the University of California at Berkeley. And in 1970, San Diego State University and Cornell University launched the first women's studies programs (Levine and Nidiffer 78; Matibag 185). In each case, the object existed before the field.

The Rise of Black Studies

The precursors of African American scholarship and teaching date to the early 1900s. Pioneering works included writings by W. E. B. DuBois, Arthur

Schomburg, Carter Woodson, J. Saunders Redding, John Hope Franklin, E. Franklin Frazier, and white scholars such as Robert Park and Melville Herskovits. Between the 1890s and World War II, numerous organizations emerged to document and analyze the experience of people of African descent, including literary and historical associations. In the 1930s, a number of historically black colleges and universities created courses on black life in America, some predominately white universities offered courses on "Negro life" or "Negro culture," and high schools in a number of states taught a course in black history. In the 1940s, Lincoln University taught a Pan-African perspective, and Fisk University began an African Studies program. The Freedom Schools in Mississippi during the summer of 1964 and 1965 may also be viewed as precursors of black studies. A systematic effort to develop an academic field, however, is linked with the growing presence of black students on campuses. Between 1964 and 1970, young blacks entered college at an unprecedented pace, increasing from 230,000 to nearly a half million by the end of that decade. One of their major roles in the Black Power movement, William Van Deberg recalls, was to help transform American higher education. To achieve that goal, they required a complete course of study that would lead to personal and group empowerment. Campus militants demanded that departments be black controlled and autonomous, that faculty be committed to the principles of the movement, and that programs be grounded in Black Power ideology (73–76). (R. L. Allen 492; Kilson 31–32; R. Harris 321; Norment xx–xxi, xxxvi, 189–90; Van Deburg 49, 51, 67–69, 73.)

The period from 1970 to 1985 was a time of growth. The first academic programs were established, a professional organization, a journal literature, and a body of knowledge with links to previous scholarship. From the outset, African American studies has been multipurpose. The academic mission focused on researching black experience, the ideological-political mission furthered cultural nationalism, and the instrumental-political mission targeted pragmatic social change in the community (R. L. Allen 493). Nathaniel Norment Jr. identified two divergent political-ideological perspectives in the early goals and direction of African American studies. One—a moderate or liberal perspective—was composed of black faculty from departments such as history, English, psychology, and sociology. Believing that black studies should be relevant to the university at large, they opposed autonomous departments and taught courses that treated African American experience within the frameworks of their own disciplines. The other—a radical nationalist perspective—was composed of black student organizations and faculty who were dissatisfied with traditional disciplinary approaches. They sought a new approach rooted in the political objectives of black cultural nationalism. Believing the field should be relevant to their communities, they linked theory and praxis in the service of alleviating social problems, and many advocated a race-specific ideology toward education (xxii–xiii).

During the late 1960s and early 1970s, the number of courses, programs, and departments increased, with estimates running as high as 1,300 institutions offering at least one course (R. L. Allen 494). The number of programs and departments is usually tallied between 130 and 250, though it reaches 500 and 700 in higher counts. Local focus varied, depending on the perceived student and community population as well as the number of faculty available to teach a course (Butler 96–97, DeSoto 302). When Little, Leonard, and Crosby examined 400 programs in 1981, 215 units were using one of three models. The "disciplinary model" offered few options that could be tailored to individual interests and addressed a limited range of concerns. The most common disciplines were history, sociology, or literature. The "interdisciplinary model" also drew on the disciplines. Courses were inclined toward special interests, and most departmental curricula focused on correcting the historical record. In contrast, the "multidisciplinary model" was based on autonomous units with faculty control. The majority of multidisciplinary curricula were structured in one of four ways: (1) social sciences and humanities courses with a double specialization, (2) social sciences or humanities courses with only a specialization in social sciences, (3) with a specialization in humanities, or (4) social science courses with specialization in a profession (699–701). Although the terms "multidisciplinary" and "interdisciplinary" are not used here in the conventional way, reversing the customary degree of integration, these categories mark the dividing line of disciplinary primacy.

When the National Council for Black Studies (NCBS) was founded in 1975, the new professional organization endorsed departmental structure. It also recommended double majors and a core curriculum that moved from an introduction to survey and advanced courses in social and behavioral sciences, history, and cultural studies to a culminating senior seminar (Alkalimat 400). NCBS favored departmental structure because it offered a more direct and permanent connection to the power structure of an institution and greater autonomy over curriculum, budget, and staffing. Programs, though, were the more typical structure. They offered greater flexibility for team teaching, multi- and interdisciplinary collaborations, and community projects. Yet, even if they offered majors and minors, programs rarely conferred degrees, there were not enough formalized programs, and they tended to rely on joint appointments, interdepartmental cooperation, and coordinators, directors, or committees lacking the authority of departmental chairs. They also exhibited the same tendencies that Little, Leonard, and Crosby found in their first and second models. Many lacked a coherent or comprehensive body of knowledge in a specific area, they rarely presented a philosophical or theoretical conceptual underpinning, and they typically did not address fundamental questions of the field (Walters, "Critical" 530–32; Hine, "Overview" 51; Adams 104; J. O. Smith 479–81; Drake 266–67; Little, Leonard, and Crosby 701–02).

Despite progress in the first era, the gains were undercut in the 1970s by a nationwide economic recession, parallel economic retrenchments in higher education, a lessened commitment to the sociopolitical objectives of black studies, and attacks on the integrity of the young field. In 1973, the percentage of black youth entering college also decreased for the first time in a decade, the movement waned as students prioritized individual career objectives, and a parallel retrenchment occurred within the larger society in social welfare, education, and housing programs (Stewart, "Field" 43, 45). In 1975, Nathan Huggins declared that the decade of ideology was over (254). At least 200 black college teachers had a primary allegiance to the field and a professional organization was in place. Yet, most programs were surviving at a bare level, and their faculty were often invisible and relegated to being outsiders in their institutions (Hayes 599–600).

From Female Studies to Women's Studies

The early years of women's studies exhibit striking parallels to the rise of black studies. Knowledge about women was historically a by-product of work in disciplinary contexts in which women and gender were traditionally minimized or ignored. Initially called "female studies," the academic field evolved from efforts to combat discrimination, to establish journals and a professional organization, and to build the first programs. In 1969, roughly sixteen courses in the United States were devoted to the subject of women and gender. By the time the National Women's Studies Association (NWSA) was founded in 1977, there were 276 programs nationwide. In scholarship, the production of knowledge followed a typical pattern in interdisciplinary fields. The first generation addressed errors, distortions, and omissions in the disciplines, accumulating data and information in order to fill gaps in existing knowledge. Elaine Showalter characterized early feminist criticism as "an empirical orphan in the theoretical storm" (180). Mere accretion of woman-centered topics and information was not enough, however. A transformation of knowledge and consciousness was needed (Coyner 349; Stimpson, "Feminist Criticism" 257; Christ 13).

In *Disciplining Feminism*, Ellen Messer-Davidow chronicles the role of three organizational fields in building resources and circulating ideas: the publishing industry, the higher education system, and the disciplines. First-generation feminists used their own venues to pry open the doors of main-stream scholarship. Their efforts counter the gatekeeping myth that femi-nist work did not appear in the mainstream because it lacked significance or quality. Disciplinary gatekeeping controlled who was allowed in and what kind of work was published. In the 1970s, commercial presses also backed away from feminist trade books that hybridized elements of aca-demic discourse and the feminist social movement. The corporatization and commodification of the publishing industry had both positive and neg-ative effects. The quest for profits and popularity of transgressive scholar-ship in some disciplines led publishers to bring out feminist books. Yet, the level of support and output in mainstream venues paled in comparison to that of feminist conferences, journals, and presses (129–34).

Verifying another pattern in the early history of interdisciplinary fields, citation data from the late 1980s indicate that most scholarship re-tained a strong disciplinary character. The deepest differences were me-thodological. Even when feminists focused on the same topic, their work often bore the stamp of a particular discipline. Dubois and colleagues' study of publications from 1966 through 1980 in history, literature, edu-cation, anthropology, and philosophy revealed uneven impact, despite a general increase in receptivity. A significant portion of scholarship also continued to appear in women's studies journals. Crucial as they are to building a literature, field-specific journals do not substitute for sustained consideration in the mainstream. Moreover, research frameworks and an-alytic concepts such as "family," "class," "race," "community," "social-ization," "social control," and "social conflict" needed to be reformu-lated to encompass new understandings of women as well as relationships between men and women.

Messer-Davidow's review of course data from 1971–72 and 1976 reveals a similar pattern in the classroom. From the beginning, feminist pedagogy prioritized an interactive learning environment, a more equal partnership of instructors and students, bridging of academic and self-knowledge, and active projects involving interaction with the community. The first generation of teachers, though, had to assemble a curriculum from courses based primarily in departments. Despite widespread talk of being "interdisciplinary," most programs consisted of a small core of introductory, senior seminar, and feminist-issues courses combined with cross-listed, department-based courses. Most introductory courses were partitioned along disciplinary lines, and cross-listed courses were oriented toward disciplines. They also tended to appear in certain departments, rather than others, especially literature, history, psychology, and sociology. The dominant pattern was a "multidisciplinary mélange" rather than an "interdisciplinary hybrid." This tendency persisted through the 1980s. Moreover, faculty were hired unevenly across departments and tended to be clustered in lower ranks and less prestigious institutions where teaching loads were heavier and part-time employment was the norm. Feminists found their status to be tenuous, their intellectual credibility impugned, and their educational agenda resisted. They aspired to be cross-disciplinary and cross-sectoral, but were contained by disciplinary and institutional limits. They sought to hybridize activist discourse and academic discourse, but the venues they used often formatted discourse along scholarly conventions (*Disciplining* 152–58).

As a body of feminist knowledge developed, Catharine Stimpson recalls, three activities supplemented, corrected, and sometimes overlapped each other: defiance of difference, celebration of difference, and recognition of differences among women. Practices ranged widely, drawing on traditions of liberal humanism while challenging established canons, crafting strategies of reading that emphasized differences within language, and using methods and theories derived from structuralism and poststructuralism, neo-Marxist theory of ideology, postcolonial experience and identity, and cultural studies. The subsequent turn into gender studies encompassed feminist interests along with lesbian and gay studies and studies of masculinity and sexuality ("Feminist Criticism" 259–67; "Women's Studies" 1978, 14–26). Like black studies, women's studies was multipurpose. Feminist practices engaged the boundaries of knowing and doing; subjective and objectified consciousness; gender, race, class, and culture; academic and other forms of knowledge; and disciplinary, professional, and interdisciplinary affiliations. In both fields, interdisciplinarity also had more than one meaning. The term connoted creating a broader and more complete approach to understanding race and gender, developing alternative curricula, borrowing disciplinary methodologies, breaking down disciplinary boundaries, providing community service, performing political work, and forging a body of knowledge based on a self-defined epistemology.

Continuing Growth and Limits

In the post-1970s, mainstream professional associations began to establish sections devoted to topics of race and gender. The movement to foster awareness of cultural diversity in the United States also widened (Butler 98). Nonetheless, African American and women's studies continued to strengthen their own fields.

Expanding African American Studies

Norment calls the period from 1985 to 2000 a time of institutionalization. In 1984, the NCBS estimated that approximately 250 schools were offering black studies programs. A resurgence of energy and productivity promised to carry the field from ad hoc experimentation to permanence. However, a lot of work remained. Innovations from the 1960s and 1970s needed to be protected and the field consolidated into a strong community. The role of the NCBS must be secured, the professional journal literature codified in the classroom, and national conferences unified (McWorter and Bailey 614–16). A stable cadre of faculty must also be established. The earliest units, Carlos Brossard recalls, tended to draw on any African American faculty, even individuals lacking pertinent intellectual interests or preparation. Young graduate students and new PhDs who taught in the first departments had to undergo a process of self-resocialization to the emerging field and to interdisciplinary work. White faculty might be involved, but, especially early on, black faculty were usually preferred (66).

Black studies gained an academic foothold as undergraduate teaching, not as research training. Akin to women's studies, developing new modes of teaching and learning was an important part of this mission, with emphasis on active learning, self-reflection, integration of knowledge and experience, the relationship of theory and praxis, and community studies (Brossard 66). By 1990, the majority of autonomous departments were awarding BA degrees. Some of the remaining units had majors and most offered minors, but the more common format was a concentration. Few units offered masters, and graduates who went on to PhDs did so in traditional disciplines. Typical of interdisciplinary fields, local programs differed in size and prestige, relation to host institution, balance of breadth versus specialization, and in the case of black studies emphasis on humanities or social sciences and orientation towards disciplines or professional programs (Hine "Overview").

Like women's studies, black studies was also confronted by its marginalization of women of color. From the beginning, feminists aimed to formulate multiple identities (Messer-Davidow, *Disciplining* 199). Yet, the founding generation of academic feminists was criticized for universalizing the nature of women's experience. African American, Chicana, Native American, and lesbian scholars undertook projects that produced a more complex understanding of differences within particular cultural groups as well as *mestiza* consciousness and transnational identities. In the 1970s and 1980s, black women's studies emerged, and black women's history and feminist literary criticism became key sites in bringing intersecting issues of race, gender, class, and sexual orientation to the forefront (Addelson and Potter 260; DuBois et al. 63). New work has encompassed theory, recovery of a black female literary tradition and popular culture, studies of the role of black women in slavery as well as the economic and political system, the church, the family, and the community. Obstacles remain, though, including lack of a critical mass of scholars, gatekeeping in the publishing industry, and the small number of courses on Africana women in their own right (Aldridge 160, 162; see also Collins).

The current status of African American studies reflects both cumulative gains and persistent limits. In 1997, NCBS reported a total of 380 programs. At least 140 were offering degrees, approximately 22 master's degrees, and 4 doctorates, with PhD programs in the works and other doctoral institutions offering concentrations in Africana studies or the African diaspora. Few historically black colleges and universities (HBCUs) offer degrees in black studies, though most of the HBCUs incorporate an African American focus into the disciplines, imbuing the curriculum with a black perspective (Moskowitz 82–83). In 2003, the NCBS website listed 250 institutional members, including school districts and community organizations, and about 2,000 individuals (http://www.nationalcouncilforblackstudies.com).

When James Stewart took stock in 1992, he judged the majority of scholarship to still be contributionist in nature. Most studies, he reported, embodied a "rationale by negation," disputing traditional claims that ancient Egyptian civilization had little connection to sub-Saharan Africa. Stewart called for a more continuous intellectual history and balancing Kemetic studies with investigations of other classical African civilizations and societies as well as communities in the Western Hemisphere ("Higher Ground" 356). In another assessment of the field, Floyd Hayes urged broadening the scope to include policy studies and advocacy, critical social theory, critical cultural studies, women's studies, social and political ethics, futures research, organizational development, and leadership preparation. He also anticipated greater "transdisciplinary" and global interests as the field responds to the postindustrial managerial society and global political economy (604). More recently, Norment judged the field to be at a crossroads. Scholars today, Norment reflected, are less concerned about justifying its place in the academy. They are working to transform the lives of everyone with Afrocentric and African-centered scholarship. Yet, he exhorts them to continue expanding the theories, methodologies, and epistemologies of African American studies while evaluating its political, intellectual, social, and cultural roles (xxxviii).

Expanding Women's Studies

Once again, women's studies exhibits striking parallels. By 1992, there were over 30,000 women's studies courses at the undergraduate level. Joan Korenman's current links to programs, departments, and centers worldwide number 700, with additional programs on the NWSA website and a count of 734 U.S. programs in 2002 (Coyner 349; Stimpson, "Feminist Criticism" 257; Christ 13; http://www.nwsa.org). The difference between 1970 and 1995 is striking. In 1970, Messer-Davidow recalls, women's studies was barely institutionalized. Roughly a hundred courses were being taught by marginal faculty, a half-dozen emerging programs existed, publications were often mimeographed, and the knowledge base consisted of little more than brief accounts of women's lives and declamations against patriarchy. By 1995, the field had an infrastructure of roughly 630 programs, hundreds of curriculum projects, more than eight campus-based research centers, national associations of feminist scholars, feminist committees and divisions in every disciplinary association, plus thousands of academic-feminist presses, book series, journals, and newsletters. The knowledge base consisted of an extensive body of data, scholarship, and theory across the full range of disciplinary and professional fields, social groups, and societies. Feminist techniques such as turn-taking, small-group discussion, and integration of everyday experience were being widely used in colleges, high schools and grade schools. Some disciplines had also been refigured and feminist subfields established in others (*Disciplining* 85).

Nonetheless, the picture remains mixed. When NWSA examined the state of the major in the late 1980s, it found more students taking courses than majoring in the field, and double majors were the norm ("Women's Studies" 214). When Messer-Davidow examined thirty programs in 1992, she also found a persistent multidisciplinary mélange. On average women's studies programs had six program-based courses and fifty cross-listed courses oriented to disciplinary subjects and methods. Most cross-listed courses appeared in disciplines that had welcomed, or at least tolerated, feminist work since 1980: namely, American studies, classics, comparative literature, composition, education, history, sociology, political science, anthropology, psychology, religion, theater, rhetoric, social work, speech, English, and German and Romance languages (*Disciplining* 158–62).

In 1997, Carol Christ reported parallel findings in scholarship. Women's studies had moved more quickly to the center of disciplines where paradigms were under discussion. The controversy over Theory in literary studies, anthropology, and to a lesser extent history legitimized the challenges posed by women's studies. Feminist interests also found a more secure home in disciplines that are "thickly descriptive," such as history, literature, and anthropology. It had easier entree into text-based disciplines, and it was more readily established in psychology and anthropology. In history, its presence and early development went hand in hand with increasing attention to social history. In philosophy, the dominance of analytic philosophy worked against a concern with gender or social relations (18, 21–22).

Even so, Messer-Davidow also found a surprising number of courses in fields that were traditionally less hospitable. Courses cross-listed with business management, criminal justice, labor studies, natural resource management, and urban planning were as numerous as cross-listings with art history, philosophy, and economics. At institutions with thriving ethnic and area studies programs, interdisciplinary courses were cross-listed with African American, Asian American, Chicano, Native American, Judaic, Near Eastern, and South Asian studies. Programs offering cross-disciplinary introductions were organized as grids with identity categories crosshatching disciplinary and/or feminist issues. Yet, introductory and advanced courses in women's studies programs exhibited a tilt toward disciplinarity. Some advanced courses—such as women's biology and feminist philosophy—facilitated feminist study in disciplines that were traditionally more resistant. Others—such as feminist literary criticism and women's history—repeated offerings available in mainstream departments. Feminist theory courses were the most immune to disciplinary tilting, and every program taught social change as a subject embedded within topics courses (*Disciplining* 159–62).

Messer-Davidow's account of interventions into the American Sociological Association and the Modern Language Association illustrates how existing infrastructures can be used to change the dominant order of knowledge. Second-wave feminists called conventional practices and precepts into question, used new methods in old paradigms, built new critical positions, formed alliances that connected dispersed groups, and situated their work inside those disciplinary organizations. Taking stock in 2002, Messer-Davidow cited significant gains in proliferating objects, knowledges, specialisms, and hybrid relations with other fields. Feminist studies reconstructed traditionally fashioned categories of "women" and "men," denaturalized "sex" and "sexuality," modeled "sex-gender systems," multiplied "identities" and "oppressions," and problematized all such categories. The transformation beckoned in theory did not pan out in practice, although not for the reasons feminists anticipated. They understood the power of academic institutions to suppress their interests, but not the power exercised by letting them go forward. The institutional–disciplinary order overdetermined feminist studies from the start. Feminist studies produced an abundance of differences, but the gap between scholarly knowledge and social activism is now entrenched in institutional structures that are largely separated from national political struggle (*Disciplining* 101–11,165–66).

Unity and Inter/Disciplinarity

Despite the pejorative taint that unity, holism, and synthesis have among proponents of critical interdisciplinarity, these concepts have a strong resonance in identity fields. Unifying disparate projects, unifying African Americans and black people across the African diaspora, unifying women, building communal solidarity, synthesizing multiple disciplinary perspectives, arriving at a holistic understanding of cultural experience, and creating common knowledge have played a central role. Identity fields also have a conflicted relationship with poststructuralism and postmodernism. Their members rejected universal knowledge, a totalizing view of history, generalizations about culture and language, and theories that minimize or ignore marginal points of view and subjects. They drew on related methods. Yet, they reformulated them for their own purposes (Christian 185), and they reformulated the conventional dichotomy of disciplinarity and interdisciplinarity.

"The Unity and Order of Blackness"

The early production of scholarship in black studies was especially strong in history, and social sciences provided the major models for conceptualizing the field. With the exception of literature, humanities courses were typically in performing arts rather than their scholarly counterparts (Adams 115, Huggins 260). In 1973, Martin Kilson argued that black studies must be "clothed in the tested scholarly and technical garment of an established discipline." He recommended tracking students through an established academic or technical discipline with a double major or concentration in the field. An economics major, for example, would take basic courses for a major along with courses that apply economic analysis to problems related to black studies, such as welfare economics, labor economics, and urban investment politics. Without the curricular control of an established discipline, Kilson maintained, interdisciplinary subjects such as black studies, African studies, American studies, Asian studies, and Middle Eastern studies could not become scholarly and intellectually viable fields. Their students would be "jack-of-all-disciplines" and "master" of none," at best "dilettantes" and at worst "charlatans" emanating from "catch-as-catch can" curricula (34–36). Others disagreed. Philip T. K. Daniel branded the argument that black studies cannot exist without the covariant presence of other disciplines "the worst kind of conjectural puerilism." They have something to offer, but, Daniel admonished, theory must be based on African-specific concepts (373). Because black studies is disciplined by the centrality of racism in American life, Ronald Walters contended, the proper foundation is the "unity and order of Blackness" (144).

From the beginning, notions of disciplinarity and interdisciplinarity have been intertwined in African American studies. Little, Leonard and Crosby advocated an "interdisciplinary discipline model" (691), and Daudi Ajani ya Azibo called black studies both "an interdisciplinary field and a singular discipline" (427). Stewart distinguished two rationales for the field. "Weak multi/interdisciplinary rationales" take the existing disciplinary structure as a given, with black/Africana studies providing "added value" by developing knowledge that represents disciplinary syntheses. Scant attention is paid, though, to underlying theoretical constructs. The "strong multidisciplinary rationale" grounds analysis in philosophy of science and subject areas, not disciplines ("Reaching" 352–53). Karenga's notion of an "interdisciplinary discipline" illustrates the strong rationale. He advocated seven interconnected and interdependent core subject areas as the basis for a curriculum: black history, black religion, black social organization, black politics, black economics, black creative production (art, music, and literature), and black psychology. Outside the field, they are taught as separate disciplines. Inside, they are transformed into subject areas that contribute to a holistic picture and approach to black experience with a dual thrust of scholarship and praxis ("Problematic 283, *Introduction*).

Karla Spurlock calls interdisciplinarity the one connecting link across differing structures, ideologies, course content, and degrees of community involvement. In specifying elements of a "truly interdisciplinary" approach, Spurlock included organizing groups into common efforts centered on common problems, engaging in continuous intercommunication, maximizing the disciplinary mix in teaching, designing a coordinated curriculum with field-specific seminars that draw on a common store of knowledge, team teaching on a wide scale, and supporting interdisciplinary journals and conferences that help to consolidate an identity and concretize a common language. The end point of the interdisciplinary continuum would be unified "trans or unidiscipinarity" in which disciplines are blended into a new discipline. Without a concerted effort to achieve interdisciplinarity, Spurlock cautioned, the field might slip back into a more multidisciplinary coexistence. Interdisciplinarity, she added, provides not only multidisciplinary breadth and a holistic vision, it stimulates creative thinking. Simply adding the word "black" to course titles or creating a curriculum of related courses from different disciplines is not enough. Creative synthesis emerges when ideas from different and potentially conflicting disciplinary methods "bang against one another." The student/scholar is put in a "virtual intellectual crossfire" (648–50).

Norment identified five major philosophical frameworks for an interdisciplinary field: traditionalist/inclusivist, self determination/nationalist, Marxist-Leninist, black feminist thought, and Afrocentricity (280). The epistemology of Afrocentricity is rooted in an organic cultural philosophy that is African-based. All elements of life are interconnected, uniting the material and the spiritual, the practical and the conceptual. Afrocentricity, though, does not ignore the diversity of experience across the diaspora. It is a metadisciplinary synthesizing framework for a variety of knowledges and projects that acknowledges the simultaneity of commonality and difference (Azibo 426). In specifying "truly interdisciplinary" elements, Spurlock identified unifying core concepts as the centrifugal force in the "interdisciplinary orbit." To illustrate, she cited James Banks's proposal that history be made truly interdisciplinary by funneling analytical concepts from separate disciplines into a historical framework. Banks identified seven concepts in social sciences: conflict (history), culture (anthropology), racism (sociology), capitalism (business), power (political science), self-concept (psychology), and region (geography). The partial disciplinary perspectives would be marshaled to focus on a particular social issue such as poverty (676–80).

The problematic of paradigm, Maulana Karenga observed, centers on the question of whether black studies would be "creature rupture" or "routine competence" ("Problematic" 292). Cornel West called for a "dedisciplinary" form of teaching that requires disciplinary critique, new institutional structures and programs, and new modes of teaching and learning. Perry Hall concurred, arguing that a "truly interdisciplinary" body of knowledge or field does not simply cross boundaries—it obliterates them. Hall demonstrated what a "truly interdisciplinary" approach would mean in the classroom with the example of the Harlem Renaissance. Teaching would not be grounded in literature but would present the Harlem Renaissance as one of several forms of cultural reflection of the urban transformation of black experience in the early twentieth century, accompanied by insights into historical and social context as well as sociodemographic and macroeconomic changes. A number of systematic and thematic principles foster a "wholly interactive and mutually transforming" understanding. The systematic principle of Transformation, for example, is the perpetual rearrangement of material and social structures that shape the ways people live, think, work, and relate. It is widely applicable and involves the global forces, factors, or conditions in which black communities emerge, develop, and transform. Interdisciplinary analysis is built around the themes of West European expansion, technologization, colonization, industrialization, and anticolonial resistance and struggle. Historical periodism is another principle. Systematic and thematic principles underscore the increased salience of double-consciousness in African American experience and identity, engaging older dichotomies such as form/essence, folk-popular/high-elite traditions, and class versus cultural frames.

When the National Council for Black Studies filed a report to the American Association for Higher Education (AAHE) in 2000, as part of AAHE's national project on rewarding faculty, NCBS representatives likened Africana studies to an Africana village. A broad ideological umbrella provides a cover for a wide variety of activities and structures. They called the current developmental trajectory of the field "postdisciplinary." It is an evolving intellectual enterprise that recognizes "indigenous cultural knowledge" outside traditional boundaries of humanistic and scientific discourse, and in visual and oral accounts. At the same time, it is a "discipline" in which the character of published research has changed as the training backgrounds of faculty have changed. The first generation was trained solely in traditional disciplines. As graduate programs produce new faculty trained in the field, alternative methodologies are being introduced in classrooms and journals. The forces of gatekeeping, though, continue in publication venues. NCBS reaffirms the importance of departmental status for control over tenure and promotion decisions and creating synergies between Africana studies and traditional disciplines (Diamond and Adam).

The "Interdisciplinary Woman"

Gloria Bowles speculated that one day the Renaissance man might be replaced by "the interdisciplinary woman" (qtd. in M. Boxer 687). In the inaugural issue of *Signs,* the editors foresaw several patterns of work, ranging from one person skilled in several disciplines and focused on one subject to several people in a discipline focused collaboratively on a subject to a group of disciplinarians publishing randomly in the same journal. Three years later, Stimpson acknowledged that the interdisciplinary promise was proving more difficult than envisioned. Resistance to moving outside of one's expertise was as strong in women's studies as in other fields. Stimpson called for translators able to "interpret the languages of one discipline to persons in another (qtd. in M. Boxer 685–87).

Women's studies illustrates one of the defining characteristics of critical interdisciplinarity. Conditions of marginality are also conditions of strength. The epistemological power of the field depends on its location in spaces where conventional boundaries are blurred ("Women's Studies" 210–11). Spatial metaphors depicted the field as the "outside within" a "fortress" or "citadel" from which women were "barred" entry. Annette Kolodny described literary criticism as a "minefield." Feminist critics had the choice of being "camped" on the edge or working to defuse the minefield, lest they be reduced to a "tributary" in the "backwater" or confined to a "ghetto."

Women's studies also illustrates the "both-and" strategy of interdisciplinary fields. Feminists work simultaneously in disciplines and in opposition to them, wielding their forms of power and authority for feminist purposes. In order to change the disciplines, one program coordinator remarked, women's studies had to be "of them, in them, and about them" (qtd. in Boxer 671, 693). Like African American studies, women's studies is both disciplinary and interdisciplinary (Wiegman, "Introduction" 3). The field offers an intellectual community and an institutional site for feminists who do most of their work in disciplines, legitimating gender as a category of analysis (Addelson and Potter 271). Within their disciplinary locations, they disperse centripetally into specializations. Within the shared space of women's studies, they move centrifugally to "cross-disciplinary" research and teaching (Hartman and Messer-Davidow 5). Most scholars Aisenberg and Harrington interviewed preferred "cross-disciplinary" to discipline-bound inquiry and were more likely to study unformulated subjects at the edges of disciplines than sharply defined subjects at the centers (qtd. in Hartman 18, 30). Sandra Coyner also found that most identify with another community—as a historian, literary critic, psychologist, or social worker. Naming tends to designate a position within a program—as women's studies faculty, student, or director—more than the kind of work performed (349–51).

Susan Stanford Friedman's description of working in two locations illustrates the lived experience of the both/and strategy. Her disciplinary home base is literary studies. It provides an intellectual anchoring and a substantive platform of knowledge and literature, narrative and figuration, representation, and a methodological base for strategies of reading texts in varied cultural contexts. Her political home base is feminism. It provides an approach to asking questions about gender, power relations, other systems of stratification, and an ethical commitment to social justice and change. Friedman travels from these two homes to other (inter)disciplinary homes, bringing back what she learned and what is most useful to her projects. Travel stimulates new ways of thinking, exposing the constructedness of what is taken for granted, dislodging unquestioned assumptions, and producing new insights, questions, and solutions to intellectual impasses at home. Like spatial travel abroad, however, the dangers of epistemological and cross-disciplinary travel are real. Misunderstanding, appropriating, and misusing or decontextualizing the "other" may result (4–5).

Diane Elam defines the space of women's studies as both a "discipline of difference" and an "interdisciplinary discipline." Reconstituting disciplinarity as cross-disciplinarity does not elevate feminism to a theoretical metalanguage or a totalizing master narrative. Borders are crossed through continuous inter- and intradisciplinary crossfertilization. Elam endorses departmental location, countering the objection that it deprives women's studies of radical politics. Departmental status harnesses funds and tenure lines for that purpose. It also draws strength from multiple disciplines without being reduced to any of them. The interdisciplinary project is defined and advanced in the space of women's studies ("Ms. en Abyme" 294–98, "Taking Account"). Mindful of the small number of full-time appointments in the field, Robyn Warhol advocates a different strategy. By paying greater attention to the changing character of disciplines, interdisciplinary teaching and scholarship can be expanded at more sites and faculty and administrators at those locations urged to ensure that new hires and tenure lines be inclusive of women's studies. Warhol's strategy of infiltration is a hedge against retrenchment and piecemeal allocations, although the dual professional life of joint appointments has a downside. A double appointment can lead to a double workload and accompanying tensions about which home is primary.

Like American studies and black studies, women's studies is also moving in new transnational and transdisciplinary directions. Caren Kaplan and Inderpal Grewal link transnational feminist practices to the changing nature of migration and global flows of media and capital. Recent scholarship differs from older modes of comparative study. It is reworking the nationalism and regionalist nature of area studies, the exceptionalism of American studies, the cultural nationalism of ethnic studies, and the domestic focus of mainstream women's studies (70, 75–76). Dölling and

Hark associate transdisciplinarity in women's studies with critical evaluation of terms, concepts, and methods that transgress disciplinary boundaries. Greater reflexivity is crucial to avoiding loss of the critical potential (1195). Women's studies also reminds us that even in a single field, all versions of interdisciplinarity may be present and in conflict. Stimpson described the field as a "portfolio of maps," not a single map ("Feminist" 251). Some see the field as filling a lacuna, others as a critique of disciplinarity. Some want women's studies to achieve the status of a discipline, with interdisciplinarity being an intermediate step. Others challenge the prevailing orientation of programs in universities. Some work to reorient disciplines to deal with issues the field raises. Others use the field as an avenue for raising questions about the very purpose and orientation of the academic and research enterprise (after Vickers; Salter and Hearn).

Like America studies, identity fields are rife with complaints about the preponderance of multidisciplinary approaches. Simply claiming that fields are "inherently" interdisciplinary is not enough. Robyn Wiegman urges greater attention to "the daily difficulty of interdisciplinary teaching and research" ("Introduction 1), and Sneja Gunew calls for learning more about "integrated interdisciplinarity" (49–51). Cindi Katz cites reading, studying, and attending conference presentations that move across disciplines as the "integrative interdisciplinary leaven." The difficulty of interdisciplinary work is compounded, however, by the bulk of parts that must be brought to the task, including both constitutive disciplines and interdisciplinary fields (11–12). Time constraints in courses, Kathleen Blee notes, rarely permit more than quick excursions or detours into intellectual genealogies. This limitation underscores the importance of theory courses that establish historical and theoretical understanding of the field, exemplary models of interdisciplinary work, and a secure location for thinking about the commonalities and differences among disciplinary approaches and jargons (180–81).

The importance of theory courses was underscored when Nancy McCampbell Grace examined exemplary syllabi from the women's studies literature and a NWSA Report to the Profession in 1991. In conducting her evaluation of the nature, strengths, and problems associated with the seven categories of courses she identified, Grace used "The Guide to Interdisciplinary Syllabus Preparation" adopted by the Association for Integrative Studies. The guide defines interdisciplinary study as a problem-focused process using two or more disciplinary perspectives, exploring the methods and assumptions of those disciplines, and integrating separate perspectives in a self-conscious manner. The seven categories of Grace's typology depict the differing balance of disciplinarity, interdisciplinarity, and transdisciplinarity.

Type 1: Single Discipline with Feminist Perspective constituted the majority of courses in women's studies programs, which were typically multidisciplinary in structure and cross-listed existing disciplinary courses. *Type 2: Multiple Disciplines with Feminist Perspectives* appeared in some introductory courses and many women and science courses. Instructors integrated feminist theory and subordinate perspectives through serial presentation of disciplines, but disciplines remained separate and their methods were not necessarily tested against feminist theory. *Type 3: Interdisciplinary* explored designated subtopics such as identity and diversity. Students gained critical interdisciplinary skills by comparing forms of evidence and evaluating competing explanations. *Type 4: Mid-Evolutionary Interdisciplinary* moved from serial presentation of disciplinary perspectives to elucidation of women's studies concepts and issues. Disciplines were blurred, but an explicit focus on integration and synthesis did not necessarily occur. *Type 5: Transdisciplinarity/New Disciplines* began outside existing disciplines with a topical focus, introducing students to recognized women's studies concepts such as gender and patriarchy, issues such as work and sexual orientation, and methods such as oral histories and connecting the personal and the political/academic. The foundational "whole" is feminist theory, but the result can be an encyclopedic entity lacking depth and clear connections. *Type 6: Feminist Interdisciplinarity* involved two or more "feminized disciplines" that are influenced by feminist theory. It was most likely to occur in upper-level theory or senior seminar/capstone courses, with proactive attention to identifying and analyzing underyling assumptions and methods. *Type 7: Feminist Transdisciplinary/Disciplinary* highlights both the complexity of feminist theory and its disciplinary character. Feminism provides a transdisciplinary umbrella for investigation of a particular feminist issue positioned apart from conventional disciplines. Such courses highlight various approaches to feminism within a new body of knowledge.

When the National Women's Studies Association filed its counterpart report in AAHE's rewarding faculty project, NWSA representatives called contemporary women's studies a "developing discipline." They highlighted differences along vectors of institutional type, local teaching cultures, the structure and degree offerings of individual programs and departments, their interface with the rest of the curriculum, the degree of control over key decisions and the curriculum, affiliations with other identity fields, and the existence of a center. Current initiatives point in four major directions: globalizing women's studies, diversifying core faculty and curriculum offerings, responding to growth in graduate education, and expanding the interdisciplinarity of research. Integration is being promoted by a critical cross-cultural interdisciplinarity that is forging *mestiza* methodology standpoints and methodologies, curriculum transformation, and program development that also advances integrative goals (Diamond and Adams).

A Question of Home

Identity fields are caught in an institutional contradiction. If the topics associated with them are only allowed in departments of those names, Stanley Bailis warns, each will have to become a virtual university and dispute teaching its subject matter in other departments. Yet, without some claim over topic domains, they may disappear as conventional departments hire their faculty and teach their courses. "Multiculturality" opened up an enormous domain conceptually, but it has a limited face. As universities hired scholars to develop emergent fields, they tended to take one of two paths—dispersing among established discipline-based departments or concentrating in new programs, departments, and schools. Both paths were contested, and people using one have blocked traffic on the other. Multiculturality expanded the meaning of culture, the study of American materials, and the scope of American Studies. Yet, it also intensified the problem of intellectual coherence ("Holism," "Babel" 95).

A new universal paradigm is not the answer. Giles Gunn likens feminist criticism to African American criticism, postcolonial criticism, and cultural critique. Feminist criticism is a composite methodological site where other interdisciplinary modes cross and recross, including reader-response criticism, semiotic analysis, psychoanalytic inquiry, cultural anthropology, other ethnic studies, and gender studies. Ultimately, Gunn suggests, interdisciplinary studies may not be a specific or united field so much as a predisposition to view all fields as potentially vulnerable to recreation in the partial image of others. Akin to Roland Barthes's notion of "transversals," their ongoing reconfiguration works to produce or recover meaning that previously configured relations tended to blur, camouflage, or efface ("Interdisciplinary Studies" 243; *Thinking* 198).

American studies has been envisioned as the place where alliances between fields might form, generating new intellectual linkages and support in a tight academic market. In her 1997 presidential address to the American Studies Association, Washington described ASA as a "principal gathering place" where ethnic studies constituencies meet annually in their own border-crossing dialogues (20). Yet, Johnella Butler finds, the cultural pluralism espoused by the multicultural movement reflects a continuing oppositional duality that—on the one hand—celebrates difference and—on the other—engages power relations and differences in a vision of a shared, cooperative, and relational pluralism. The growing presence in ASA of scholars of color and scholars interested in ethnic studies underscores the importance of exploring how American studies and ethnic studies can coexist in mutually supportive ways (97–98). Vicki Ruiz called ASA the home of choice for most Chicano/a scholars. Yet, there are limits. Steve Sumida called ASA a "dormitory" more than a "home" (qtd. in Washington 6). Native American studies is a particularly compelling case because it is usually neglected and, in its greater marginality, underscores the problematics of inclusion and exclusion.

A Home for the Native Other?

A panel on American Indian studies at the 2002 ASA meeting and subsequent special section of *American Quarterly* addressed the question of home. Philip Deloria recalled Washington asking, as she prepared for her 1997 presidential address to ASA, why so few Indian American scholars found ASA to be the same type of intellectual home as scholars of other fields. Demography is one answer. The 2000 census listed American Indian and Alaska Native populations as less than 1% of the total U.S. population. As a result, the pool of academic intellectuals is smaller. Indian people are also qualitatively different from other groups. Because they have ongoing treaty relationships with the federal government, they must understand and negotiate forms of tribal governance that hybridize local knowledge with external American constitutional models. Given this reality, a significant number of prospective Native academic intellectuals choose a law degree or master's in public policy over a six-year PhD program. Hence, "'Interdisciplinary' might mean political science, law, education, health, and language as much as it does history, literature, film, performance studies, and cultural theory." The core concepts of "America" and "culture" are also shaped by social and intellectual orders that were not of their making. Even the hybrid construction of American (sub)cultures may point Native scholars away from the central ideas and theoretical interests of American studies. The social and cultural content of Indian nations rests on traditional governance and other intellectual, cultural, political, and legal sovereignty. Could ASA be both an intellectual home and a place of border-crossing dialogues? "Home," Deloria suggested, is a shifty metaphor. One version might be a "house," with tight-knit residents asking similar questions about similar subjects with similar goals and some shared sense of vocabulary and method. Another vision is a "community" in which the kind of border-crossing dialogue Washington envisioned might take place. Both are needed, Deloria concluded, and American studies must reach out to Native scholars from multiple positions without proffering a new form of intellectual imperialism or assimilation.

Taking stock, Robert Warrior reported that despite the accomplishments of stand-alone departments, some graduate degree programs, many undergraduate programs, and significant research and writing, Native American studies does not have its own academic association, annual meeting, or a single "must read" journal. Scholars are scattered across ASA, the Western History Association, the American Anthropological Association, the Modern Language Association, and the American Society for Ethnohistory. Jean O'Brien agreed, adding that, with the exception of the American Anthropological Association, more Native scholars go to ASA meetings, although they also attend other smaller forums. Their multiple presence makes the field more visible. Yet, Warrior commented, it is hard to keep track of currents in the field, and Native scholars must navigate the identity politics of those organizations. ASA offered refuge from "intellectual homelessness," but attention to Native topics has been irregular. Like other identity fields, Native American studies needs a regular space to define and develop its interests. O'Brien deemed American studies more than a mere refuge, but observed that ASA is only an "occasional visit" for many and a "completely foreign country" for most Indian scholars. American studies came to be a logical home because of its lenses of multiculturalism, interdisciplinarity, and postnationalism. Yet, underlying assumptions about "nation" and sovereignty as a category of analysis must be constantly tested. Warrior stressed the importance of a "provocative presence" in ASA, challenging both old and new orthodoxies. Convergences already exist in method, subject matter, and interdisciplinary graduate training. Yet, lack of critical mass means that Native studies are still marginal. In actual practice, O'Brien concluded, ASA is more of a "shelter" or "umbrella" for ethnic studies than a "truly transformative space" and many scholars find shelter elsewhere.

Commenting on the 2002 forum, Washington underscored the limitations and possibilities inherent in her call for change. Listening to the others speak, she was struck initially by the thought that intellectual homelessness is not so much a problem as a sign of progressive and radical politics. Recalling Sumida's remark about still feeling like an outsider in the "dormitory" of ASA, she questioned the supposition that ethnic studies has found a ready place. Washington crafted her presidential speech in the mode of a conciliator envisioning change and collaboration. While admitting she may have engaged in naïve celebration of the prospects, Washington closed her commentary on the forum by listing concrete strategies for going beyond token inclusion. They include nominating Native American scholars to influential committees, using the ASA newsletter to call attention to Native American issues, petitioning for annual conference sites near centers of American Indian studies, increasing the number of proposals at conferences with cultural themes, organizing joint meetings of ASA and institutions where Native scholars are most involved, and critiquing the theoretical paradigms that do not serve Native scholarship. In his own presidential address to ASA that year, Sumida acknowledged that ethnic studies has not assumed a central role in American studies, but new initiatives at the committee level are working toward making it more centrally interactive. He likened the effort to the elevation to standing committee status of the once ad hoc MLA Commission on the Status of Women in the Professions and the Commission on the Literature and Languages of America (347–48).

Jeffrey Peck's reflection on German studies contributes another parallel insight into the question of home. Academic and scholarly territories are dominated by a repertoire of spatial metaphors of boundaries, borders, domains, regions, fields of demarcated interests, territories, the cultures that inhabit those territories, intellectual surfaces, and academic contours. The nations and the disciplines that aim describe, explain, analyze, interpret, and legitimate the entity of Germany—and by extension American regions and cultural groups—are constituted by categories, taxonomies, and statements that are governed in turn by rules of organization and formation that divide geographical and intellectual territories. Peck imagines the topography of German studies as an alternative interdisciplinary space for reflection on itself and its critical and academic practices. The various discourses about Germany—and, by extension, "America"—are situated at the in-between space where the clash of multiple subjectivities can foreground difference. This middle-of-the-road position does not produce a harmonious resolution or transcendence. It calls for a more hermeneutic vision that acknowledges the oppositional potential in the friction between borders.

Boundaries are not dissolved, Peck adds. They are continually crossed, reconfiguring disciplinary and academic territories so that different forms of knowledge continue to emerge and engage. Whether national or regional, disciplinary or interdisciplinary, cultures are not bounded objects that are complete and finished. The idea of a knowledge boundary encompasses both stasis and flux, fixing and permeating, identity and relation, formation and navigation, structure and ecology. The word "ecology," Michael Winter reminds us, derives from the Greek word *oikeos,* meaning household or settlement. The verbs associated with *oikeos* suggest inhabiting, settling, governing, controlling, managing, and other activities in a complex interweaving of fields of social action. Spatial dynamics of place and organic dynamics of production are not mutually exclusive, however. They operate simultaneously. Spatial metaphors highlight formation and maintenance. Organic metaphors—crossing, interdependence, and interrelation—highlight connection. Spatial and organic models may even be combined, Winter suggests, to form a third type, highlighting interactions between social groups and their environments. Organism and environment imply one another mutually. Both are territorial, competitive, and expansionist. The underlying idea is to make and reinforce jurisdictional claims, analogous to the territorial claims that humans and animals make in ecological niches. At the same time, organisms, environment, and knowledge communities exploit resources to produce new life-forms and settlements. Territories blur and shift, intersecting, merging, fusing, and producing new hybrid forms (343–44).

Given that they have been part of the academic system for only three and a half decades, identity fields have accomplished a lot. Yet, they face new threats in the current economic retrenchment of higher education. Departments may be reduced to programs, programs trimmed to crossdepartmental committees, and all interdisciplinary studies lumped together.

Speaking in 2002, NCBS President James Stewart admonished professors to continue defending African American studies. In many institutions it is still tenuous, despite programs and departments at roughly 200 colleges and universities. Black studies has gained academic acceptance, Christopher Lucas affirmed. Yet, it is still charged with being both too narrow, with its focus on one group, and too broad, with its wise compass of disciplines. They will always be on the periphery, but, Lucas exhorted, black studies programs will survive because of dedicated faculty ("Black Studies").

Similar caveats are voiced in women's studies. The history of identity fields, Gunew concludes, is marked by underfunding, marginalization, and lacking the time and resources to articulate interdisciplinarity fully in intellectual and pedagogical terms (50–51). Robyn Wiegman concurs, adding that identity-based knowledges which used interdisciplinarity as one of their primary explanatory arguments are still working to achieve equal footing with disciplinary projects. Interdisciplinarity continues to exist more at the level of the student, and disciplines dominate in upper–division and graduate training, leaving fields reliant on cross-listed courses. Even if they achieve autonomy, they may be reduced to" solo engines" for undergraduate education, especially multicultural breadth requirements ("Introduction" 8–9). Their viability depends on defining interdisciplinary cores of knowledge and education with a rigor that does not derive from generalist distribution or disciplinary accumulation. Otherwise, they will be a dependent variable rather than a category of knowledge that informs other categories and the concept of "America."

CONCLUSION

CRAFTING HUMANITIES FOR A NEW CENTURY

Jerry Gaff likens scholarship to the molten mass of radioactive material that forms the core of the earth. Periodically, it erupts in a volcano or the tectonic plates shift, changing the shape of the earth's crust. Inevitably, it also finds its way into the intellectual landscape of the constantly shifting curriculum ("Tensions" 701). The final chapter returns full circle to the origin of humanities. Since many of the earliest pronouncements were on education, it is appropriate to ask in closing what impact new interdisciplinary scholarship has had on the undergraduate curriculum and, in particular, on general education. The original curriculum of the American college was a common core of undergraduate studies that was deeply rooted in humanities and the ideals of the generalist model. New scholarship challenged the generalist model and the modern system of disciplinarity. The pace and impact, though, were not as sudden or uniform as the rhetoric of "revolution" implies in debates on the canon and the core curriculum.

The aim of this chapter is not an encyclopedic account of examples that are readily available in numerous directories, case studies, and reports on higher education. Rather, the chapter reflects on the changing character of humanities education and the implications. Several questions follow from that objective. What kinds of changes have been occurring? What are the imperatives of change in general education? What are the major trendlines in the humanities portion of general education cores? How is the representation of culture changing? What are the limits of recent reforms? And, in the way of conclusion, what are the prospects for humanities?

The Changing Curriculum

In 1984, the head of the National Endowment for Humanities (NEH), William Bennett, called attention to a general decline in humanities enrollment and required courses in history, literature, philosophy, languages, and the study of classical civilizations. He blamed the decline on inadequate undergraduate teaching, excess freedom of choice, anti-Western and ideological pressures of political radicals, and a new guiding principle of subjective relativism. The title of Bennett's report—*To Reclaim a Legacy*—pointed the way to a solution. He called for a common core of works from the Western heritage supplemented by a foreign language, familiarity with at least one non-Western culture, and some awareness of art, architecture, and music. Four years later, Bennett's successor, Lynn Cheney, reported continuing difficulties. In *Humanities in America,* she blamed politics, the relegation of timeless truths to transitory constructs, and the addition of non-Western and ethnic studies at the expense of American and Western culture. Cheney's positive exemplars featured strong historical cores, close reading of texts, and substantial requirements in Western civilization. The Bennett and Cheney reports, along with Allan Bloom's 1987 book *The Closing of the American Mind,* became flashpoints in national debate on humanities, the canon, and the core curriculum.

By the 1990s, some pundits declared the end of the culture wars. Yet, tension between the old and the new continues. In his 2001 book *Humanism Betrayed,* Graham Good posted a litany of contemporary ills. Good charged that English is collapsing under the weight of Theory. Cultural studies is swallowing up literature and language while moving toward neighboring disciplines and older interdisciplinary programs. Art is being turned into a new holism of "culture" defined by social practices that challenge the older holism of "civilization." The emancipatory capacity of creative imagination is being lost. Transcendent identity is being sealed into compartments of identity, period, culture, and class. And, the keyword "global" is replacing the keyword "universal," displacing perennial questions about God, fate, death, and the human condition (40, 55, 59, 74, 84–88, 100). The same year, Victor Davis Hanson, John Heath, and Bruce Thornton took aim in *Bonfire of the Humanities* at "the motley crew of Marxists, squishy leftists, radical feminists, deconstructionists, social constructionists, multiculturalists, and other postmodernist warriors against patriarchal corporate hegemony." They blamed the decline of humanities on preoccupation with personal war stories, an all-inclusive cultural studies, the jargon-ridden and antihumanist bent of postmodern research, and the extremes of philological research. To remedy these problems, they exhorted "old-style" humanists to uphold the singular distinction of the Greeks and timeless, universal ideas and values.

These and similar defenses of tradition are often dismissed by new-style humanists as ranting diatribes. To be fair, some charges ring true. Preoccupation with academic careerism has come at the expense of undergraduate education, and the pressure of being au courant in Theory did deprivilege other forms of scholarship. However, the allegation that multicultural courses are increasingly replacing courses in Western tradition does not stand up to the evidence. Hanson, Heath, and Thornton alleged the tradition "hardly is taught at all anymore" (26). Yet, the principle author of a study of trendlines, Arthur Levine, found the notion that multiculturalism is replacing the historic canon to be "untenable" (Levine and Cureton 29). After examining the literature and national surveys, Francis Oakley likewise concluded that the bulk of critical commentary is characterized by sweeping and sensationalist claims and a "disheveled anecdotalism" about what is happening at probably no more than a dozen leading research universities and liberal arts colleges. Selective representation is all the more problematic because, Gaff observes, most of the elite 200 or so institutions have not been leaders in curriculum change ("Tensions" 692). The image of the professoriate abandoning teaching for research is also countered by studies that indicate a majority of academics view teaching as their primary mission (Oakley, "Ignorant Armies" 65, 67–68; "Academic Profession" 51).

Even in the face of data to the contrary, however, stark polarities persist in the popular and the academic press. Scholarship is pitted against teaching, past against present, Europe against America, Western heritage against other cultures, and a preservationist campaign to restore tradition against a reformist campaign to forge a critical alternative. The actual practice of humanities education is far more variegated across the roughly 4,000 postsecondary institutions currently operating in the United States.

The Changing Humanities

A study of college transcript samples by the National Center for Education Statistics provides a baseline for talking about change. It produced a quantitative map of undergraduate enrollment patterns from 1972 through

1993. The author of the study defined the largest percentage of total credits as an "empirical core curriculum" that represents 37.7% of all credits generated in colleges, community colleges, and trade schools. The "core-of-the-core" was composed of English composition, college-level mathematics, basic lab science, history, and Spanish. The eleven humanities categories included in the study appear in order of frequency of enrollment, with the first five items ranking within the top fifteen college credits overall (Adelman *New College Course Map*).

1. English Composition
2. Spanish: Introductory and Intermediate
3. U.S. History Surveys
4. World/Western Civilization
5. U.S. Government
6. French: Introductory and Intermediate
7. Art History
8. Introduction to Literature
9. Introduction to Philosophy
10. English Literature
11. American Literature

Looking back on the study in her 1997 report on humanities for the *Handbook of the Undergraduate Curriculum*, Lynn Maxwell White concluded that a significant share of credits are still being earned in traditional course categories. Based as it was on transcript categories, though, the study did not reveal changes in design, content, or approaches in response to new scholarship and debate on the civic purposes of humanities, let alone relationships among courses. White went a step further. She examined trends in curriculum innovation based on a Higher Education in the Humanities Program sponsored by NEH from 1985 to 1995 and the 1995 program book from the Fund for the Improvement of Postsecondary Education (273–74). Projects differed, but as a group they exhibited the following tendencies. They were:

• collaborative across departments, institutions, and sectors
• comparative in their approach to culture
• designed around engaging pedagogies and using technology
• inclusive of both new and traditional materials
• selectively focused rather than aiming for coverage

- successful in engaging faculty and students in new learning
- related to institutional strengths, missions, and directions

(White 274)

These trends, White asserts, constitute another empirical reality defined by actions rather than numbers. White's exemplary practices document the variety of those actions. Oregon State University developed a program allowing undergraduates in any discipline to obtain an international degree concurrent with courses in foreign languages and international studies. At Clark Atlanta University, English department faculty expanded a two-semester general education survey of world literature. Eckerd College strengthened core offerings with a required first course comparing Western and Asian texts and perspectives. Global perspectives courses on topics such as Japanese family life and Asian fiction are also available at sophomore and junior levels, and a required capstone course focuses on moral and religious issues in the cultural heritages of the West and East Asia. Lewis and Clark College created a two-semester core course on *Inventing America* to replace a one-semester course called *Basic Studies*. Southwest Texas State University put together a two-semester upper-division sequence on the relationship of the region's geography and physical ecology to its history and the interaction of Anglo, Chicano, and Indian cultures. Students can earn a minor in interdisciplinary and intercultural regional studies.

The same year White presented her report, Oakley published results of his own comparative study of course catalogues for 1969–70 and 1994–95. Oakley's data reveal five major changes:

1. an increase in the number of courses listed and presumably offered on a cyclical basis
2. a change in the nature of courses and the ways they tend to be described
3. a marked and well-distributed increase in the number of interdepartmental and/or interdisciplinary programs offering either majors or minor concentrations
4. accelerated globalization of the curriculum
5. an increase in offerings pertaining to American minority populations and ethnic groups and, above all, to women's studies and gender-related issues

(Oakley," Ignorant Armies" 69–70)

Attributing the first change to more than a simple increase in the size of the professoriate, Oakley suggested that course proliferation might in part stem from widespread loosening of requirements and a greater variety of electives. The second change reflects a shift from standardized coverage based on genres or historical periods to thematic courses. The third and fourth changes in the direction of greater interdisciplinarity and globalization are evident in foreign languages, history, religion, art history, English, music, and philosophy. Preoccupation with postcolonial theory and writing is growing as well. The third and fourth changes are occurring across institutional types. The fifth is more evident in research universities and leading liberal arts colleges, though its reverberations are evident in other sectors. English and history have been the leading departments in introducing a multicultural element. In addition, Oakley found a modest growth of course offerings in subjects such as film, peace studies, business, medical and environmental ethics, and the literature of religious mysticism.

Taken together, these reports counter allegations that the enduring ideas and texts of Western heritage and the United States have been jettisoned. Change is occurring, but through addition more than drastic substitutions (Oakley, "Ignorant Armies" 71, 73). A similar pattern appears in the place where the greatest number of undergraduate students come into contact with humanities—general education.

General Education

General education has always been part of the American undergraduate experience. It is the place where all students are acquainted with "essential" knowledge and skills regardless of their chosen specialties. The most recent national report, *The Status of General Education in the Year 2000,* indicates that not only does general education remain a high priority on the majority of campuses, in 55% of cases interdisciplinary courses were reported and in 49% common learning experiences (Ratcliff, Johnson, La Nasa, and Gaff 59). In 1999, Jerry Gaff identified thirteen major trends in general education. Renewed emphasis is being placed on liberal arts and science subject matter. Greater attention is being paid to skills. Core programs are being strengthened and standards raised. Interest in interdisciplinarity and integration is expanding. The study of domestic diversity is a growing priority. Global studies and international themes are being incorporated across the curriculum. Moral and ethical dimensions of every field are being explored. The first and senior years are being targeted, and general education is extending across all four years. There is heightened interest in active, experiential, technological, and collaborative methods of learning. New approaches are being taken to assessment of learning, and administrators are supporting faculty collaboration in curriculum planning, course development, and teaching core courses (*General Education* 1–2).

Interdisciplinarity is not simply one more item on the list. It intersects with every trendline. As liberal arts and science subject matter are being updated, new interdisciplinary scholarship is being incorporated. Synthesis and the capacity to work with multiple forms of knowledge have become essential skills. The teaching of diversity and international themes as well as moral and ethical issues draws on new scholarship. Many first-year seminars are organized around integrative study of themes and problems. Senior capstone seminars afford opportunities to make connections with other disciplines, general education, and the "real world." Four-year programs move from a multidisciplinary overview to higher-level synthesis. Collaborative learning and other innovative pedagogies such team teaching stimulate connections. Assessment increasingly includes interdisciplinary outcomes. The needs of interdisciplinary teaching are being recognized in faculty development. Interdisciplinary cores are replacing distribution models based on a menu of existing disciplinary courses. Courses are being clustered and linked, and learning communities are being formed across the curriculum.

Humanities is not isolated to a single place on the list either. As renewed emphasis is being placed on liberal arts and science subject matter, new scholarship is being incorporated into older humanities courses and new curricula in general education and disciplinary majors. Heightened attention is being paid to skills of communication and critical thinking in skill-intensive courses and across-the-curriculum initiatives. The study of domestic diversity and international themes is incorporating new understandings of culture in humanities courses, general education, and interdisciplinary fields with a strong humanities orientation. The study of moral and ethical dimensions of all fields is extending the teaching of skills of reflective judgment and civic responsibility beyond philosophy departments. And, integrative cores are often organized around theme-based study of history and culture that draw on humanities texts. More generally, Beth Casey adds, the greatest growth in subject matter of general education has encouraged interdisciplinary approaches in such areas as international studies, multicultural and gender studies, and historical and ethical understanding ("Administration" 56).

Undergraduates typically encounter humanities in three places: disciplinary majors, humanities programs, and general education. Humanities programs serve three major purposes. They are administrative homes for disciplines and interdisciplinary fields, catalysts for new interdisciplinary curricula, and providers of general education. Some programs also offer a broad humanities major. In his 1996 directory of *Interdisciplinary Undergraduate Programs,* Alan Edwards Jr. included programs with the specialized foci of comparative literature, a variety of period studies, religious studies, applied ethics, and history and literature. The most common function, though, is general education. The amount of time devoted to humanities varies. Some institutions offer courses only in the first and second years. Others have tiered programs, culminating in a senior seminar. Some have common curricula. Others offer alternative tracks on a voluntary basis or for designated populations such as honors students, future teachers, or cohort groups in particular disciplines or preprofessional tracks. The distribution model is still the most common structure, but more campuses are introducing interdisciplinary cores.

The Humanities Core

The four principal models of core curricula in humanities are 1. great books; 2. major historical periods or junctures; 3. overarching themes, ideas, and motifs; and 4. ways of knowing (Shattuck 360–61). Anne Brooks and Un-chol Shin's survey of 100 humanities programs in the early 1980s provides a baseline for talking about change. They identified four major goals from the responses, in order of priority:

1. helping students acquire knowledge of great works of literature, art, music, philosophy, and religion
2. introducing students to the great ideas of Western civilization
3. helping students develop a philosophy of life or worldview
4. helping students realize their individual human potential.

(Brooks and Shin 6)

No single educational philosophy prevailed, but classical essentialism and pragmatism were prominent, and the leading curricular approaches were cultural history and aesthetics (7). These trends continued throughout the 1980s and 1990s, but the variety of programs expanded and new approaches to knowledge and culture were incorporated into integrative cores.

As faculty, administrators, and curriculum committees design integrated cores, they address several common questions:

- How much time should be devoted to humanities? How much to particular disciplines?
- How much time should be devoted to non-Western and multicultural perspectives?
- How much time should be devoted to particular "essential" texts? How much to historical versus contemporary works?
- What role should new critical approaches play?
- What is the ideal balance of breadth and depth? Of uniformity and flexibility? Of disciplinary and interdisciplinary emphasis?
- How much time should be devoted to skills?

The answers vary from campus to campus, although, broadly speaking, the changes that are being implemented are occurring more by addition than sudden transformation. A recent collection of case studies provides a fuller picture based on commissioned reports by members of thirteen humanities-based general education programs. The papers formed the basis for a national conference in 1998 on "Teaching the Humanities" and the book *Alive at the Core*. The exemplary programs range from small secular and religious-affiliated liberal arts colleges to public and private universities, including well-known models such as Columbia University's "Introduction to Contemporary Civilization" and Stanford University's Area One Program "Introduction to the Humanities." The variety of program types, locations, and duration make this collection and examples in Edwards's directory important gauges of change.

Together, the two sets of examples reveal that the West and textual humanities still dominate. Non-Western content is increasingly being included, though, along with a wider representation of women and American cultural groups. The concept of textuality is broadening to include multiple kinds of texts, from literary works and historical documents to works of art, music, and film to monuments and advertisements. Interdisciplinary focus is being heightened through theme- and problem-based study, and the concept of context is moving from an inert background to sustained engagement of interactive aesthetic and social forces. The historical spine remains prominent, but the scope varies from selected historical periods to a broad overview whimsically dubbed the "Plato to NATO" approach. Titles in period-based surveys are often deceptive. On the surface, many titles suggest an older great books approach to "civilization." Yet, the inner content and approaches to teaching it are changing.

Reflecting on the current state of humanities-based general education, Michael Nelson stressed its variety. Some programs center on the West. Others are global in scope. Some are traditional, others nontraditional. They also reflect the trade-offs that occur between competing goals. Depth versus breadth is perhaps the most familiar one. No program can teach the whole of humanities, so decisions must be made about the length of reading lists and corresponding trade-off between comprehensiveness and more intensive engagement of a smaller number of works. The competing claims of the generalist and the expert are no less vexing. No faculty member has degrees in all areas, but instructors who teach in new areas model the idea that a good life encompasses breadth of knowledge and lifelong learning ("Preface" xxiii, "Alive" 17–19). In introducing *Alive at the Core,* Martha Nussbaum hearkened back to Seneca's notion of liberal education as an occasion for liberating the mind to lead the Socratic notion of the "examined life" and to be a reflective critic of traditional practices. Most of the thirteen programs in the book have chosen a great books approach, but they disagree on whether Seneca's preference for Socratic questioning should take precedence over traditional acculturation (xii–xvi).

One of the most important changes that is occurring is the representation of culture as diversity, not a homogeneous unity. Initial efforts to teach diversity, Debra Humphreys recalls, tended to concentrate on remedying inaccuracies or omissions in core curricula and disciplines. African American, ethnic, and women's studies were primary locations, but campuses often limited opportunities for examining the variety of cultural identities and traditions to these locations. Many courses focused on a single discipline, programs tended to serve a small number of students, and institutional structures inhibited greater cooperation and integration. At present, diversity courses are expanding across the curriculum, and they have an increasingly interdisciplinary character (*General Education* 5, "Interdisciplinarity" 124).

The transformative capacity of diversity is evident in Olguin and Schmitz's report on "multicultural humanities" in the *Handbook of the Undergraduate Curriculum.* Courses have begun to incorporate texts and topics introducing students to the political and legal histories of different people; their literature, art, and music; and their worldviews and definitions of self and community. Most departments now have at least one course that covers these topics, either by focusing on particular groups or by offering comparative studies cross-listed with identity fields. In general education, there are three models of incorporating cultural pluralism, each with advantages and disadvantages. The first—specialized courses from interdisciplinary fields—contributes new scholarship on the traditions, cultures, and histories of previously marginalized groups. It facilitates in-depth study with faculty skilled in analysis and pedagogy of race, class, and gender. If a specialized course is not reinforced by a broader transformation, however, it remains isolated. The second model—incorporating cultural pluralism across the curriculum or a curricular transformation—confers wider acknowledgement. This model, though, requires extensive faculty development. The third model—new interdisciplinary courses on cultural pluralism—provides courses outside the current framework, greater freedom to develop courses, and sites for collaboration on learning goals and skills. Yet, it is costly because faculty need to work together on curriculum and staffing (449–51).

More broadly across the curriculum, James A. Banks found, four approaches to integrating multicultural content have evolved since the 1960s. Many instructors and programs move from the simplest to the most complex, though others mix and blend two or more approaches depending on their needs and possibilities. *Level I: The Contributions Approach* inserts discrete cultural artifacts and information into the curriculum, using criteria similar to those used in selecting mainstream elements. *Level II: The Additive Approach* adds content, concepts, themes, and perspectives to the curriculum without changing its primary structure, purposes, and characteristics. New content, materials, and issues are appendages, not integral parts of instruction. *Level III: The Transformation Approach* entails a fundamental alteration of curriculum goals, structure, perspectives, and assumptions. Students are able to view concepts, issues, themes, and problems from several ethnic and cultural perspectives and points of view. The emphasis is not on the ways various cultural and ethnic groups contributed to mainstream culture and society. It is on how a common culture and society emerged in the United States from a complex synthesis and interaction of diverse cultural elements that originated with various cultural, racial, ethnic, and religious groups who make up U.S. society. *Level IV: The Social Action Approach* includes all the traits of the transformation approach and adds components requiring students to make decisions and take actions related to the concept, issue, or problems studied in a particular unit. They become reflective social critics and eventually agents of change (Banks, "Approaches" 195–214; Humphreys, "Interdisciplinarity" 125–26).

Banks's typology of change in multicultural content parallels Toombs and Tierney's general framework of curricular change in the academy.

Every campus does not respond in the same fashion or at the same pace. The first strategy—*Modification*—adds new knowledge, techniques, and practices to existing disciplines and professional fields. Connections and metareflections on the disciplines are also fostered, but they are often limited to special programs. Accretion may eventually result in significant change, but this strategy unfolds on the ground of disciplinary logic. Hence, it tends to preserve existing compartmentalizations. Content, topics, concepts, and theories expand, but the basic structure, purposes, and characteristics of culture and knowledge are not challenged. The second strategy—*Integration*—provides a sense of unity, a larger scope of study, and connections between disciplines and throughout the curriculum. Its impact, though, is often partial, and marginalized interdisciplinary programs are "only suffered to exist." The third strategy—*Transformation*—moves beyond while encompassing elements of modification and integration. It recognizes that new issues must be addressed, such as gender equity, ethnicity, multiculturalism, globalism, ethics, and environmental, health, and educational policy. Yet, these issues pose questions and make demands that are only partly engaged and defined at present, compelling colleges and universities to create new structures and practices (Tombs and Tierney, qtd. in Reardon and Ramley 515–16).

One of the added developments in the new scholarship of culture witnessed in earlier chapters is also apparent in the curriculum. Once a marginal activity, internationalizing became a "leading imperative" of reform in the 1990s. Global problems are often endorsed as the primary impetus for international education. Yet, Joseph Johnston and Jane Spalding suggest, the strongest rationale arises from interpreting the aims of liberal education rather than forces external to the university. An educated person needs general knowledge of the larger world, some understanding of the individual cultures that constitute the world, their interdependence, and the place of their own culture among the others. International education may also be the best context in which to learn multidisciplinarity and comparative thinking, since categories such as "religion" or "feudalism" are not identical across cultures (417–18).

Many campuses treat domestic and international diversity separately. Yet, Grant Cornwell and Eve Stoddard define multicultural learning as a form of "interculturalism" that works at the intersections of both disciplines and cultures. Interculturalism fosters an understanding of global processes that dismantles the boundaries between domestic and international diversity. It also goes beyond most visions of interdisciplinarity. A new "cross-disciplinary," "transnational" paradigm emerges for understanding the epistemological and ideological assumptions undergirding disciplines and cultures and for critiquing the notion of universal forms of truth and knowledge without erasing commonalties (28–30). The older metaphor of unity assumed consistency in the sense of logical relations in a linear framework. The alternative metaphor of coherence allows for many kinds of connection in an evolving social construct. The difference is apparent, James Ratcliff observes, in the way that an institution deals with multiculturalism. Understood as an added imperative, it complicates the curriculum. It is a contradiction. Understood as a task in integration and coherence, it does not mean simply adding to a curriculum or creating a false unity. It requires constructing a logical sequencing of courses in a new matrix that recognizes both the multicultural nature of American society and the multidimensional nature of knowledge (146–47).

The Changing American Academy

In 1998, Carol Geary Schneider and Robert Shoenberg called the most recent period in the history of higher education a time of transformative change. Emerging conceptualizations and practices point in a new direction across the entire curriculum, from restructuring majors and general education to expanding the role of interdisciplinary fields and related programs to widening the focus on diversity and deepening the engagement of a learner-centered curriculum. Curricular reforms are drawing on the wisdom of the past while placing prior understandings in the context of the challenges students face today. Humanities disciplines are being rejustified in epistemological and civic terms, and older questions of culture and identity are being resituated. A complete transformation has not occurred, but every element of a "New Academy" is visible across the country. In *Liberal Learning and the Arts of Connection for the New Academy,* Elizabeth Minnich defined the New Academy as a broad-based movement that has grown up around the edges and increasingly within the departments of the "old academy." It is composed of new ways of thinking, reconfigurations of disciplines, new modes of teaching and assessment, and new forms of scholarship. These developments did not appear *de novo*. They were informed by "multiversities" that already existed and are themselves being changed by new developments. Together they are reconfiguring the social and cognitive space of the academy into a relational pluralism and contextualized form of knowing.

Humanities is central to the New Academy. However, humanities education is confronted by the continuing pressures of specialization and new declines in resources. The narrowing of time and space in the curriculum means that humanities winds up carrying more weight than it can bear. It is expected to transmit cultural heritage, to explore our common humanity, to equip students to be critical thinkers and reflective members of society, to acquaint them with disciplinary and interdisciplinary understandings of knowledge and culture, to train them in basic literacies, and, if there is time left over or the inclination to go beyond prioritizing the verbal, to incorporate the visual, the auditory, and the kinetic. No campus can do all of that. John Churchill likens curricular design to politics: it is "the art of the possible" (311). The state of humanities education lies in a thousand daily decisions on campuses across the country as national trendlines are tested in the forge of local needs, interests, and capabilities.

Casey calls the cumulative effect of change in scholarship a "quiet revolution" that has transformed humanities disciplines, fostering reintegration with each other and with social science (72). While less sanguine about the change, Gertrude Himmelfarb also speaks of a revolution dominated by postmodernism. It does not constitute one more wave of revisionism, Himmelfarb declares. It is a new way of thinking about all subjects and all disciplines (143). The limits, though, are as striking as claims of radical change. Pro and con, the rhetoric of "crisis" continues to cut across debate on the future of humanities. The word "crisis," Stephen McKnight points out, comes from the vocabulary of medicine. It refers to the turning point in an illness when therapy might take effect and restore the health of a patient, or a disease may go unchecked and destroy the body. The problem with the language of crisis, McKnight objected, is that it only implies an either/or turning point. The condition of humanities is more ambiguous than the either/or dichotomy allows. It also implies a time, if the patient recovers health, when the disease is gone for good. A return to history is instructive.

Wither Humanities?

Without a doubt, McKnight admitted, humanities faces serious challenges. However, to portray recent decades as the only era of troubles reflects a short-sighted view of history. The liberal arts were born in a time of social upheaval and conflict. In the classical era, their content and objectives were subject to controversy, debate, conflict, and even ridicule. As the Latin *humanitas* developed into the modern humanities, disciplines shared the epistemological function of defining the meaning and purpose of human life. The various symbolic modes that were their platforms of exploration, though, contained contradictory modes of thought and expression with differing truth claims. Over the course of the history of humanities, Platonists clashed with Aristotelians, scholastics with humanists, theologians with natural philosophers, disciplinarians with generalists, disciplinarians with other disciplinarians, disciplinarians with interdisciplinarians, and traditionalists with postmodernists (22–27).

In *The Opening of the American Mind* Lawrence Levine also reminds us that college curricula do not exist apart from the culture in which they develop: "they are products of that culture and both reflect and influence it." Significant curricular changes are invariably and inextricably linked to significant changes in the general society and culture as well as the shifting landscape of knowledge. They are not concocted by a single group or the source of agreement within broad groups (67–68). Tension between the old and the new, he adds, has been a thematic of humanities throughout their history. Much of the nostalgia for a lost past exhibits a faulty sense of the history of the American university that masks prior controversies, minimizing the expansion and alteration of canons and curricula and stripping tradition of its own historical context and controversies. "Obsolete models and the clamor of archaic debates" prevail, and the current period is constructed as an aberrant product of a debased society. To the contrary, the state of humanities today is "the current chapter of a much older and continuing discussion about values, meanings, perspectives, and ways of comprehending ourselves and those around us." Moreover, multiculturalism may be a relatively new term, but the debate over multiculturalism has occurred since the beginning of humanities.

In the 1997 book *What's Happened to the Humanities?*, leading scholars weighed in on the present and future prospects of humanities. In introducing the volume, Alvin Kernan commented that the "tectonic shifts" in higher education over the past several decades have had an indisputable impact on liberal arts in general and on humanities in particular (47). The most important trends include the rise of new fields of knowledge, increasing interdisciplinarity, and the widening appeal of cultural studies. Yet,

Lynn Hunt remarked in her contribution, these developments are not framed by "the atmosphere of buoyant expansion" in the 1960s. They are framed by a "fiercely contested zero-sum game" in which new positions jockey for place with older ones. New forms of knowledge are not a symptom of decline, Hunt avers. They signal the robustness of contemporary humanities. Yet, they may coexist with declines in the status, prestige, and power of humanities. Demographic change played a productive role in the intellectual transformation marked by an increasingly multiethnic and female student population. In an era of declining resources, however, economic constraints, the feminization of labor in humanities, and greater reliance on part-time employment have been creating a kind of class or caste system within universities. Hunt also joins others in warning about the danger of cultural studies becoming an administrative convenience for amalgamating humanities departments under a single roof and reducing their size. Interdisciplinarity may likewise be used to make the case that all humanities faculty are interchangeable and therefore many are expendable.

Claims of a sudden and radical transformation humanities are further checked by the realities of implementing change. Civian, Arnold, Gamson, Kanter, and London found that faculty are typically more willing to make changes in teaching if their disciplines are moving in certain new directions. Yet, there is still no guarantee that individuals will want to change (648). Generally speaking, change is more likely to take hold if it is the result of a long-term process. In a study of the art and science of changing minds, Howard Gardner reports that a change of mind results more often from a slow and even unidentifiable shift of viewpoint, not a single argument or a sudden epiphany. Suddenness often masks subtler processes that have jelled over a longer period of time. Mental representations play a key role. The content of the mind is by its nature open and infinitely expandable. Yet, certain concepts, stories, theories, and skills carry a larger proportion of the cognitive weight. A more powerful concept, a compelling story, a robust theory, or an effective practice may displace entrenched mental representations. Still, it is more difficult to replace a simple way of thinking about a matter with a more complex way. "Simpler mind changes," Gardner counsels, "tend to trump more complex ones." Mind changes due to indirect creations also take longer, although their effects have the potential to last longer.

In the current complexity of knowledge and culture, faculty development becomes all the more important. The rate and complexity of knowledge growth," James Farmer advises, "means that frequent and perhaps continuous curriculum redesign becomes increasingly necessary" (480). Faculty development today often means new skill areas such as doing interdisciplinary teaching and generalizing, serving in general education, developing interdisciplinary core courses and senior seminars or projects, and teaching themes or practices across the curriculum, including ethics or values, global studies, cultural pluralism, gender issues, writing, and computer literacy (Civian, Arnold, Gamson, Kanter, and London 664). It also means grappling with one of the primary themes of this book—the changing relationship of disciplinarity and interdisciplinarity.

In 1984, Stanley Bailis lamented that a significant part of the problem of interdisciplinarity was the way disciplinarity is understood. Disciplines were often presumed to be topically coalescent, solidified, and monolithic. In actuality, they are highly differentiated, and practices are contested. Worse, disciplines were rarely taught with reference to each other, and the bridges built between them tended to become separate domains or subdisciplines ("Social Sciences" 206). Today, though, shifts in disciplinary boundaries and new interdisciplinary practices are scrambling traditional knowledge taxonomies, organizational charts, and library classification schemes. New disciplinary histories from the professional organizations and the literature on change in higher education depict an astonishing array of changes in the content and structure of disciplines as they respond to new scholarship. In surveying the literature on interdisciplinary education in both K-12 and college, Fiscella and Kimmel also found the "contemporary life" of disciplines and school subjects to be a major topic of discussion across subjects (10). Yet, an astonishing number of faculty are not familiar with the latest state-of-the-art reports from their professional organizations that document changing mental representations of knowledge, culture, and higher education.

This book took 1636 as the starting point and the turn of the nineteenth and twentieth centuries as the pivotal turn into a new era of humanities. The original humanities-based core curriculum was replaced by a system of disciplines that grew in complexity over the course of its first century. New interdisciplinary fields emerged and new webs of relation with traditional disciplines. The principle of unitary knowledge was challenged by the knowledge explosion and new intellectual problematics, concepts, and methods. The principle of unitary culture was challenged by the changing demography of the United States and a family of cross-secting approaches to the study of culture. The boundary line dividing intrinsic work from external forces was crossed, and the responses of readers, viewers, and listeners became part of the meaning of a work. We will not reach a state of nirvana or a fixed condition at the end of history, Jerry Gaff advises. As long as society is changing, student backgrounds and interests are shifting, and scholars are creating new knowledge, frames of reference, interpretations, and methodologies, it will be necessary to critically examine the best way to educate students (704). It will be equally necessary to scrutinize all generalizations about the health or crisis of humanities. To borrow Mieke Bal's formulation in art history, the question is not whether they are "sick or in the pink," or both. They are evolving in response to new conditions of knowledge and culture. They always have.

WORKS CITED

Note: The journals *Humanities Education* and *Interdisciplinary Humanities* are the same publication of the National Association for Humanities Education. Page numbers in the body of the text for works reprinted in the Norment anthology on African American studies refer to that book, since some originals are difficult to obtain. Original citations are included where available. For guides to literature on interdisciplinarity and compilations of bibliography, see the link to Publications on the website of the Association for Integrative Studies (http://www.units.muohio.edu/aisorg/). See also Fiscella and Kimmel's *Interdisciplinary Education: A Guide to Resources* and bibliographies in Julie Thompson Klein's *Interdisciplinarity* and *Crossing Boundaries*. For models of interdisciplinary humanities education, consult James Davis, Alan Edwards, Jr., and Michael Nelson (all listed below).

AAC[&U]. *Liberal Learning and the Arts and Sciences Major.* Washington, DC: Association of American Colleges [and Universities]. 1990. Volume I: *The Challenge of Connecting Learning;* Volume II: *Reports from the Fields: Project on Liberal Learning, Study-in-Depth, and the Arts and Sciences Major.*

AAR. "Religion." In AAC[&U]. *Liberal Learning and the Arts and Sciences Major* V. II: 169–83.

Abrams, M. H. "The Transformation of English Studies: 1930–1995." Bender and Schorske, *American Academic Culture* 123–49.

Adams, Russell L. "African-American Studies and the State of the Art." Norment, *Reader* 103–21.

Addelson, Kathryn Pyne, and Elizabeth Potter. "Making Knowledge." Hartman and Messer-Davidow 259–77.

Adelman, Clifford. *A New College Course Map and Transcript Files: Changes in Course-Taking and Achievement, 1972-1993; Based on the Postsecondary Records from Two National Longitudinal Studies.* Washington, DC: U.S. Department of Education, 1995.

Aisenberg, Nadya, and Mona Harrington. *Women of Academe: Outsiders in the Sacred Grove.* Amherst: U of Massachusetts P, 1988.

Aldridge, Delores P. "Womanist Issues in Black Studies: Towards Integrating Africana Womanism into Africana Studies." Norment, *Reader* 157–66; revised version of original in *Journal of the National Council for Black Studies* 1. 1 (1992): 167–82.

Alkalimat, Abdul et al. "Toward a Paradigm of Unity in Black Studies." Norment, *Reader* 391–407.

Allen, Paula Gunn. "The Intersection of Gender and Color." In Gibaldi, *Introduction* 303–19.

Allen, Ray. "Folk Musical Traditions." In Kurian, Orvell, Butler, and Mechling V. II: 184–90.

Allen, Robert L. "Politics of the Attack on Black Studies." *Black Scholar* 6. 1 (1974): 2–7. Rpt. in Norment, *Reader* 491–96.

Allert, Beate. "Introduction." Allert, *Languages* 1–25.

———, ed. *Languages of Visuality: Crossings between Science, Art, Politics, and Literature*. Detroit: Wayne State UP, 1996.

Altieri, Charles. "Ideal and Ideal." In *CANONS*. Ed. Robert van Hallberg. Chicago: U of Chicago P, 1984. 41–64.

Amariglio Jack, Stephen Resnick, and Richard Wolff. "Division and Difference in the 'Discipline' of Economics." In *Knowledges: Historical and Critical Studies in Disciplinarity*. Ed. Ellen Messer-Davidow, David R. Shumway, and David J. Sylvan. Charlottesville: UP of Virginia, 1993. 150–84.

Anderson, Charles. "Knowledge, Politics, and Interdisciplinary Education." In *Reinventing Ourselves: Interdisciplinary Education, Collaborative Learning, and Experimentation in Higher Education*. Ed. Barbara Leigh Smith and John McCann. Bolton, MA: Anker, 2001. 454–65.

APA. 1991. "Philosophy." AAC[&U]. *Liberal Learning and the Arts and Sciences Major* V. II: 97–115.

Arac, Jonathan. "Shop Window or Laboratory: Collection, Collaboration, and the Humanities." Kaplan and Levine 116–26.

Aronowitz, Stanley. 1990. "On Intellectuals." Robbins, *Intellectuals* 3–56.

Arthurs, Alberta. "The Humanities in the 1990s." In *Higher Learning in America, 1980-2000*, Ed Arthur Levine. Baltimore: The Johns Hopkins UP, 1993. 259–72.

Asante, Molefi. *The Afrocentric Idea*. Philadelphia: Temple UP, 1987.

Azibo, Daudi Ajani ya. "Articulating the Distinction Between Black Studies and the Study of Blacks: The Fundamental Role of Culture and the African Centered Worldview." *The Journal of the National Council for Black Studies* (n.d.). Rpt. in Norment, *Reader* 420–41.

Bailey, Ronald. "Black Studies in Historical Perspective." Norment, *Reader* 229–38.

Bailis, Stanley. "The Culture of Babel: Interdisciplinarity as Adaptation in Multicultureland." *Issues in Integrative Studies* 14 (1996): 87–98.

———. "Holism, Pluralism and the Interdisciplinary Persuasion in American Studies." Paper presented at the American Studies Association annual meeting. Boston, Massachusetts. 5 November. 1993.

———. "The Social Sciences in American Studies: An Integrative Conception." *American Quarterly* 26. 3 (1974): 202–24.

Bal, Mieke. "Introduction." In *The Practice of Cultural Analysis: Exposing Inter-disciplinary Interpretation*. Ed. Mieke Bal. Palo Alto, CA: Stanford UP, 1999. 1–14.

———. *Reading "Rembrandt": Beyond the Word-Image Opposition*. Cambridge: Cambridge UP, 1991.

———. *Travelling Concepts in Humanities*. Toronto: U of Toronto P, 2002.

Bal, Mieke, and Norman Bryson. "Semiotics and Art History." *Art Bulletin* 73. 2 (1991): 174–208.

Banks, James A. "Approaches to Multicultural Curriculum Reform." In *Multicultural Education: Issues and Perspectives*. 2nd ed. Eds. James A. Banks and Cherry A. McGee Banks. Boston: Allyn and Bacon, 1993. 195–214.

———. "Teaching Black Studies for Social Change." Excerpted from "Teaching Black History with a Focus on Decision-Making." *Social Education* 35 (November 1971): 740–45 ff, 820–21; and paper presented at the First Congress of Blacks in Higher Education. University of Texas at Austin, 5–7 April 1972. Rpt. in Norment, *Reader* 672–90.

Banta, Martha. "Working the Levees: Building Them Up or Knocking Them Down?" *American Quarterly* 43. 3 (1991): 375–91.

Baraka, Amiri. "Jazz and the White Critic." O'Meally, *Jazz Cadence* 137–42.

Barkan, Elazar. "History and Cultural Studies." Cohen and Roth 349–69.

Barricelli, Jean-Pierre, and Joseph Gibaldi, eds. *Interrelations of Literature*. New York: Modern Language Association, 1982.

Barricelli, Jean-Pierre, Joseph Gibaldi, and Estella Lauter, eds. *Teaching Literature and Other Arts*. New York: Modern Language Association, 1990.

Barthes, Roland. "From Work to Text." In *Image, Music, Text*. Trans. Stephen Heath. New York: Hill and Wang, 1977. 155–64.

Bate, W. Jackson. "The Crisis in English Studies." *Harvard Magazine* 85 (1982): 46–53.

Bates, Marsha J. "Learning about the Information Seeking of Interdisciplinary Scholars and Students." *Library Trends* 45.1 (1996): 155–64.

Bathrick, David. "Cultural Studies." In Gibaldi, *Introduction to Scholarship*, 1992, 320–40.

Bazerman, Charles. *Shaping Written Knowledge: The Genre and Activity of the Experimental Article in Science*. Madison: U of Wisconsin P, 1988.

Becher, Tony. "The Counter-Culture of Specialization." *European Journal of Education* 25. 2 (1990): 333–46.

Bender, John. 1992. "Eighteenth-Century Studies." In Greenblatt and Gunn, *Redrawing the Boundaries* 79–99.

Bender, Thomas. "The Erosion of Public Culture: Cities, Discourses, and Professional Disciplines." In *The Authority of Experts*. Ed. Thomas Haskell. Bloomington: Indiana UP, 1984. 84–106.

———. "Locality and Worldliness." In *The Transformation of Humanistic Studies in the Twenty-First Century: Opportunities and Perils*. ACLS Occasional Paper, No. 40. New York: American Council of Learned Societies, 1997. 1–10.

———. "Politics, Intellect, and the American University, 1945–1995." Bender and Schorske, *American Academic Culture* 17–54.

Bender, Thomas. "Public Intellectuals: Kazin: Debate About Topics That Matter." *Los Angeles Times*, 14 June 1998: M1.

———. "Wholes and Parts: The Need for Synthesis in American History." *The Journal of American History* 73. 1 (1986): 120–36.

Bender, Thomas, and Carl E. Schorske, eds. *American Academic Culture in Transformation: Fifty Years, Four Disciplines*. Princeton: Princeton UP, 1997.

———. "Introduction." In Bender and Schorske, *American Academic Culture* 3–13.

Bennett, Douglas C. "Innovation in the Liberal Arts and Sciences." In *Education and Democracy: Re-imagining Liberal Learning in America*. Ed. Robert Orrill. New York: The College Board. 1997. 131–49.

Bennett, William. *To Reclaim a Legacy: A Report on the Humanities in Higher Education*. Washington, DC: National Endowment for the Humanities, 1984.

Bercovitch, Sacvan, and Myra Jehlen, eds. *Ideology and Classic American Literature*. Cambridge: Cambridge UP, 1987.

Bergeron, Katherine. "Prologue: Disciplining Music." In Bergeron and Bohlman, *Disciplining Music* 1–9.

Bergeron, Katherine, and Philip Bohlman, eds. *Disciplining Music: Musicology and Its Canons*. Chicago: U of Chicago P, 1992.

———. "Preface." In Bergeron and Bohlman, *Disciplining Music* ix–xi.

Bergonzi, Bernard. *Exploding English: Criticism, Theory, Culture*. Oxford: Clarendon Press, 1990.

Berkhofer, Robert F. Jr. "A New Context for a New American Studies?" *American Quarterly* 41. 4 (1989): 588–613.

Berkin, Carol. "'Dangerous Courtesies': Assault on Women's History." *Chronicle of Higher Education* 11 December 1991: A44.

Berman, Art. *From the New Criticism to Deconstruction: The Reception of Structuralism and Post-Structuralism*. Urbana: U of Illinois P, 1988.

Bernstein, Basil. *The New Constellation*. Cambridge: Polity, 1990.

Bhabha, Homi K. "Postcolonial Criticism." In Greenblatt and Gunn, *Redrawing the Boundaries* 437–65.

Bizzell, Patricia, and Bruce Herzberg, eds. *The Rhetorical Tradition*. Boston: Bedford, 1990.

Black, Brian. "Borderlands." In Kurian, Orvell, Butler, and Mechling V. I: 252–54.

"Black Studies: Fighting for Respect." CNN.COM: Education. 21 January 2002 <http://fyi.cnn.com/2002/fyi/teachers.ednews/01/21/black.studies.ap/>.

Blee, Kathleen. "Contending with Disciplinarity." In Wiegman, *Women's Studies* 178–82.

Bogue, E. Grady, and Jeffrey Aper. *Exploring the Heritage of American Higher Education: The Evolution of Philosophy and Policy*. Phoenix: Oryx, 2000.

Bohlman, Philip V. "Epilogue: Musics and Canons." In Bergeron and Bohlman, *Disciplining Music* 197–210.

———. "Ethnomusicology's Challenge to the Canon: The Canon's Challenge to Ethnomusicology." In Bergeron and Bohlman, *Disciplining Music* 116–36.

Bohman, James F., David R. Hiley, and Richard Shusterman. "Introduction: The Interpretive Turn." In *The Interpretive Turn: Philosophy, Science, and Culture.* Ed. David R. Hiley, James F. Bohlman, and Richard Shusterman. Ithaca: Cornell UP, 1991.

Boudreau, Thomas E. *Universitas: The Social Restructuring of American Undergraduate Education.* Westport, CT: Praeger, 1998.

Boutet, Danielle. "Interdisciplinarity in the Arts." *Harbour* 6 (1993): 66–72.

Boxer, Marilyn J. "For and About Women: The Theory and Practice of Women's Studies in the United States." *Signs* 7. 3 (1982): 661–95.

Boyer, Ernest. 1. "The Quest for Common Learning." In *Common Learning: A Carnegie Colloquium on General Education.* Washington, DC: The Carnegie Foundation for the Advancement of Learning, 1981. 3–21.

Brantlinger, Patrick. *Crusoe's Footprints: Cultural Studies in Britain and America.* New York: Routledge, 1990.

Brilliant, R. "What Has Happened in Art History?" *Humanities* 6. 1 (1985): 204.

Bronner, Simon J. "Introduction" to "Beyond Interdisciplinarity: The New Goals of American Studies Programs." *American Studies Association Newsletter* 28.1 (March 2005): 1–5.

Brooks, Ann, and Un-chol Shin. "Past, Present, and Future of Interdisciplinary Humanities." *Humanities Education.* I, 3 (September 1984): 3–9.

Brossard, Carlos. "Classifying Black Studies Programs." *The Journal of Negro Education.* n.d. Rpt. in Norment, *Reader* 65–78.

Broude, Norma, and Mary Garrard. "Preface" and "Introduction." In *The Expanding Discourse: Feminism and Art History.* Ed. Norma Broude and Mary Garrard. New York: Icon Editions, Imprint of Harper Collins. 1992. ix–x, 1–25.

Bryson, Norman. *Word and Image: French Painting of the Ancient Regime.* Cambridge: Cambridge UP, 1981.

Buell, Lawrence. "Commentary" [on Henry Nash Smith, "Can 'American Studies' Develop a Method?"] In Maddox 13–16.

Burke, Kenneth. *Language as Symbolic Action: Essays on Life, Literature, and Method.* Berkeley: U of California P, 1966.

Burke, Peter. "Overture: The New History, Its Past and Its Future." In *New Perspectives on Historical Writing.* Ed. Peter Burke. University Park: Pennsylvania State UP, 1991. 1–23.

Burkholder, J. Peter. "Music Theory and Musicology." *The Journal of Musicology* 11. 1 (1993): 11–23.

Butler, Johnnella E. "Ethnic Studies." In Kurian, Orvell, Butler, and Mechling V. II: 96–98.

Buttigieg, Joseph. "Introduction: Criticism without Boundaries." In *Criticism without Boundaries: Directions and Crosscurrents in Postmodern Critical Theory.* Ed. Joseph A. Buttigieg. South Bend: U of Notre Dame P, 1987. 1–22.

Cain, William. "English in America Reconsidered: Theory, Criticism, Marxism, and Social Change." In *Criticism in the University*. Ed. Gerald Graff and Reginald Gibbons. Evanston: Northwestern UP, 1985. 85–104.

Caldwell, Lynton K. "Environmental Studies: Discipline or Metadiscipline?" *Environmental Professional* 5 (1983): 247–59.

Campbell, Colin. "Scholarly Disciplines: Breaking Out." *New York Times* 25 April 1986: A18.

Campbell, Neil, and Alasdair Kean. *American Cultural Studies: An Introduction to American Culture*. London: Routledge, 1997.

Caponi-Tabery, Gena. "Music: An Overview." In Kurian, Orvell, Butler, and Mechling V. III: 164–70.

Carlisle, Barbara. "Music and Life." *American Music Teacher* 44 (June/July1995): 10–13.

Carnochan, W. B. *The Battleground of the Curriculum: Liberal Education and American Experience*. Stanford: Stanford UP, 1993.

Carp, Richard. "Interdisciplinary Humanities." Paper presented at annual meeting of Association for Integrative Studies. Eastern Michigan University. Ypsilanti, Michigan. 5 October 1996.

Casey, Beth A. "The Administration and Governance of Interdisciplinary Programs." In *Interdisciplinary Studies Today*. No. 58 in New Directions for Teaching and Learning. Ed. Julie Thompson Klein and William Doty. San Francisco: Jossey Bass, 1994. 53–67.

———. "The Quiet Revolution: The Transformation and Reintegration of the Humanities." *Issues in Integrative Studies* 4 (1996): 71-92.

Cassidy, Donna M. *Painting The Musical City: Jazz and Cultural Identity in American Art, 1910-1940*. Washington, DC: Smithsonian Institute P, 1997.

Chambers, Iain. *Culture After Humanism: History, Culture, Subjectivity*. London: Routledge, 2001.

Chapin, Lloyd. "The Core Curriculum at Eckerd College." In Nelson, *Alive* 96-122.

Cheney, Lynne V. *Humanities in America: A Report to the President, the Congress, and the American People*. Washington, DC: National Endowment for the Humanities, 1988.

Chodorow, Stanley. "Taking the Humanities Off Life Support." In *The Transformation of Humanistic Studies in the Twenty-First Century: Opportunities and Perils*. ACLS Occasional Paper, No. 40. New York: American Council of Learned Societies, 1997. 11-19.

Christ, Carol T. "The American University and Women's Studies." *Tulsa Studies in Women's Literature* 16. 1 (1997): 13-25.

Christian, Barbara. "But Who Do You Really Belong to—Black Studies or Women's Studies." *Women's Studies* 17. 2 (1988): 147-53. Rpt. in Norment, *Reader* 183-86.

Churchill, John. "Western Intellectual Traditions at Hendrix College." In Nelson, *Alive* 302-28.

Civian, Jan. T., Gordon Arnold, Zelda Gamson, Sandra Kanter, and Howard B. London. "Implementing Change." Gaff and Ratcliff, *Handbook* 647-60.

Clayton, Keith. "The University of East Anglia." *Inter-Disciplinarity Revisited: Re-Assessing the Concept in Light of Institutional Experience.* Ed. L. Levin, and I. Lind. OECD/CERI, Swedish National Board of Universities and Colleges, Linköping U, 1985. 189–96.

Cluck, Nancy Anne. "Reflections on the Interdisciplinary Approaches to the Humanities." *Liberal Education* 66. 1 (1980): 67–77.

Cohen, Ralph. "Afterthoughts: Historical Intervention and the Writing of History." Cohen and Roth 396–409.

Cohen, Ralph, and Michael S. Roth, eds. *History and . . . Histories within the Human Sciences.* Charlottesville: UP of Virginia, 1995.

Cohen, Walter. "Marxist Criticism." In Greenblatt and Gunn, *Redrawing the Boundaries* 320–48.

Collins, Patricia Hill. "Learning from the Outsider Within: The Sociological Significance of Black Feminist Thought." Hartman and Messer-Davidow *(En)Gendering Knowledge* 40–65.

Connor, Steve. *Postmodernist Culture: An Introduction to Theories of the Contemporary.* Oxford: Basil Blackwell, 1989.

Cornwall, Grant, and Eve Stoddard. *Globalizing Knowledge: Connecting International and Intercultural Studies.* No. 4 in The Academy in Transition series. Washington, DC: Association of American Colleges and Universities, 1999.

Covach, John. "We Won't Get Fooled Again: Rock Music and Musical Analysis." In Schwarz, Kassabian, and Siegel 75–89.

Cowan, Michael. "American Studies: An Overview." In Kurian, Orvell, Butler, and Mechling V. I: 105–17.

Coyner, Sandra. "Women's Studies." *NWSA Journal* [National Women's Studies Association] 3. 3 (1991): 349–54.

Crane, R. S. *The Idea of the Humanities and Other Essays Critical and Historical.* Chicago: U of Chicago P, 1967.

Crouchett, Lawrence P. "Early Black Studies Movements." *Journal of Black Studies* 2 (1971): 189–200. Rpt. in Norment, *Reader* 192–98.

Culler, Jonathan. "Literary Theory." In Gibaldi, *Introduction to Scholarship* 201–35.

Curzan, Anne, and Priscilla Wald. "Americanization." Kurian, Orvell, Butler, and Mechling V. I: 118–21.

Daniel, Philip T. K. "Theory Building in Black Studies." *The Black Scholar* 12, 13 (1981): 29–36. Rpt. in Norment, *Reader* 372–79.

D'Arms, John. "Pressing Issues for a New Generation of Humanists." *The Chronicle of Higher Education* 2 (July 1999): B6–7.

Davis, James R. *Interdisciplinary Courses and Team Teaching: New Arrangements for Learning.* Phoenix, AZ: American Council on Education, Oryx, 1995.

Dawidoff, Robert. "History . . . But." In Cohen and Roth 370–82.

Deloria, Philip J. "American Indians, American Studies, and the ASA." *American Quarterly* 55. 4 (2003): 669–687.

Denning, Michael. *Cultural Front: The Laboring of American Culture in the Twentieth Century.* New York, London: Verso, 1997.

———. "Work and Culture in American Studies." In Pease and Wiegman 419–40.

Denzin, Norman K. *Symbolic Interactionism and Cultural Studies: The Politics of Interpretation*. Cambridge: Blackwell, 1992.

Derrida, Jacques. "The Principle of Reason: The University in the Eyes of its Pupils." *Diacritics* (Fall 1983): response section 3–20.

DeSoto, Aureliano Maria. "Chicanos." Kurian, Orvell, Butler, and Mechling V. I: 299–304.

Deveaux, Scott. "Constructing the Jazz Tradition." In O'Meally, *Jazz Cadence* 483–512. Rpt. from Scott Deveaux. "Constructing the Jazz Tradition: Jazz Historiography." *Black American Literature Forum* 25. 3 (1991): 525–60.

Dhareshwar, Vivek. "The Predicament of Theory." Kreiswirth and Cheetham, *Theory* 231–50.

Diamond, Robert M., and Bronwyn E. Adam, eds. *The Disciplines Speak II: More Statements on Rewarding the Scholarly, Professional, and Creative Work of Faculty*. Washington, DC: American Association of Higher Education, 2000. "Defining Women's Studies Scholarship" 125–51. "Africana Studies: Past, Present, and Future" 153–78.

Dogan, Mattei, and Robert Pahre. *Creative Marginality: Innovation at the Intersections of Social Sciences*. Boulder: Westview Press, 1990.

Dölling, Irene, and Sabine Hark. "She Who Speaks Shadow Speaks Truth: Transdisciplinarity in Women's and Gender Studies." *Signs* 25. 4 (2000): 1195–98.

Drake, St. Clair. "What Happened to Black Studies?" *New York University Education Quarterly*. n.d. Rpt. in Norment, *Reader* 265–76.

Dubois, Carol Ellen, Gail Paradise Kelly, Elizabeth Lapovsky Kennedy, Carolyn W. Korsmeyer, and Lillian S. Robinson. *Feminist Scholarship: Kindling in the Groves of Academe*. Urbana: U of Illinois P, 1987.

Durbin, Paul T. "Encyclopedias and the Integration of Knowledge." *Social Epistemology*. 10. 1 (1996): 123–33.

Early, Gerald. "Black Studies: An Education or the Reflection of a Crisis?" *Academic Questions* 11. 4 (1998): 12–20.

Easton, David. "The Division, Integration, and Transfer of Knowledge." In *Divided Knowledge: Across Disciplines, Across Cultures*. Ed. David Easton and Corinne S. Schelling. Newbury Park: Sage, 1991. 7–36.

Edwards, Alan F. Jr. *Interdisciplinary Undergraduate Programs: A Directory*. 2nd ed. Acton, MA: Copley, 1996.

Edwards, Brent. "The Seemingly Eclipsed Window of form: James Weldon Johnson's Prefaces." O'Meally, *Jazz Cadence* 580–601.

Elam, Diane. "Ms. en Abyme: Deconstruction and Feminism." *Social Epistemology* 4. 3 (1990): 293–308.

———. "Taking Account of Women's Studies." Wiegman, *Women's Studies* 218–23.

Elbow, Peter. *What Is English?* New York: Modern Language Association, 1990.

Elliott, Mary Jane Suerro. "Chicano Literature." In Kurian, Orvell, Butler, and Mechling V. I: 304–308.

———. "Mestiza Consciousness." In Kurian, Orvell, Butler, and Mechling V. III: 106–07.

Ellis, John. *Literature Lost: Social Agendas and the Corruption of the Humanities.* New Haven: Yale UP, 1997.

Farrell, James J. "What Are American Studies For? Some Practical Perspectives." *American Studies* 40. 2 (1999): 183–97.

Featherstone, Mike. "In Pursuit of the Postmodern: An Introduction." *Theory, Culture, and Society* 5. 2–3 (1988): 195–215.

Ferren, Anne. "Achieving Effectiveness and Efficiency." In Gaff and Ratcliff, *Handbook* 533–57.

Finke, Laurie A., and Martin B. Shichtman. "Profiting Pedants: Symbolic Capital, Text Editing, and Cultural Reproduction." Shumway and Dionne, *Disciplining English* 159–78.

Fiscella, Joan, and Stacey Kimmel. *Interdisciplinary Education: A Guide to Resources.* New York: The College Board, 1998.

Fischer, Michael M. J. [Comment on] "Knowledge Collaborations in the Arts, the Sciences, and the Humanities. Part 3: The Humanities and Social Sciences." *Knowledge* 14, 1 (1992): 124–28.

Fish, Stanley. "Being Interdisciplinary Is So Very Hard To Do." *Profession* 89 (1985): 15–22. [Modern Language Association].

———. *Professional Correctness: Literary Studies and Political Change.* Cambridge, MA: Harvard UP, 1995.

Fisher, Philip. "American Literary and Cultural Studies Since the Civil War." In Greenblatt and Gunn, *Redrawing the Boundaries* 232–50.

Fiske, John. "Cultural Studies and the Culture of Everyday Life." Grossberg, Nelson and Treichler 154–73.

Flexner, Hans. "The Curriculum, the Disciplines, and Interdisciplinarity in Higher Education: A Historical Perspective." Kockelmans, *Interdisciplinarity* 93–122.

Fluck, Winfried. "The Humanities in the Age of Expressive Individualism and Cultural Radicalism." In Pease and Wiegman 211–30.

Folley-Cooper, Marquette, Deborah Macanic, and Janice McNeil. *Seeing Jazz: Artists and Writers on Jazz.* San Francisco: Chronicle Books, in association with the Smithsonian Institution Traveling Exhibition Service, 1997.

"Forum: Defining Interdisciplinarity." *PMLA* 111. 2 (1996): 271–311.

Fowler, Alastair. "Periodization and Interart Analogies." *New Literary History* 3. 3 (1972): 487–509.

Fox-Genovese, Elizabeth. "Between Individualism and Fragmentation: American Culture and the New Literary Studies of Race and Gender." *American Quarterly* 42. 1 (1990): 7–34.

Frank, Roberta. "'Interdisciplinary': The First Half-Century." In *WORDS: For Robert Burchfield's Sixty-Fifth Birthday.* Ed. E. G. Stanley and T. F. Hoad. Cambridge: D. S. Brewer, 1988. 91–101

Fresonke, Kris. "Regionalism." In Kurian, Orvell, Butler, and Mechling V. IV: 12–18.

Frey, Gerhard. "Methodological Problems of Interdisciplinary Discussions." *RATIO* 15. 2 (1973): 161–82.

Friedensohn, Doris. "Towards a Post-Imperial, Transnational American Studies: Notes of a Frequent Flier." *American Studies* 38.2 (1997): 69–85.

Friedman, Susan Stanford. "Academic Feminism and Interdisciplinarity." *Feminist Studies* 27. 2 (2001): 499–531.

Frith, S. "Towards an Aesthetic of Popular Music." In *Music and Society: The Politics of Composition, Performance, and Reception*. Ed. R. Leppert and S. McClary. Cambridge: Cambridge UP, 1987. 133–49.

Frye, Northrup. *Anatomy of Criticism: Four Essays*. Princeton: Princeton UP, 1997.

Fuller Steve. "The Position: Interdisciplinarity." In *Philosophy, Rhetoric, and the End of Knowledge*. Madison: U of Wisconsin P, 1993. 33–64.

Furhmann, Barbara S. "Philosophies and Aims." Gaff and Ratcliff, *Handbook* 86–99.

Gabbard, Krin. "Acknowledgments" and "Introduction." Gabbard, *Jazz* vii–viii, 1–28.

———, ed. *Jazz among the Discourses*. Durham: Duke UP, 1995.

Gaff, Jerry G. *General Education: The Changing Agenda*. Washington, DC: Association of American Colleges and Universities, 1999.

———. "Tensions Between Tradition and Innovation." Gaff and Ratcliff, *Handbook* 684–705.

Gaff, Jerry G., and James L. Ratcliff, eds. *Handbook of the Undergraduate Curriculum: A Comprehensive Guide to Purposes, Structures, Practices, and Change*. San Francisco: Jossey Bass, 1997.

———. "Preface." Gaff and Ratcliff, *Handbook* xii–xxxii.

Gallagher, Catherine. "The History of Literary Criticism." Bender and Schorske, *American Academic Culture* 151–71.

Gallagher, Chris W. "REVIEW: Remodeling English Studies." *College English* 63. 6 (2001): 780–89.

Garber, Marjorie. *Academic Instincts*. Princeton: Princeton UP, 2001.

Gardner, Howard. *Changing Minds: The Art and Science of Changing Our Own and Other People's Minds*. Boston: Harvard Business School P, 2004.

Garcia, Mildred, and James L. Ratcliff. "Social Forces Shaping the Curriculum." Gaff and Ratcliff, *Handbook* 118–36.

Gates, Henry Louis Jr. "African American Criticism." Greenblatt and Gunn, *Redrawing the Boundaries* 303–19.

———. "'Ethnic and Minority' Studies." Gibaldi, *Introduction* 288–302.

Geertz, Clifford. "Blurred Genres: The Refiguration of Social Thought." *American Scholar* 42. 2 (1980): 165–79.

Gendron, Bernard. "'Moldy Figs' and Modernists: Jazz at War (1942–1946)." Gabbard, *Jazz* 31–56.

Germano, William. "Why Interdisciplinarity Isn't Enough." In *The Practice of Cultural Analysis: Exposing Interdisciplinary Interpretation*. Ed. Mieke Bal. Stanford: Stanford UP, 1999. 327–34.

Gibaldi, Joseph, ed. *Introduction to Scholarship in Modern Languages and Literatures*. New York: Modern Language Association of America, 1981.

————. *Introduction to Scholarship in Modern Languages and Literatures*. New York: Modern Language Association of America, 1992.

Gibbons, Michael et al. *The New Production of Knowledge: The Dynamics of Science and Research in Contemporary Societies*. London: Sage, 1994.

Giles, Paul. "Virtual Americas: The Internationalization of American Studies and the Ideology of Exchange." *American Quarterly* 50. 3 (1998): 523–47.

Gilroy, Paul. "Cultural Studies and the Crisis in Britain's Universities." *The Chronicle of Higher Education* 26 July 2002: B20.

Ginzburg, Carol. "Vetoes and Compatibilities." *The Art Bulletin* 77. 4 (1995): 534–36.

Giroux, Henry. *Schooling and the Struggle for Public Life*. Minneapolis: U of Minnesota P, 1988.

Giroux, Henry, David Shumway, and James Sosnoski. "The Need for Cultural Studies: Resisting Intellectuals and Oppositional Public Spheres." *Dalhousie Review* 64 (1984): 472–86.

Glick, Walter. "A Functional Definition of Humanities." *Humanities Education* 4. 4 (1987): 7–12.

Goldman, Harvey. "Innovation and Change in the Production of Knowledge." *Social Epistemology* 9. 3 (1995): 211–32.

Good, Graham. *Humanism Betrayed: Theory, Ideology, and Culture in the Contemporary University*. Montreal: Mc-Gill-Queen's UP, 2001.

Goodwin, Andrew, and Janet Woolf. "Conserving Cultural Studies." In *From Sociology to Cultural Studies: New Perspectives*. Ed. Elizabeth Long. Malden, MA and Oxford, UK: Blackwell, 1997. 123–49.

Grace, Nancy McCampbell. "An Exploration of the Interdisciplinary Character of Women's Studies." *Issues in Integrative Studies* 16 (1996): 59–86.

Graff, Gerald. *Professing Literature: An Institutional History*. Chicago: U of Chicago P, 1987.

Graff, Gerald and Bruce Robbins. "Cultural Criticism." Greenblatt and Gunn, *Redrawing the Boundaries* 419–36.

Grafton, Anthony, and Lisa Jardine. *From Humanism to the Humanities: Education and the Liberal Arts in Fifteenth- and Sixteenth-Century Europe*. Cambridge: Harvard UP, 1986.

Graubard, Stephen. "Foreword." Bender and Schorske, *American Academic Culture* vii–x.

Gray, Louise. "Music Education through the Contemporary Classics." *Interdisciplinary Humanities* 9. 3 (1992): 13–22.

Green, Jon D. "Determining Valid Interart Analogies." In *Teaching Literature and Other Arts*. Ed. Jean-Pierre Barricelli, Joseph Gibaldi, and Estella Lauter. New York: Modern Language Association, 1990. 8–15.

Greenblatt, Stephen. *Shakespearean Negotiations: The Circulation of Social Energy in Renaissance England*. Berkeley: U of California P, 1988.

Greenblatt, Stephen, and Giles Gunn. "Introduction." Greenblatt and Gunn, *Redrawing the Boundaries* 1–11.

————, eds. *Redrawing the Boundaries: The Transformation of English and American Literary Studies*. New York: Modern Language Association, 1992.

Greene, David B. "Music and the Humanities: Coming to New Questions." *Interdisciplinary Humanities* 9 4 (1992): 55–64.

Greene, Maxine. *The Dialectic of Freedom*. New York: Teachers College P, 1988.

Gross, Robert. A. "The Transnational Turn: Rediscovering American Studies in a Wider World." *Journal of American Studies* 34. 3 (2000): 373–93.

Gross, Ronald. "Columbia's University Seminars—Creating a 'Community of Scholars.'" *Change* 14. 2 (1982): 43–45.

Grossberg, Lawrence, Cary Nelson, and Paula Treichler, eds. *Cultural Studies*. New York: Routledge, 1992.

Guillory, John. "Literary Study and the Modern System of the Disciplines." In *Disciplinarity at the Fin de Siècle*, Ed. Amanda Anderson and Joseph Valente. Princeton: Princeton UP, 2002. 20–43.

Gunew, Sneja, "Feminist Cultural Literacy: Translating Differences, Cannibal Options." Wiegman, *Women's Studies* 47–65.

Gunn, Giles. "Interdisciplinary Studies." Gibaldi, *Introduction to Scholarship*, 1992, 239–61.

————. "Introduction: Globalizing Literary Studies." *PMLA* 116. 1 (2001): 16–31.

————. *Thinking Across the American Grain: Ideology, Intellect and the New Pragmatism*. Chicago: U of Chicago P, 1992.

Habell-Pallán, Michelle. "Chicano Performing and Graphic Arts." Kurian, Orvell, Butler, and Mechling V. I: 308–12.

Hall, Perry. "Introducing African American Studies: Systematic and Thematic Principles." *Journal of Black Studies* 26. 6 (1996): 713–34.

Hall, Stuart. "Cultural Studies and the Center: Some Problematics and Problems." In *Culture, Media, Language: Working Papers in Cultural Studies*. Ed. Stuart Hall et al. London: Hutchison. 1979. 16–47.

————. "Cultural Studies and Its Theoretical Legacies." Grossberg, Nelson, and Treichler 270–94.

Hamilton, Charles V. "The Challenge of Black Studies." *Social Policy* 1. 2 (1970): 16.

Hanson, Victor Davis, John Heath, and Bruce S. Thornton. *Bonfire of the Humanities: Rescuing the Classics in an Impoverished Age*. Wilmington, DE: ISI Books, 2001.

Hare, Nathan. "Questions and American about Black Studies." *The Massachusetts Review* (1970). Rpt. in Norment, *Reader* 13–21.

Harkin, Patricia. "Child's Ballads: Narrating Histories of Composition and Literary Studies." Shumway and Dionne, *Disciplining English* 21–37.

Harris, Ellen T. "The Arts." Gaff and Ratcliff, *Handbook* 320–40.

Harris, Robert Jr. "The Intellectual and Institutional Development of Africana Studies." In *Three Essays, Black Studies in the United States*. Ed. Robert Harris, Darlene Clark Hine, and Nellie McKay. New York: The Ford Foundation. 1990. Rpt. in Norment, *Reader* 321–26.

Harrison, Frank. "American Musicology and the European Tradition." In *Musicology*. Ed. Harrison, Hood, and Palisca. Englewood Cliffs, NJ: Prentice-Hall, 1963. 1–86.

Harth, Phillip. "Clio and the Critics." In *Studies in Eighteenth-Century Culture*. Vol. 10. Madison: U of Wisconsin P, for American Society for Eighteenth-Century Studies, 1981. 3–16.

Hartley, John. "Introduction: 'Cultural Exceptionalism.'" In *American Cultural Studies: A Reader*. Ed. John Hartley and Robert E. Pearson with Eva Vieth. Oxford: Oxford UP, 2000. 1–13.

Hartman, Joan E. "Telling Stories: The Construction of Women's Agency." Hartman and Messer-Davidow *(En)Gendering Knowledge* 11–39.

Hartman, Joan E., and Ellen Messer-Davidow, eds. *(En)Gendering Knowledge: Feminists in Academe*. Knoxville: U of Tennessee P, 1991.

———. "Introduction: a Position Statement." Hartman and Messer-Davidow *(En)Gendering Knowledge* 1–7.

Hastings Center. *On the Uses of the Humanities: Vision and Application*. Hastings-on-Hudson: Institute of Society, Ethics, and the Life Sciences, 1984.

Hawthorne, Elizabeth M. "Institutional Contexts." Gaff and Ratcliff, *Handbook* 30–52.

Hayes, Floyd. "Taking Stock: African American Studies at the Edge of the 21st Century." *Western Journal of Black Studies*. Rpt. in Norment, *Reader* 593–608.

Hayles, N. Katherine. *Chaos Bound: Orderly Discourse in Contemporary Literature and Science*. Ithaca: Cornell UP, 1990.

Haynes, Carolyn, ed. *Innovations in Interdisciplinary Teaching*. Westport, CT: Oryx Press/American Council on Education, 2002.

Hendershott, Anne Barnhardt, and Sheila Phelan Wright. "The Social Sciences." Gaff and Ratcliff, *Handbook* 301–19.

Henderson, Mae H. "Introduction: Borders, Boundaries, and Frame(work)s." In *Borders, Boundaries, and Frames: Cultural Criticism and Cultural Studies*. Ed. Mae Henderson. New York: Routledge, 1995. 2–30.

Herbert, James D. "Masterdisciplinarity and the Pictorial Turn." *The Art Bulletin* 77. 4 (1995): 537–40.

Herman, Martin M. "A Shared Methodology: Gothic Architecture, Scholastic Philosophy, and Notre-Dame Organum." *Interdisciplinary Humanities* 9. 4 (1992): 35–54.

Hermand, Jost, and Evelyn Torton Beck. *Interpretive Synthesis: The Task of Literary Scholarship*. New York: Ungar, 1968.

Higham, John. "The Matrix of Specialization." In *The Organization of Knowledge in Modern America, 1860-1920*. Ed. Alexandra Oleson and John Voss. Baltimore: The Johns Hopkins UP, 1979. 3–18.

Himmelfarb, Gertrude. *The New History and the Old*. Cambridge: Harvard UP, 987.

Hine, Darlene Clark. "Black Studies: An Overview." In *Three Essays: Black Studies in the United States*. Ed. Robert Harris, Darlene Clark Hine and

Nellie McKay. New York: The Ford Foundation, 1990. Rpt. in Norment, *Reader* 50–57.

———. "The Black Studies Movement: Afrocentric-Traditionalist-Feminist Paradigms for the Next Stage." In *Afro-American Studies: A Report to the Ford Foundation*. Ed. Nathan I. Huggins. New York: The Ford Foundation, 1985. Excerpted in Norment, *Reader* 239–64.

Hirst, Paul H. *Knowledge and the Curriculum: A Collection of Philosophical Papers*. London: Routledge, 1974.

Hite, Molly. "Inventing Gender: Creative Writing and Critical Agency." Shumway, and Dionne, *Disciplining English* 149–58.

Hoagland, Sarah. "On the Reeducation of Sophie." In *Women's Studies: An Interdisciplinary Collection*. Ed. Kathleen O'Connor Blumhagen and Walter Johnson. Westport, CT: Greenwood. 1978. 13–20.

Hollinger, David A. "The Disciplines and the Identity Debates, 1970–1995." Bender and Schorske, *American Academic Culture* 353–71.

Holquist, Michael. "A New Tour of Babel: Recent Trends Linking Comparative Literature Departments, Foreign Language Departments, and Area Studies Programs." *ADFL Bulletin* 27. 1 (1996): 6–12.

Hood, William. "The State of Research in Italian Renaissance Art." *The Art Bulletin* 69. 2 (1987): 174–86.

Hooker, Richard. "The Invention of American Musical Culture: Meaning, Criticism, and Musical Acculturation in Antebellum America." Schwarz, Kassabian, and Siegel 107–26.

Horn, T. C. R. and Harry Ritter. "Interdisciplinary History: A Historiographical Review." *History Teacher* 19. 3 (1986): 427–48.

Horwitz, Richard. "American Studies: Approaches and Concepts." Kurian, Orvell, Butler, and Mechling V. I: 112–18.

———. "To Kvetch and Define a Field." *American Studies* 38.2 (1997): 49–68.

Hoskins, Christopher B. "From Bridges to Text: *Brooklyn Bridge,* Myth and Symbol, American/Cultural Studies." *American Studies* 40. 1 (1999): 101–14.

Howard, June. *Publishing the Family*. Durham: Duke UP, 2001.

Howe, Florence. "Breaking the Disciplines." In *The Structure of Knowledge: A Feminist Perspective*. Ed. Beth Reed. Ann Arbor: Great Lakes Colleges Association Women's Studies Program, 1978. 1–10.

Huggins, Nathan I. "Afro-American Studies." *A Report to the Ford Foundation on Afro-American Studies*. New York: The Ford Foundation, 1985. Rpt. in Norment, *Reader* 248–64.

Hulsether, Mark. "Three Challenges for the Field of American Studies: Relating to Cultural Studies, Addressing Wider Publics, and Coming to Terms with Religions." *American Studies* 38. 2 (1997): 117–46.

The Humanities in American Life. Berkeley: U of California P, 1980.

Humphreys, Debra. *General Education and American Commitments: A National Report on Diversity Courses and Requirements*. Washington, DC: Association of American Colleges and Universities, 1997.

———. "Interdisciplinarity, Diversity, and the Future of Liberal Education." Haynes 122–38.

Hunt, Lynn Maxwell. "Democratization and Decline? The Consequences of Demographic Change in the Humanities." Kernan, *What Happened* 17–31.

Hutcheon, Linda "Disciplinary Formation, Faculty Pleasures, and Student Risks." *ADE Bulletin* 117 (Fall 1997): 19–22.

———. "Introduction: *Plus ça change*" *PMLA* 155. 7 (2000): 1719–27.

Hutcheon, Linda, and Michael Hutcheon. "A Convenience of Marriage: Collaboration and Interdisciplinarity." *PMLA* 116. 5 (2001): 1364–76.

Hutcheson, Philo A. "Structures and Practices." Gaff and Ratcliff, *Handbook* 100–17.

Interdisciplinarity: Problems of Teaching and Research in Universities. Paris: Organization for Economic Cooperation and Development, 1972.

Jaffa, Arthur. "Black Visual Intonation." O'Meally, *Jazz Cadence* 264–68.

Jardine, Alice A. 1. *Gynesis: Configurations of Woman and Modernity.* Ithaca: Cornell UP, 1985.

Jay, Martin. "Name-Dropping or Dropping Names?: Modes of Legitimation in the Humanities." Kreiswirth and Cheetham, *Theory* 19–34.

Jay, Paul. "Beyond Discipline? Globalization and the Future of English." *PMLA* 116. 1 (2001): 32–47.

Jefferson, Margo. 1. "'Noise' Taps a Historic Route to Joy." O'Meally, *Jazz Cadence* 381–85.

Johnston, Joseph S. Jr., and Jane Spalding. "Internationalizing the Curriculum." Gaff and Ratcliff, *Handbook* 416–35.

Kann, Mark. "The Political Culture of Interdisciplinary Explanation." *Humanities in Society* 2. 3 (1979): 185–300.

Kaplan, Caren, and Inderpal Grewal. "Transnational Practices and Interdisciplinary Feminist Scholarship: Refiguring Women's and Gender Studies." In *Women's Studies on Its Own: A Next Wave Reader in Institutional Change.* Ed. Robyn Wiegman. Durham: Duke UP, 2002. 66–81.

Kaplan, E. Ann, and George Levine. "Introduction." *The Politics of Research.* Ed. E. Ann Kaplan and George Levine. New Brunswick: Rutgers UP, 1997. 1–18.

Karenga, Maulana Ron. "Black Studies and the Problematic of a Paradigm: The Philosophical Dimension." *Journal of Black Studies* 18. 4 (1988): 395–414. Rpt. in Norment, *Reader* 282–94.

———. *Introduction to Black Studies.* Los Angeles: Kawaida, 1982.

Kassabian, Anahid. "Introduction: Music, Disciplinarity, and Interdisciplinarities." Schwarz, Kassabian, and Sigel 1–10.

Katz, Cindi. "Disciplining Interdisciplinarity." *Feminist Studies* 27. 2 (2001): 499–531.

Katz, Stanley. "Beyond the Disciplines." Address at a meeting on "The Role of the New American College in the Past, Present, and Future of American Higher Education." Saint Mary's College of California. Moraga, California, 17 June 1996.

Kearney, Michael. "Borders and Boundaries of State and Self at the End of Empire." *The Journal of Historical Sociology* 4.1 (1991): 52–74.

Kellner, Douglas. *Media Culture: Cultural Studies, Identity, and Politics Between the Modern and the Postmodern.* London: Routledge, 1995.

———. "Postmodernism as Social Theory: Some Challenges and Problems." *Theory, Culture, and Society* 5. 2–3 (1988): 239–69.

Kelly, James. "Wide and Narrow Interdisciplinarity." *Journal of General Education* 45. 2 (1996): 95–113.

Kelly, R. Gordon. "Literature and the Historian." *American Quarterly* 26 (May 1974): 141–59.

Kennedy, G. A. "Classics and Canon." In *The Politics of Liberal Education.* Ed. D. J. Gless and B. H. Smith. Durham: Duke UP, 1992. 223–31.

Kerber, Linda. "Diversity and the Transformation of American Studies." *American Quarterly* 41. 3 (1989): 415–32.

Kerman, Joseph. *Contemplating Music: Challenges to Musicology.* Cambridge: Harvard UP, 1985.

Kernan, Alvin. *The Death of Literature.* New Haven: Yale UP, 1990.

———, ed. *What's Happened to the Humanities?* Princeton: Princeton UP, 1997.

Kilson, Martin. "Reflections on Structure and Content in Black Studies." *The Journal of Black Studies* 1. 2 (1973): 297–313. Rpt. in Norment, *Reader* 31–40.

Kimball, Bruce A. "Toward Pragmatic Liberal Education." In *The Condition of American Liberal Education.* Ed. Robert Orrill. New York: The College Board, 1995. 3–122.

Kirby, John T. "Classical Greek Origins of Western Aesthetic Theory." Allert, *Languages* 129–45.

Klein, Julie Thompson. *Crossing Boundaries: Knowledge, Disciplinarities, and Interdisciplinarities.* Charlottesville: UP of Virginia, 1996.

———. *Interdisciplinarity: History, Theory, and Practice.* Detroit: Wayne State UP. 1990.

———. "Unity of Knowledge and Transdisciplinarity: Contexts of Definition, Theory, and the New Discourse of Problem Solving." In *Encyclopedia of Life Support Systems.* Oxford: EOLSS, 2003. Online resource at <http://www.eolss.net/>.

Klein, Julie Thompson, and William H. Newell. "Advancing Interdisciplinary Studies." Gaff and Ratcliff, *Handbook* 393–415.

Kleiner, Elaine. "Romantic" [Review of Matthew Brennan, *Wordsworth, Turner, and Romantic Landscape: A Study of the Traditions of the Picaresque and the Sublime*]. *Humanities Education* 6. 1 (1989): 31–32.

Kockelmans, Joseph J. "Science and Discipline: Some Historical and Critical Reflections." Kockelmans, *Interdisciplinarity* 11–48.

———. "Why Interdisciplinarity?" Kockelmans, *Interdisciplinarity* 123–60.

Kolodny, Annette. "Dancing Through the Minefield: Some Observations on the Theory, Practice, and Politics of a Feminist Literary Criticism." *Feminist Studies* 6 (1980): 1–25.

Koltai, Leslie. "Editor's Notes." *Merging the Humanities*. Number 12 in New Directions for Community Colleges. Ed. Leslie Koltai. San Francisco: Jossey Bass, 1975.

Kraft, Selma. "Interdisciplinarity and the Canon of Art History." *Issues in Integrative Studies* 7 (1989): 57–71.

Kreiswirth, Martin, and Mark A. Cheetham. "Introduction: 'Theory-Mad Beyond Redemptions'(?)." Kreiswirth and Cheetham, *Theory* 1–16.

———. *Theory Between the Disciplines: Authority, Vision, Politics*. Ann Arbor: U of Michigan P, 1990.

Kreiswirth, Martin, and Thomas Carmichael. "Introduction." In *Constructive Criticism: The Human Sciences in the Age of Theory*. Ed. Martin Kreiswirth and Thomas Carmichael. Toronto: U of Toronto P, 1995. 3–11.

Krieger, Murray, ed. *The Aims of Representation: Subject/Text/History*. New York: Columbia UP, 1987.

Kroker, Arthur. "Migration Across the Disciplines." *Journal of Canadian Studies* 15 (Fall 1980): 3-10.

Kuczynski, Janusz. "Diversity and Unity of Sciences as the Foundation of Universalism." *Dialogue and Humanism* 4. 4 (1994): 143–75.

Kuhn, Kathryn E., and Wynne Walker Moskop. "Free Riders or Front Runners? The Role of Social Scientists in the American Studies Movement." *American Studies* 40. 2 (1999): 115–36.

Kuklick, Bruce. "The Emergence of the Humanities." In *The Politics of Liberal Education*. Ed. Darryl J. Gless and Barbara Herrnstein Smith. Durham: Duke UP, 1992. 201–12.

———. "Myth and Symbol in American Studies." *American Quarterly* 24 (1972): 435–50.

———. "The Professionalization of the Humanities." In *Applying the Humanities*. Ed. Daniel Callahan, Arthur L. Caplan, and Bruce Jennings. New York: Plenum Press, 1985. 41–54.

Kurian, George T., Miles Orvell, Johnnella E. Butler, and Jay Mechling, eds. *Encyclopedia of American Studies*. 4 vols. New York: Grolier Education, Scholastic Incorporated, 2001.

Kuspit, Donald. "Traditional Art History's Complaint Against the Linguistic Analysis of Visual Art." *Journal of Aesthetics and Art Criticism* 45. 4 (1987): 345–49.

LaCapra, Dominick. "Criticism Today." In *The Aims of Representation: Subject/Text/ History*. Ed. Murray Krieger. New York: Columbia UP, 1987. 235–55.

———. *Soundings in Critical Theory*. Ithaca: Cornell UP, 1989.

Lansford, Tom. "Popular Culture." Kurian, Orvell, Butler, and Mechling V. III: 366–72.

Lattuca, Lisa. *Creating Interdisciplinarity: Interdisciplinary Research and Teaching among College and University Faculty*. Nashville: Vanderbilt UP, 2001.

Lauer, Janice. "Studies of Written Discourse: Dappled Discipline." Address to the Rhetoric Society of America. 34th Meeting of the Conference on College Composition and Communication. Detroit, Michigan. 17 March 1983.

Lauter, Paul. *From Walden Pond to Jurassic Park: Activism, Culture, and American Studies*. Durham: Duke UP, 2001.

———. "Reconfiguring Academic Disciplines: The Emergence of American Studies." *American Studies* 40. 2 (1999): 23–38.

Leitch, Vincent. *American Literary Criticism from the Thirties to the Eighties*. New York: Columbia UP, 1988.

Lenz, Gunther H. "American Studies—Beyond the Crisis?: Recent Redefinitions and the Meaning of Theory, History, and Practical Criticism." *Prospects, Annual of American Cultural Studies* 7 (1982): 53–113.

———. "Periodization and American Studies." Kurian, Orvell, Butler, and Mechling V. III: 293–96.

Lepenies, Wolf. "Toward an Interdisciplinary History of Science." *International Journal of Sociology* 8. 1–2 (1978): 45–69.

Lerner, Gerda. *The Majority Finds Its Past: Placing Women in History*. New York: Oxford UP, 1979.

Levin, Harry. "The Modern Humanities in Historical Perspective." In *The Future of the Modern Humanities*. Ed. J. C. Laidlaw. Cambridge: The Modern Humanities Research Association, 1969. 1–17.

Levine, Arthur, and Jana Nidiffer. "Key Turning Points in the Evolving Curriculum." Gaff and Ratcliff, *Handbook* 53–85.

Levine, Arthur, and Jeanette Cureton. "The Quiet Revolution: Eleven Facts about Multiculturalism and the Curriculum." *Change* 24 (January–February 1992): 25–29.

Levine, George. "Introduction" and "Epilogue." In *One Culture: Essays in Science and Literature*. Ed. George Levine. Madison: U of Wisconsin P, 1987. 3–32, 339–42.

———. "Victorian Studies." Greenblatt and Gunn, *Redrawing the Boundaries* 130–53.

Levine, George, Peter Brooks, Jonathan Culler, Marjorie Garber, E. Ann Kaplan, and Catharine R. Stimpson. *Speaking for the Humanities*. ACLS Occasional Papers No. 7. New York: American Council of Learned Societies. 1989.

Levine, Lawrence W. "Jazz and American Culture." O'Meally, *Jazz Cadence* 431–47.

———. *The Opening of the American Mind: Canons, Culture, and History*. Boston: Beacon Press, 1996.

Levy, Alan, and Barbara L. Tischler. "Into the Cultural Mainstream: The Growth of American Music Scholarship." *American Quarterly* 42. 1 (1990): 57–73.

Limerick, Patricia. "Insiders and Outsiders: The Borders of the USA and the Limits of the ASA." *American Quarterly* 49. 3 (1997): 449–69.

Lipsitz, George. *American Studies in a Moment of Danger*. Minneapolis: U of Minnesota P, 2001.

———. "Listening to Learn and Learning to Listen: Popular Culture, Cultural Theory, and American Studies." Maddox 310–31.

———. "No Shining City on a Hill: American Studies and the Problem of Place." *American Studies* 40. 2 (1999): 53–69.

———. "'Sent for You Yesterday, Here You Come Today': American Studies Scholarship and the New Social Movements." Pease and Wiegman 441–60.

Little, William A., Carolyn M. Leonard, and Edward Crosby. "Black Studies and Africana Studies Curriculum Model in the United States." *The Journal of the National Council of Black Studies*. n.d. Rpt. in Norment, *Reader* 691–711.

Lornell, Kip, and Anne K. Rasmussen. "Music and Community in Multicultural America." In *Musics of Multicultural America: A Study of Twelve Musical Communities*. Ed. Kip Lornell and Anne K. Rasmussen. New York: Schirmer Books, 1997. 1–23.

Lubin, David M. "Art, Society, and Culture." Kurian, Orvell, Butler, and Mechling V. I: 173–82.

Lyon, Arabella. "Interdisciplinarity: Giving Up Territory." *College English* 54. 6 (1992): 681–93.

Lyotard, Jean-Francois. *The Postmodern Condition: A Report on Knowledge*. Trans. G. Bennington and B. Massumi. Minneapolis: U of Minnesota P, 1988.

Mackey, Nathaniel. "Sound and Sentiment, Sound and Symbol." O'Meally, *Jazz Cadence* 602–28.

McClary, Susan. "Terminal Prestige: The Case of Avant-Garde Music Composition." Schwarz, Kassabian, and Sigel 54–73.

McCorison, Marcus. "The Nature of Humanistic Societies in Early America." In *The Pursuit of Knowledge in the Early American Republic: American Scientific and Learned Societies from Colonial Times to the Civil War*. Ed. Alexandra Oleson and Sanborn C. Brown. Baltimore: Johns Hopkins UP, 1976. 248–60.

McCreless, Patrick. "Rethinking Contemporary Music Theory." In Schwarz, Kassabian, and Sigel 13–53.

McKeon, Michael. "The Origins of Interdisciplinary Studies." *Eighteenth-Century Studies* 28. 1 (1994): 17–28.

McKeon, Richard P. "The Liberating and Humanizing Arts in Education." In *Humanistic Education and Western Civilization*. Ed. Arthur A. Cohen. New York: Holt, Rinehart, and Winston, 1964. 159–81.

McLeod, Susan, and Aline Maimon. "Clearing the Air: WAC Myths and Realities." *College English* 62. 5 (2000): 573–83.

McWorter, Gerald, and Ronald Bailey. "Black Studies Curriculum Development in the 1980s: Its Patterns and History." *The Black Scholar* (March–April. 1984). Rpt. in Norment, *Reader* 614–30.

Maddox, Lucy, ed. *Locating American Studies: The Evolution of a Discipline*. Baltimore: Johns Hopkins UP, 1999.

Matibag, Eugenio. "Asian Americas." Kurian, Orvell, Butler, and Mechling V. I: 182–86.

Marcell, David. "Characteristically American: Another Perspective on American Studies." *Centennial Review* 21. 4 (1977): 388–400.

Marx, Leo. "Reflections on American Studies, Minnesota, and the 1950s." *American Studies* 40. 2 (1999). 39–51.

Maus, Fred Everett. "Introduction: A Symposium. Music Theory and Other Disciplines: Three Views." *Journal of Musicology* 11. 1 (1993): 7–10.

Mayville, William V. *Interdisciplinarity: The Mutable Paradigm.* AAHE-ERIC/ Higher Education Research Report No. 9. Washington, D.C.: ERIC Clearinghouse on Higher Education, 1978.

Mechling, Jay. "Commentary." [On Gene Wise, "Paradigm Dramas."] Maddox 211–14.

———. "Some [New] Elementary Axioms for an American Cultur[al] Studies." *American Studies* 38. 2 (1997): 9–30.

Mechling, Jay, Robert Meredith, and David Wilson. "American Culture Studies: The Discipline and the Curriculum." *American Quarterly* 25. 4 (1973): 363–89.

Mehl, James V. "Liberal Arts, Fine Arts, Humanities." *Humanities Education* (January 1985): 37–43.

———. "Towards a Postmodern Humanism: Challenges for Humanists at the Century's End." *Interdisciplinary Humanities* 10. 2 (1993): 3–12.

———. "Why Define?" *Humanities Education* (Fall 1987): 3–7.

Melville, Stephen. "Basic Concepts of Art History." Melville and Readings, *Vision and Textuality* 31–37.

Melville, Stephen, and Bill Readings. "General Introduction." Melville and Readings, *Vision and Textuality* 3–28.

———, eds. *Vision and Textuality.* Durham: Duke UP, 1995.

Menand, Louis. "Re-imagining Liberal Education." In *Education and Democracy: Re-imagining Liberal Learning in America.* Ed. Robert Orrill. New York: The College Board, 1997. 1–19.

———. "Undisciplined." *The Wilson Quarterly* 25. 4 (Autumn 2001): 51–59.

Messer-Davidow, Ellen. *Disciplining Feminism: From Social Activism to Academic Discourse.* Durham Duke UP, 2002.

———. "Whither Cultural Studies?" In *From Sociology to Cultural Studies: New Perspectives.* Ed. Elizabeth Long. Malden, MA and Oxford: Blackwell, 1997. 489–522.

Middleton, Ann. "Medieval Studies." Greenblatt and Gunn, *Redrawing the Boundaries* 12–40.

Miller, J. Hillis. "Cultural Studies and Reading." *ADE Bulletin* 117 (Fall: 1997): 15–18.

———. "The Function of Rhetorical Study at the Present Time." In *Teaching Literature: What Is Needed Now.* Ed. James Engell and David Perkins. Cambridge: Harvard UP, 1988. 87–109.

———. *Illustration.* Cambridge: Harvard UP, 1992.

———. "The Role of Theory in the Development of Literary Studies in the United States." In *Divided Knowledge: Across Disciplines, Across Cultures.* Ed. David Easton and Corinne S. Schelling. Newbury Park: Sage. 1991. 118–38.

Miller, Raymond. "Varieties of Interdisciplinary Approaches in the Social Sciences." *Issues in Integrative Studies* 1 (1982): 1–37.

Minnich, Elizabeth. *Liberal Learning and the Arts of Connection for the New Academy.* Washington, DC: Association of American Colleges and Universities, 1995.

Mirzoeff. Nicholas. *An Introduction to Visual Culture.* London and New York: Routledge, 1999.

———. *The Visual Culture Reader*. London and New York: Routledge, 1998.

———. "What Is Visual Culture?" Mirzoeff, *Reader* 3–13.

Mitchell, W. J. T. "Against Comparison: Teaching Literature and the Visual Arts." In *Teaching Literature and Other Arts*. Ed. Jean-Pierre Barricelli, Joseph Gibaldi, and E. Lauter. New York: Modern Language Association, 1990. 30–37.

———. "Interdisciplinarity and Visual Culture." *The Art Bulletin* 77. 4 (1995): 540–44.

———. *Picture Theory: Essays on Verbal and Visual Representation*. Chicago: U of Chicago P, 1994.

Montrose, L. W. "Professing the Renaissance: The Poetics and Politics of Culture." In *The New Historicism*. Ed. H. A. Vesser. New York: Routledge, 1989. 15–36.

Moran, Joe. *Interdisciplinarity*. London and New York: Routledge, 2002.

Morgan, Robert P. "Rethinking Musical Culture: Canonic Reformulations in a Post- Tonal Age." Bergeron and Bohlman, *Disciplining Music* 44–63.

Moskowitz, Milton. "The Status of Black Studies at the Nation's Highest-Ranked Universities." *The Journal of Blacks in Higher Education* 16 (Summer 1997): 2–91.

Murphey, Murray G. "American Civilization as a Discipline?" *American Studies* 40. 2 (1999): 5–21.

———. "American Civilization at Pennsylvania." *American Quarterly* Summer Supplement (1970): 489–502.

Murray, Albert. "The Visual Equivalent of the Blues." In *Romare Bearden, 1970–1980*. Charlotte, NC: Mint Museum, 1980.

Nehamas, Alexander. "Trends in Recent American Philosophy." Bender and Schorske, *American Academic Culture* 227–41.

Nelson, Cary, and Michael Bérubé. "Introduction." In *Higher Education Under Fire: Politics, Economics, and the Crisis of the Humanities*. Ed. Michael Bérubé and Cary Nelson. New York: Routledge, 1995. 1–32.

Nelson, Cary, Paul Treichler, and Lawrence Grossberg. "Cultural Studies: An Introduction." Grossberg, Nelson, and Treichler 1–22.

Nelson, Michael, ed. *Alive at the Core: Exemplary Approaches to General Education in the Humanities*. San Francisco: Jossey Bass, 2000.

———. "Alive at the Core: Programs and Issues." Nelson, *Alive* 1–19.

Newell, William. "Professionalizing Interdisciplinarity: Literature Review and Research Agenda." In *Interdisciplinarity: Essays from the Literature*. Ed. William Newell. New York: The College Board, 1998. 529–63.

Norment, Nathaniel Jr., ed. *The African American Studies Reader*. Durham: Carolina Academic Press, 2001.

———. "Introduction" and editorial bridges. Norment, *Reader* xix–vlii, passim.

Nussbaum, Martha. *Cultivating Humanity: A Classical Defense of Reform in Liberal Education*. Cambridge: Harvard UP, 1997.

———. "Historical Conceptions of the Humanities and Their Relationship to Society." In *Applying the Humanities*. Ed. Daniel Callahan, Arthur L. Caplan, and Bruce Jennings. New York: Plenum Press. 1985. 3–28.

Oakley, Francis. "The Elusive Academic Profession: Complexity and Change." *Daedalus* (Fall 1997): 43–66.

———. "Ignorant Armies and Nighttime Clashes: Changes in the Humanities Classroom, 1970–1995." Kernan, *What's Happened* 63–83.

O'Brien, Jean M. "Why Here? Scholarly Locations for American Indian Studies." *American Quarterly* 55. 4 (2003): 689–96.

Ohmann, Richard. 2002. "Afterword." Shumway and Dionne, *Disciplining English* 213–19.

Oleson, Alexander, and John Voss. "Introduction." *The Organization of Knowledge in Modern America, 1860–1920.* Ed. Alexandra Oleson and John Voss. Baltimore: Johns Hopkins U P, 1979. vii–xxi.

Olguin, Enrique "Rick," and Betty Schmitz. "Transforming the Curriculum Through Diversity." Gaff and Ratcliff, *Handbook* 436–56.

———. "Preface," "Introductions," and chapter bridges. O'Meally, *Jazz Cadence* ix–xvi, 3–4, passim.

O'Meally. Robert, ed. *The Jazz Cadence of American Culture.* New York: Columbia University Press, 1998.

Orrill, Robert. "An End to Mourning: Liberal Education in Contemporary America." In *The Condition of American Liberal Education: Pragmatism in a Changing Tradition.* Ed. Robert Orrill. New York: The College Board. 1995. ix–xxiii.

Orvell, Miles, Johnnella Butler, and Jay Mechling. "Preface." Kurian, Orvell, Butler, and Mechling V. I: vii–xii.

Palmer, Carole L., and Laura J. Neumann. "The Information Work of Interdisciplinary Humanities Scholars: Exploration and Translation." *Library Quarterly* 72. 1 (2002): 85–117.

Parker, Roger. "Literary Studies: Caught Up in the Web of Words." *Acta Musicologica* 69. 1 (1997): 10–15.

Parker, William Riley. "The Future of the 'Modern' Humanities." In *The Future of the Modern Humanities.* Ed. J. C. Laidlaw. Cambridge: The Modern Humanities Research Association, 1969. 106–26.

Pasler, Jann. "Directions in Musicology." *Acta Musicologica* 69. 1 (1997): 16–21.

Patterson, Annabel M. "Historical Scholarship." Gibaldi, *Introduction* 182–200.

Paxson, Thomas D. "Modes of Interaction between Disciplines." *Journal of General Education* 45. 2 (1996): 79–94.

Pease, Donald E., and Robyn Wiegman, eds. *The Futures of American Studies.* Durham: Duke UP, 2002.

Peck, Jeffrey. "There's No Place Like Home? Remapping the Topography of German Studies." *The German Quarterly* 62. 2 (1989): 178–87.

Pedelty, Mark. "Jenny's Painting: Multiple Forms of Communication in the Classroom." In *Reinventing Ourselves: Interdisciplinary Education, Collaborative Learning, and Experimentation in Higher Education.* Ed. Barbara Leigh Smith and John McCann. Bolton, MA: Anker, 2001. 230–52.

Peters, Michael. "Preface." In *After the Disciplines: The Emergence of Cultural Studies.* Ed. Michael Peters. Westport, CT: Bergin & Garve, 1999. xi–xiii.

Pollock, Griselda. "Beholding Art History: Vision, Place, and Power." Melville and Readings, *Vision and Textuality* 38–66.

Porter, Carolyn. "History and Literature: 'After the New Historicism.'" Cohen and Roth 23–43.

Powell, Richard J. "Art History and Black Memory: Toward a 'Blues Aesthetic.'" O'Meally, *Jazz Cadence* 182–95.

Pratt, Linda. "In a Dark Wood: Finding a New Path to the Future of English." *ADE Bulletin* 131 (Spring 2002): 27–33.

Preziosi, Donald. "Constru(ct)ing the Origins of Art History." *Art Journal* 42. 4 (1982): 320–27.

———. "The Question of Art History." *Critical Inquiry* 18. 2 (1992): 363–86.

———. *Rethinking Art History: Meditations on a Coy Science.* New Haven: Yale UP, 1989.

Putnam, Hilary. "A Half Century of Philosophy, Viewed from Within." Bender and Schorske, *American Academic Culture* 193–226.

Putzell, Ed. "The Humanities and the Image of Man." In *The Crisis in the Humanities: Interdisciplinary Responses.* Ed. Sara Putzell-Korab and Robert Detweiler. Potomac, MD: Studia Humanitatis, 1983. 193–212.

Rabb, Theodore K. "The Historian and the Climatologist." In *The New History: The 1980's and Beyond. Studies in Interdisciplinary History.* Ed. Theodore K. Rabb, Robert I. Rotberg, and Thomas Glick. Princeton: Princeton UP, 1983. 251–58.

Radway, Janice. "'What's in a Name?' Presidential Address to the American Studies Association, November 20, 1998." *American Quarterly* 51. 1 (1999): 1–32.

Randel, Don Michael. "The Canons in the Musicological Toolbox." Bergeron and Bohlman, *Disciplining Music* 10–22.

Rasula, Jed. "The Media of Memory: The Seductive Menace of Records in Jazz History." Gabbard, *Jazz* 134–62.

Ratcliff, James L. "Quality and Coherence in General Education." Gaff and Ratcliff, *Handbook* 151–69.

Ratcliff, James I., D. Kent Johnson, Steven M. La Nasa, and Jerry G. Gaff. *The Status of General Education in the Year 2000: Summary of a National Survey.* Washington, DC: Association of American Colleges and Universities, 2001.

Raynor, Deirdre. "African American Literature." Kurian, Orvell, Butler, and Mechling V. I: 22–27.

Readings, Bill. "For a Heteronomous Cultural Politics: The University, Culture, and the State." Kreiswirth and Carmichael *Constructive Criticism* 169–89.

———. *The University in Ruins.* Cambridge: Harvard UP, 1996.

Reardon, Michael F., and Judith A. Ramaley. 1. "Building Academic Community While Containing Costs." Gaff and Ratcliff, *Handbook* 513–32.

Reed, T. V. "Class and Culture." Kurian, Orvell, Butler, and Mechling 358–65.

Reese, Thomas F. "Mapping Interdisciplinarity." *The Art Bulletin* 77. 4 (1995): 544–49.

Rich, Daniel, and Robert Warren. "The Intellectual Future of Urban Affairs: Theoretical, Normative, and Organizational Options." *Social Science Research* 17. 2 (1980): 53–66.

Richards, Donald G. "Meaning and Relevance of 'Synthesis' in Interdisciplinary Studies." *Journal of General Education* 45. 2 (1996): 114–28.

Robbins, Bruce, ed. *Intellectuals: Aesthetics, Politics, Academics.* Minneapolis: U of Minnesota P, 1990.

———. "Introduction: The Grounding of Intellectuals." Robbins, *Intellectuals* xi–xxvii.

———. "Less Disciplinary Than Thou: Criticism and the Conflict of the Faculties." Kaplan and Levine, *Politics* 93–115.

Roberts, Jon H., and James Turner. *The Sacred and the Secular University.* Princeton: Princeton UP, 2000.

Rogoff, Irit. "Studying Visual Culture." Mirzoeff, *Reader* 14–26.

Ross, Dorothy. *The Origins of American Social Science.* Cambridge: Cambridge UP, 1991.

Rowe, John Carlos. "Postmodernist Studies." Greenblatt and Gunn, *Redrawing the Boundaries* 179–208.

Rudolph, Frederick. "Heritage and Traditions." In *Common Learning: A Carnegie Colloquium on General Education.* Washington, DC: The Carnegie Foundation for the Advancement of Learning, 1981. 57–73.

Ruiz, Nicholas, III. "Theory, Interdisciplinarity, and the Humanities Today: An Interview with Vincent B. Leitch." *Interculture.* 2 (May 2005). e-journal at <http://www.fsu.edu_proghum/interculture/homepage.html> ISSN 1552-5910.

Russell, David R. "Institutionalizing English: Rhetoric on the Boundaries," Shumway and Dionne, *Disciplining English* 39–58.

Ryan, Barbara. "Harlem Renaissance." Kurian, Orvell, Butler, and Mechlng V. II: 290–94.

Ryan, Michael. "Cultural Studies: A Critique." Cited in Leitch 404, 438n34.

Sabin, Margery. "Evolution and Revolution: Change in the Literary Humanities, 1968–1995." Kernan, *What's Happened* 84–103.

Salter, Liora, and Alison Hearn, eds. *Outside the Lines: Issues in Interdisciplinary Research.* Montreal and Kingston: McGill-Queen's UP, 1996. See also Salter and Hearn "On Interdisciplinarity." Report to the SSHRC of Canada.

Sawhney, Sabina. "Strangers in the Classroom." Wiegman, *Women's Studies* 341–67.

Sayre, Gordon. "Early America." Kurian, Orvell, Butler, and Mechling V. II: 58–60.

Schleifer, Ronald. "A New Kind of Work: Publishing, Theory, and Cultural Studies." Shumway and Dionne, *Disciplining English* 179–94.

Schneider, Carol Geary, and Robert Shoenberg. *Contemporary Understandings of Liberal Education.* Number 1 in The Academy in Transition series. Washington, DC: Association of American Colleges and Universities, 1998.

Scholl, Sharon. "The Trouble with Music. . . ." *Interdisciplinary Humanities* 9. 3 (1992): 5–12.

Scholle, David. "Resisting Disciplines: Repositioning Media Studies in the University." *Communication Theory* 5 (1995): 130–43.

Schor, Naomi A. "Feminist and Gender Studies." Gibaldi, *Introduction*, 1992, 262–87.

Schorske, Carl E. "The New Rigorism in the Human Sciences, 1940–1960." Bender and Schorske, *American Academic Culture* 309–29.

Schwartz, Richard B. "Contextual Criticism and the Question of Pedagogy." *Eighteenth-Century Life* 5. 3 (1979): 95–100.

Schwarz, David. "On Music and Disciplinarity" [Review Essay]. *Stanford Humanities Review* 5. 2 (1993): 180–86.

Schwarz, David, Anahid Kassabian, and Lawrence Siegel, eds. *Keeping Score: Music, Disciplinarity, Culture*. Charlottesville: UP of Virginia, 1997.

Scott, Joan. "The Rhetoric of Crisis in Higher Education." In *Higher Education Under Fire: Politics, Economics, and the Crisis of the Humanities*. Ed. Michael Bérubé and Cary Nelson. New York: Routledge, 1995. 293–304.

Scouten, Arthur H. "The Limitations of the Interdisciplinary Approach." *Eighteenth- Century Life* 5. 3 (1979): 101–8.

Searle, John R. "Politics and the Humanities." *Academic Questions* 12. 4 (1999): 45–50.

Seaton, James. "On the Future of the Humanistic Tradition in Literary Criticism." *Humanitas* 11. 1 (1998): 4–13.

Seidman, Steven. "Relativizing Sociology: The Challenge of Cultural Studies." In *From Sociology to Cultural Studies: New Perspectives*. Ed. Elizabeth Long. Malden, MA and Oxford: Blackwell, 1997. 37–61.

Seyhan, Azade. "Visual Citations: Walter Benjamin's Dialectic of Text and Image." Allert, *Languages* 229–41.

Shank, Barry. "The Continuing Embarrassment of Culture: From the Culture Concept to Cultural Studies." *American Studies* 38. 2 (1997): 95–116.

———. "Culture and Cultural Studies." Kurian, Orvell, Butler, and Mechling V. I: 443–48.

Shapin, Steven. "Discipline and Bonding: The History and Sociology of Science as Seen Through the Externalism-Internalism Debate." *History of Science* 30. 4 (1992): 333–69.

Shattuck, Roger. "Conclusion: What Now Shall We Teach?" Nelson, *Alive* 348–65.

Sheehan, David. "Pope and Palladio, Hogarth and Fielding: Kinds of Discipline in Inerdisciplinary Studies." *Eighteenth-Century Life* 5. 3 (1979): 76–82.

Shepherd, G. J. "Building a Discipline of Communication." *Journal of Communication* 43 (1993): 83–91.

Shepherd, John. *Music as Social Text*. Cambridge, UK: Polity Press. 1991.

Showalter, Elaine. "Feminist Criticism in the Wilderness." *Critical Inquiry* 8. 2 (1981): 179–205.

Shumway, David. "Emerson and the Shape of American Literature." Shumway and Dionne, *Disciplining English* 99–114.

———. "The Interdisciplinarity of American Studies." Unpublished manuscript, 1988.

Shumway, David, and Craig Dionne, eds. *Disciplining English: Alternative Histories, Critical Perspectives.* Albany: State U of New York P, 2002.

———. "Introduction." Shumway and Dionne, *Disciplining English* 1-18.

Sibbald, Mary Jo. "The Search for a Humanistic Approach to Music Education." *Interdisciplinary Humanities* 9. 4 (1992): 17-21.

Sill, David J. "Integrative Thinking, Synthesis, and Creativity in Interdisciplinary Studies." *Journal of General Education* 45. 2 (1996): 129-51.

Sklar, Robert. "The Problem of an American Studies 'Philosophy': A Bibliography of New Directions." *American Quarterly* 16 (1975): 245-62.

Skura, Meredith. "Psychoanalytic Criticism." Greenblatt and Gunn, *Redrawing the Boundaries* 340-73.

Smith, Henry Nash. "Can 'American Studies' Develop a Method?" *American Quarterly* 9. 2, pt. 2 (1957): 197-208.

Smith, J. Owens. "The Political Nature of Black Studies Departments and Programs." *Western Journal of Black Studies* n.d. Rpt. in Norment, *Reader* 472-83.

Smith, William D. "Black Studies: A Survey of Models and Curricula." *Journal of Black Studies* 10. 3 (1971): 269-77. Rpt. in Norment, *Reader* 631-40.

Snea, James A. "Repetition as a Figure of Black Culture." O'Meally, *Jazz Cadence* 62-81.

Solie, Ruth A. "Sophie Drinker's History." Bergeron and Bohlman, *Disciplining Music* 23-43.

"Special Topic: Performance." *PMLA* 107. 3 (1992): 432-607.

Spurlock, Karla J. "Toward the Evolution of a Unitary Discipline: Maximizing the Interdisciplinary Concept in African/Afro-American Studies." *Western Journal of Black Studies.* n.d. Rpt. in Norment, *Reader* 647-52.

Stafford, Barbara Maria. "The Eighteenth-Century: Towards an Interdisciplinary Model." *The Art Bulletin* 70. l (1988): 6-24.

Steiner, Wendy. *The Colors of Rhetoric: Problems in the Relations between Modern Literature and Painting.* Chicago: U of Chicago P, 1982.

Stewart, James B. "The Field and Function of Black Studies." Paper presented to the William Monroe Trotter Institute for the Study of Black Culture at the University of Massachusetts. July 1987. Rpt. in Norment, *Reader* 41-49.

———. "Reaching for Higher Ground: Toward an Understanding of Black/Africana Studies." *The Afrocentric Scholar* l. 1 (1992): l-63. Rpt. in Norment, *Reader* 349-66.

Stimpson, Catharine R. "Feminist Criticism." Greenblatt and Gunn, *Redrawing the Boundaries* 251-70.

Stone, James H. "Integration in the Humanities: Perspectives and Prospects." *Main Currents in Modern Thought* 26. 1 (1969): 14-19.

Suleiman, Susan. "Introduction: Varieties of Audience-Oriented Criticism." In *The Reader in the Text: Essays on Audience and Interpretation.* Ed. Susan Suleiman and Inge Crosman. Princeton: Princeton UP, 1980. 3-45.

Swoboda, Wolfram W. "Disciplines and Interdisciplinarity: A Historical Perspective." Kockelmans, *Interdisciplinarity* 49-92.

Sykes, Richard E. "American Studies and the Concept of Culture: A Theory and Method." *American Quarterly* Summer supplement (1963): 253–70.

"Theatre and Interdisciplinarity." *Theatre Research International*. Special Focus 26. 2 (2001): 129–98.

Thomas, Brook. *The New Historicism and Other Old-Fashioned Topics*. Princeton: Princeton UP, 1991.

Thomas, Lorenzo. "Music and the Black Arts Movement." Gabbard, *Jazz* 256–74.

Thorne, Barrie. "A Telling Time for Women's Studies." *Signs* 25. 4 (2001): 1183–87.

Thorpe, James, ed. *The Aims and Methods of Scholarship in Modern Languages and Literatures*. New York: Modern Language Association, 1963.

———. *The Aims and Methods of Scholarship in Modern Languages and Literatures*. 2nd ed. New York: Modern Language Association, 1970.

———. *Relations of Literary Study: Essays on Interdisciplinary Contributions*. New York: Modern Language Association, 1967.

Tichi, Cecelia. "American Literary Studies to the Civil War." Greenblatt and Gunn 209–31.

Toombs, William, and William Tierney. *Meeting the Mandate: Renewing the College and Departmental Curriculum*. ASHE-ERIC Higher Ed Report # 6, 1991.

Treitler, Leo. "History and Music." Cohen and Roth 209–30.

Turner, Richard. "Trading Tunes with Stanley Fish: Grand Unification Theories and the Practice of Literature and Science." *Issues in Integrative Studies* 9 (1991): 113–25.

Turner, Stephen. *Brains/Practices/Relativism: Social Theory after Cognitive Science*. Chicago: U of Chicago P, 2002.

Tuve, Rosemond. *Essays by Rosemond Tuve: Spenser, Herbert, Milton*. Ed. Thomas R. Roche. Princeton: Princeton UP, 1970.

Umberger, Daryl. "Myth and Symbol." In Kurian, Orvell, Butler, and Mechling V. III: 180–84.

Van Deburg, William L. *New Day in Babylon: The Black Power Movement and American Culture, 1965-1975*. Chicago: U of Chicago P, 1992.

Van Den Toorn, Pieter C. *Music, Politics, and the Academy*. Berkeley: U of California P, 1995.

Van Dusseldorp, Dirk, and Seerp Wigboldus. "Interdisciplinary Research for Integrated Rural Development in Developing Countries: The Role of Social Sciences." *Issues in Integrative Studies* 12 (1994): 93–138.

Veysey, Laurence R. *The Emergence of the American University*. Chicago: U of Chicago P, 1965.

———. "The Plural Organized Worlds of the Humanities." In *The Organization of Knowledge in Modern America, 1860-1920*. Ed. Alexandra Oleson and John Voss. Baltimore: The Johns Hopkins UP, 1979. 51–106.

Vickers, Jill. "'[U]framed in open, unmapped fields': Teaching and the Practice of Interdisciplinarity." *Arachné: An Interdisciplinary Journal of the Humanities* 4. 2 (1997): 11–42.

248 *Works Cited*

Vosskamp, Wilhelm. "From Scientific Specialization to the Dialogue Between the Disciplines." *Issues in Integrative Studies* 4 (1986): 17–36.

———. "Crossing of Boundaries: Interdisciplinarity as an Opportunity for Universities in the 1980's?" *Issues in Integrative Studies* 12 (1994): 43–54.

Wager, Willis J., and Earl J. McGrath. *Liberal Education and Music.* New York: Teachers College, Columbia University, 1963.

Wald, Pricilla. "The Idea of America." Kurian, Orvell, Butler, and Mechling V. II: 82–86.

Wallace, Jo-Ann. "English Studies versus the Humanities? Cultural Studies and Institutional Power." *University of Toronto Quarterly* 64. 4 (1995): 506–13.

Wallace, Robert K. "Chasing the Loon: The Crazy Pleasures of Comparing the Arts." *Interdisciplinary Humanities* 12. 1 (1995): 17.

Walser, Robert. 1995. "'Out of Notes': Signification, Interpretation, and the Problem of Miles Davis." Gabbard, *Jazz* 165–88.

Walters, Ronald. "Critical Issues on Black Studies." n.d. Rpt. in Norment, *Reader* 528–37.

———. "The Discipline of Black Studies." *Negro Educational Review* 21. 4 (1970): 138–44.

Ward, John William. "Introduction." In *A Report to the Congress of the United States on The State of the Humanities and the Reauthorization of the National Endowment for the Humanities by the American Council of Learned Societies.* New York: The American Council of Learned Societies, 1985. v–xv.

Warhol, Robyn R. "Nice Work If You Can Get It—and If You Can't? Building Women's Studies Without Tenure Lines." Wiegman, *Women's Studies* 224–32.

Warrior, Robert. "A Room of One's Own at the ASA: An Indigenous Provocation." *American Quarterly* 55. 4 (2003): 681–87.

Washington, Mary Helen. "Commentary." *American Quarterly* 55. 4 (2003): 697–702.

———. "'Disturbing the Peace': What Happens to American Studies If You Put African American Studies at the Center?" Presidential Address to the American Studies Association, October 19, 1997. *American Quarterly* 50, 1 (1998): 1–23.

Watts, Steve. "American Studies and Americans: A Crank's Critique." *American Studies* 38. 3 (1997): 87–93.

Weber, Samuel. *Institution and Interpretation.* Minneapolis: U of Minnesota P, 1987.

Weingart, Peter. "Interdisciplinarity: The Paradoxical Discourse." In *Practicing Interdisciplinarity.* Ed. P. Weingart and N. Stehr. Toronto: U of Toronto P, 2000. 25–41.

Weisstein, Ulrich. "Literature and the Visual Arts." Barricelli and Gibaldi, *Interrelations* 251–77.

White, Lyn Maxwell. "The Humanities." Gaff and Ratcliff, *Handbook* 262–79.

Wiegman, Robyn. "Introduction: On Location." Wiegman, *Women's Studies* 1–44.

———. "Women's Studies: Interdisciplinary Imperatives." *Feminist Studies* 27. 2 (2001): 514–18.

——, ed. *Women's Studies on Its Own: A Next Wave Reader in Institutional Change*. Durham: Duke UP, 2002.

Williams, Jeffrey. "The Posttheory Generation." In Shumway and Dionne, *Disciplining English* 115–34.

Williams, Raymond. *Keywords: A Vocabulary of Culture and Society*. Rev. ed. New York: Oxford UP, 1983.

Wilson, Elizabeth. "A Short History of a Border War: Social Science, School Reform, and the Study of Literature." Shumway and Dionne, *Disciplining English* 59–82.

Wise, Gene. "Paradigm Dramas in American Studies." *American Quarterly* 31. 3 (1979): 293–337.

——. "Some Elementary Axioms for an American Culture Studies." *Prospects: The Annual of American Cultural Studies* 4 (1978): 517–47.

Wissocker, Ken. "Negotiating a Passage Between Disciplinary Borders: A Symposium." *ITEMS* [Social Science Research Council] (Fall 2001): 1, 5–7.

Wolff, Janet. "Excess and Inhibition: Interdisciplinarity in the Study of Art." Grossberg, Nelson, and Treichler 706–18.

"Women's Studies." In AAC[&U]. *Liberal Learning and the Arts and Sciences Major* V. II: 207–24.

"Women's Studies: An Overview." *University of Michigan Papers in Women's Studies* (May 1978): 14–26.

Yu, Pauline. "The Course of the Particulars: Humanities in the University of the Twenty-First Century." In *The Transformation of Humanistic Studies in the Twenty-First Century: Opportunities and Perils*. ACLS Occasional Paper No. 40. New York: American Council of Learned Societies, 1997. 21–29.

INDEX

African-American; and American studies, 159, 175,76; arts, 111, 188; and cultural studies approach in literature, 171–72; increased attention to race in mainstream post-1970s, 183; and music, 113, 132, 140, 148; precursors of scholarship and teaching, 177–78; and psychology, 178; subfield of history, 160

African American studies: assessments of field, 185, 201; borrowing in, 6; centers, 75; community activism in, 6, 54, 178; and cultural studies, 51; emergence of black women's studies, 184; expansion of, 183–85; global and transdisciplinary interests in, 196; holism in, 187–88; and literary studies, 92–93, 172; marginalization of women of color in, 184; National Council for Black Studies, 178–180, 183, 184, 191; and New Interdisciplinarity, 41; paradigm of Afrocentricity, 190; pedagogies, 6, 178; as postdisciplinarity, 127; preview of, 6; rise of, 177–180; and Stony Brook humanities center, 76; and Theory, 43; and women's studies, 186, 192, 196. See also African American; identity fields

America, concept of: in American studies, 3, 154, 174, 201; in debates on curriculum, 205; in Indian American studies, 198; in women's studies, 201

American studies: American Studies Association, 72, 153, 155, 168, 172–76, 197–99; appraisals of early history, 156–59; and art history, 112; assessments of, 171–75; call for critical interdisciplinarity in, 57–58; case study of field, 153–76; and community, 174; concept of American cultural studies, 3, 6, 50–53, 160–68; 196; concept of place, 164–68; counterpressure of identity fields, 175–77; critical and cultural turns, 154, 159–68, 161; and ethnic studies, 174; as exemplar of interdisciplinary studies, 77; future of, 174; global and transnational interests, 167–68, 174; and history, 154, 159; holism, 154–56, 159, 174; as home for study of American and popular music, 139, 141; Indian American studies, 197–99; journal *American Quarterly,* 74, 156–57; and *mestiza* consciousness, 166; and multiculturalism, 197; multidisciplinary nature of, 169, 171, 194; new anthropological and historical approaches in, 6, 177; new historicism in, 171; origin and early history of field, 2, 154–56; popular and non-Western culture in, 163–64, 174; preview, 6; and psychology, 159; scholarship on regionalism, 165; social scientific understandings of American life, 159; talk of interdisciplinarity, 61; types of scholars today, 172–73; at Yale Humanities Center, 76; and women's studies, 186. See also America